CONQUERORS OF THE AIR

CONQUERORS

TEXT BY HEINER EMDE

ILLUSTRATED BY CARLO DEMAND

OF THE AIR

THE EVOLUTION OF
AIRCRAFT 1903-1945

A STUDIO BOOK · THE VIKING PRESS · NEW YORK

AN EDITA BOOK LAUSANNE

The Viking Press wishes to acknowledge the valuable assistance of Hartley A. Soulé, former Research Airplanes Projects Leader for the National Advisory Committee for Aeronautics, in the preparation of this edition.

Technical data: Hans Redemann

Published in 1968 by The Viking Press, Inc.
625 Madison Avenue, New York, N.Y. 10022
Library of Congress catalog card number: 68-9283

Printed and bound in Switzerland

CONTENTS

INTRODUCTION

"The great magic in flying lies in the exceptional fascination coming from the countless problematic aspects of flight—and every single one of these aspects is interesting." Aviation was only ten years old when Algernon E. Berriman, the English aviator and writer, wrote these words. He described man's triumph in conquering the air; a triumph hardly matched by the invention of the wheel. Man had moved over the earth, then he had conquered water, and now he was flying as well. That was in 1913. Aviation had no administration, no brilliant managers. Anyone who flew was a pioneer.

Today, flying is taken so much for granted that a report such as "the day is not far off when jet aircraft will replace the last of the propeller planes in air travel," which appeared in the travel section of a large newspaper in 1968, goes largely unheeded.

When the Wright brothers soared into history with their first flight on December 17, 1903, they laid the first milestone in motorized aviation history. The spell preventing men from conquering the third dimension had been broken. Inventors and pseudo-inventors, unimaginative technicians and laymen of genius, plunged into the great adventure. They all had one thing in common: the enthusiasm with which they pursued the new paths, whether they were the right ones or not.

"I was floating along in a blue-white sea and saw nothing but the goal," the flying Brazilian, Alberto Santos-Dumont said, recalling one of his first flights. His sensation was shared by all those who flew: Orville and Wilbur Wright, William E. Boeing, and Glenn Curtiss in the United States; Charles and Gabriel Voisin and Louis Blériot in France; the Russians Igor Sikorsky and Andrei Nikolayevitch Tupolev; the Germans Claudius Dornier, Ernst Heinkel, and Willy Messerschmitt; Geoffrey De Havilland and Frederick Handley-Page in Britain; Anthony Fokker of the Netherlands; and countless other pioneers.

Famous or forgotten, successful or unfortunate—these pioneers saw nothing but the goal in man's quest for wings. What they designed, built and flew between 1903 and 1945 were technical milestones. Orville Wright's twelve second flight paved the way for long, routine, long-range flights in highly sophisticated aircraft. And in 1945, when World War II ended, American, British, German, Japanese, Italian, and Soviet designers could look back on an impressive number of milestones that had marked the way.

In the very beginning, practical experience and flair, courage to face the unknown, and the will to progress, were the dominating characteristics of the pioneers of flight. But mathematics and physics, meteorology and economy soon followed, and then man's new toy became a weapon. In World War I the doves became birds of prey, and the pioneers, once bound by a common interest, suddenly found themselves enemies.

Once again war became the mother of invention. The global conflict gave incitement to the development of the airplane: national need spurred on new inventions, discoveries, and the establishment of hitherto unknown laws of theoretical and practical physics. Emphasis was on the superlative: faster, farther, higher, longer, stronger. And deadlier.

The romantic epoch in aviation was brief. From then on aviation was divided—flying for war and for peace. The interest of military leaders in practical war machines—fighters and interceptors, bombers and reconnaissance planes—which still holds true today—continued unabated. They recognized the importance of the airplane for their purposes and promoted every further development.

But to weary civilians in the years directly following World War I, the airplane was associated with the idea of a deadly, dangerous, and, above all, economically useless device. Nevertheless, a number of aviation companies were established to transport mail, freight, and passengers on a commercial basis. Conservative officials gave little recognition and no support to civil air transport—until they suddenly recognized its economic importance, whereupon they tried to put all civil aviation under state control.

Meanwhile, the pioneer designers, whose knowledge and accomplishments had grown with unparalleled rapidity during the war years, switched over to the development and construction of machines for peacetime use. Neither hidebound officials nor technical setbacks clouded their vision of the future course of aviation: globe-circling air passenger service.

During a short transitional period, unarmed military machines were flown for the use of civilians. Masked passengers, who were considered very brave (and indeed they were), rode in windy cockpits and in the gunner's or observer's positions in bombers and reconnaissance planes which had been stripped of their weapons. Anyone who designed or flew an aerial machine was still a pioneer. But designers and fliers had set clearly outlined goals for themselves. Their objectives in civil aeronautics were naturally more ambitious than those of the pre-war pioneers, and more realistic. They foresaw dense traffic networks, complicated international agreements, but above all the transport of unlimited passengers without risk in large and comfortable giant airplanes at high speeds, with costs within reach of both the airline companies and customers.

Years were to pass before these bright prospects became a reality. Disadvantages and technical setbacks had to be overcome, and it was not until after 1923 that an airline was spoken of as the final and genuine task of aviation, creating significant links between nations. France, especially, took an active part in officially promoting this new means of transport; the French government smoothed the way with direct expenditures of money. Britain, on the other hand, placed aviation—military and civil—under a joint state high command; she put military facilities at the disposal of commercial aviation but refrained from giving direct financial support. The United States, today the leading nation in commercial air transport, allowed its civil aviation to eke out a precarious economic existence without any subsidies whatsoever. "Barnstormers," former combat pilots who earned their living from aerial acrobatics, managed to maintain public interest in flying through spectacular stunts. Even as late as 1927, the year that Charles Lindbergh flew the Atlantic, Washington officialdom still refused to give open recognition to civil aviation. But when the politicians finally did act, they acted swiftly and they did a good, businesslike job. By 1929, planes from more than 40 regular airlines were flying in the United States. Almost overnight, the lead that other nations thought they had secured in civil aviation had vanished.

Within a few years, civil aviation had expanded into a lucrative, independent, respected, and highly prospective commercial enterprise. Aviation became a matter of national prestige. Apart from military demands, designers of civil machines also received favors from the government. Ulterior motives frequently influenced state investments: cargo and passenger aircraft could, as a rule, also be tested for their usefulness as troop transporters, bombers, or reconnaissance machines.

In the early thirties, many changes came about in aviation: aircraft were no longer built individually but were manufactured in series by large companies such as Boeing, Fokker, De Havilland, Heinkel, and Messerschmitt. Aircraft production became a part of the national product; new vocations—pilot, navigator, radioman, flight engineer, steward, ground mechanic, and even aviation salesman—were created in addition to those of designer and aeronautical engineer. The airplane in the sky still evoked wonder, but no longer disbelief or astonishment. The words "air fleet" now crept into the vocabulary, and every country was proud of its own. In August 1936, the major air-minded countries ranked as follows: the United States was first with 445 commercial airliners (a total of 9,037 civil aircraft). France was second with 193 airliners (a total of 2,186 civil aircraft), and Britain was third with 166 airliners (a total of 1,758 aircraft). Germany, in fourth place, had 1,809 civil planes, but her 150 airliners were less than England's passenger and cargo planes. Italy had more than 82 airliners (a total of 385 civil aircraft), and finally Czechoslovakia—always open to all technical progress—had 227 civil aircraft, 36 of which were airliners.

As air travel became big business, a significant new vocabulary developed: aviation policy, aviation law, aviation authority, flight research. Nor were these merely words. Under aviation policy, organizational principles as well as the position of the state regarding aviation and aircraft industry were understood; it took international regulations into consideration and strove to gain influence over commercial aviation. Long before aviation's thriving years in the thirties, organization and administration involved legal considerations. The first international congress for aviation law had been held in Paris in 1911. This resulted in an international code of aviation law which—among other points, some of them amazing, some of them farseeing—laid down the following: "Airspace is free, with the rights of countries reserved, in the airspace over their territory, to adopt more qualified measures which they might deem necessary to protect their own security as well as that of their inhabitants and their properties."

Article 6 of Chapter II in Book One of this book of rules likewise set down a basic principle: "Every proprietor of an aircraft can only leave his private airfield after registering the airplane with the proper authority. Every country will formulate the necessary regulations itself for registration within its territory." However, in 1911 many things were unforeseeable, such as the power and range limitations of aircraft. Landing in open fields was allowed, but in other cases had to be controlled: "Apart from Acts of God, it is forbidden to land a) in fortresses and near fortified areas within the districts stipulated by the military authorities; b) within inhabited areas apart from places designated by official authority."

Today, nearly 60 years later, some of these early regulations sound quaint—such as Article 13 in Chapter IV, which reads: "Apart from cases of urgent danger, it is forbidden to throw overboard any object that could lead to personal or property damage." Even lost planes were not overlooked in the rules: "Whoever should find a damaged or abandoned aircraft or a part of such must inform the competent authority."

The early regulations indicate an awareness on the part of the pioneers that aviation without regulations would never prove to be practicable. Nevertheless, as the transport of passengers, goods, and mail increased rapidly in the years following World War I, the regulations adopted by the forefathers had to be adapted and extended. A globe-spanning network was developing from the many crudely flown short runs, and by 1925 the world's network amounted to 18,800 miles in Europe, 5,300 miles in America, 4,500 miles in Africa, 3,655 miles in Asia and 3,522 miles in Australia.

The I.A.T.A. (International Air Transport Association) was founded in 1919. It covered air transport and soon developed into a rate and price commission. At first, only the Netherlands, Britain, and Germany were members, but soon all air-conscious nations joined the organization. The I.C.A.O. (International Civil Aviation Organization) later coordinated international air traffic. Weather service and aircraft companies remained—despite all efforts to coordinate joint interests in joint organizations—under the charge of individual states.

When World War II broke out in 1939, the manufacture of aircraft again underwent a drastic change. Certainly none of the great powers had been unprepared for this eventuality. In fact, between the two wars, designers and engineers had been just as busy solving problems of military aircraft construction as they had in designing civil aircraft.

Between 1939 and 1945 an unbelievable number of aviation milestones was achieved. Never before had planes been so fast, so powerful, so enduring; and never before had they been so feared. Armament appropriations resulted in the manufacture of huge airplanes and long-range bombers, in fighters and interceptors with a performance undreamed of earlier. Deadly machines rolled off the assembly lines; production figures in the United States, the Soviet

Union, and Germany reached gigantic proportions. World War II was to usher in two new ages; the rocket age, potentially the mass transport means of tomorrow, and the jet age, without which aviation in its present form, be it civil or military, would be inconceivable. After the war, the airplane conquered the skies in a double sense; mankind had developed a new means of transport, a new weapon, and a new dimension.

The speed of aircraft development has been so great that chroniclers and historians attempting to piece together the history of motorized flight have had a hard time pinning down many of the facts. Sources considered to be impeccable have sometimes supplied varying technical data and measurements for one and the same airplane. Inexact figures on times and dates have been given out by official sources, and factory spokesmen admit that some records on old aircraft are missing. The reason for these gaps and errors is understandable. For example, during the early years of flight, engine performance could often be issued only in an inexact form. Few engines of the same design and series compared precisely to the next. Thus seemingly absurd differences arose between the meaning of horsepower and PS (the abbreviation of the German word "Pferdestärke" meaning horsepower). Modifications often changed the aircraft itself, certain types becoming longer or shorter, higher or lighter, or changing their wingspan or weight. Sometimes figures were difficult to reconstruct exactly, since there was a time when detail designs of an airplane were chalked in on the factory floor in a 1:1 scale, so that they could be taken directly to the construction unit. Some designers provided data other than that given by contemporary sources, because of faulty memories. In addition many sources of information were destroyed during the war.

Thus it is easier to obtain a true sketch of Leonardo da Vinci's flight device than the exact measurements of a certain World War I aircraft, which could have been buried and lost among the papers of its designer. More information was supplied on Karl Jatho, say, the claimant to the world's first motorized flight, than on a renowned French giant plane of the thirties. Gustave Whitehead (alias Gustav Weisskopf), an inventive Frank from Leuthershausen, Germany, who wanted to be fledged in America and who then contributed more to other branches of technology than to aeronautics, left behind a far more complete biography than the most significant Soviet designer of the recent past. Professor Samuel Pierpont Langley, the mathematical genius whom America laughed at (although he was on the right track) because of his experimental failures, is less known than Otto Lilienthal, who succeeded in the first controlled glider tests, and some of Langley's students, who later became pioneers. However, after compiling, selecting, sometimes discarding, and checking all known data, this book has at last emerged as a brief history of the years 1903 to 1945.

The airplane, the one-time flying box, has in an incredibly short time developed from an astonishing phenomenon in the skies to an integrated part of the machine world of the twentieth century. It serves in peace and war. It can benefit and it can destroy; it contributes to research as well as progress. And every day sees more designs of these heavier-than-air machines.

August 1968   HEINER EMDE   CARLO DEMAND

ALBERTO SANTOS-DUMONT

A man and his dream

A Brazilian in Paris plans a "Volkswagen of the air"

Alberto Santos-Dumont is one of the most fascinating figures in the history of human flight. He was born into a wealthy Brazilian family on July 20, 1873, in São Paulo, and was later to make good use of his financial independence in Paris. In September, 1898, at the age of 25, Santos-Dumont piloted the first of many airships he built. On July 13, 1901, he won the 100,000 franc prize which Henry Deutsch de la Meurthe, a leading member of the Aero Club de France, had offered the first person to fly the 6.75 mile stretch from Saint-Cloud to the Eiffel Tower in 30 minutes. On October 19, 1906, he climbed into another of his aircraft to win a cup offered by the great flying patron Ernest Archdeacon for a 656 ft. long flight. His aircraft on this occasion, the "Santos No. 14 bis," subsequently underwent several alterations. Santos-Dumont's greatest achievement was a small aircraft which he called "Santos No. 20" or "Demoiselle" (which can mean both "Young Lady" or "Dragonfly"), an attractive monoplane made of bamboo, linen, and wire, with a wingspan of 16 ft. 5 in. On September 13, 1909, powered by a 24 h.p. engine, the "Demoiselle" flew the slightly more than five miles from Saint-Cyr to Bue, near Paris, in five minutes. Santos-Dumont exhibited it in Paris afterward. In 1910 "Little Santos," as he was then called, holder of licenses for flying free balloons, dirigibles, monoplanes, and biplanes, withdrew from the aviation scene. "My dreams have all come true, and others will continue my work. I attach no importance at all to making a fortune from this development of mine," said this warm-hearted man who donated thousands of francs to the poor. "Mankind has always wanted to fly—now it can. And quite cheaply!" Santos-Dumont told a reporter from the British aviation journal "Flight."

The first "Volkswagen of the air" had made its appearance. "Santos-Dumont further emphasizes that he has concluded arrangements with a Mr. Clement and a Mr. Charron whereby a run of 1,000 of these ' Voiturettes ' will shortly be offered for sale at a reasonable price," "Flight" reported. But Santos-Dumont's dream of an airplane for every man never became reality, nor to date have any other of the projects seeking this same objective. Nevertheless, the "Demoiselle" has an assured place as a milestone in the history of "heavier-than-air flying devices."

Santos-Dumont traveled a long and expensive road to his "No. 20," a road full of triumphs and disappointments. Admittedly the backbiters (and there was no lack of them among aircraft manufacturers and pilots) accused the coffee millionaire of being a showman and a spendthrift. In actual fact the Brazilian had only one idiosyncrasy: he insisted on being dressed in the latest fashion, from the highly polished toecaps of his shoes to his sportsman's cap, on every occasion and particularly when carrying out his breakneck maneuvers above the roofs of Paris.

After hazardous flights in hot-air and free balloons, and after suffering some minor crashes, the pioneering aviator built his first aircraft. He was familiar with the successful flights in a dirigible by the French Army officers Charles Renard and A.C. Krebs in 1884, and in 1898 he built an airship 82 ft. long. It was yellow and had a wickerwork gondola with a fuel engine attached to the back end.

The "Santos-Dumont I" first became airborne on September 20, 1898. It rose against the wind—and against the advice of experienced balloonists, who were then surprised to see the dirigible struggle upward and fly slowly but surely toward Longchamp at a height of 1,300 ft. Later the dirigibles "Santos-Dumont II", "III," and "IV" appeared. Parisians grew accustomed to their madcap favorite as he clattered over their heads. They finally became so fond of him that a jury was forced to declare him winner (against its own judgment but in favor of public demand) following the flight for the Deutsch de la Meurthe Prize.

Santos-Dumont was far more interested in progress than in fame or the 100,000 franc prize. He built fourteen more

A familiar sight in the Paris skies early in the century: Alberto Santos-Dumont in his light aircraft "Demoiselle," which he hoped to make into a popular airplane.

dirigibles, gave demonstration flights, ranked as the leading aviator in Europe, and spared no effort to interest the skeptical public in conquering the air.

In the summer of 1903, the Brazilian was making one of his familiar flights over Paris, when sudden explosions terrified the spectators. Flames spurted from the exhaust and licked the dirigible's hydrogen-filled body. People waited helplessly, expecting complete disaster and the end of Little Santos. For this flight the aviator had abandoned his stylish check cap. He was wearing a straw hat, which he quickly removed from his head and used to beat out the flames. Shouts of encouragement rose from the crowd. Little Santos waved his white-gloved hand, lifted his soot-covered straw hat, and calmly flew on!

For a long time, even his successful dirigible aircraft had failed to satisfy Santos-Dumont; he could not regard it as the ideal fulfillment of his dream for flight. A few months after his near disaster, Paris was startled by sensational news from the United States: two brothers, Wilbur and Orville Wright, planned to fly in heavier-than-air machines.

While Paris had its doubts, Ernest Archdeacon, President of the Aero Club de France, offered a cup for the first pilot to fly a distance of 82 ft. As might be expected, Alberto Santos-Dumont was among the competitors.

As early as September 13, 1906, the audacious aviator launched a box kite-like monstrosity which he had designed according to Hargrave kite principles. Everything was "odd" about this machine which the Voisin brothers had built to Santos-Dumont's order; the rudder was in front and the engine behind. On October 23, more than a thousand spectators watched the Brazilian's 197 ft. flight in this new creation at Saint-Cloud, for which he won a cup. However, November 12 is the date given by Her Majesty's Stationery Office, London, in a table of "powered takeoffs and flights" quoting an official flight distance of 722 ft. by the modified "Santos-Dumont No. 14 bis," which took 21.5 seconds to cover it. Little Santos had already covered more than twice the distance required by the Aero Club.

Santos-Dumont honestly believed that he was the first man to fly in a heavier-than-air mechanically propelled machine, and some of the press, particularly the Paris "Matin," supported him in this belief. But Santos-Dumont eventually had to accept the kind of disappointment that pursues most inventors; someone else had claimed the same honor. Certainly, to Santos-Dumont went the honor of having been the first man in Europe to make a powered flight in anything but a dirigible, but the Wright brothers had already beaten him to it in America. A year later, Louis Blériot flew 604 ft. in his "Blériot VI," and on November 9, 1907, the Frenchman of English ancestry, Henry Farman, flew 3,380 ft. in his "Voisin-Farman I."

Henry Farman, who, along with the Voisin brothers and Blériot was one of Little Santos' keenest and hardest-working competitors, rapidly became one of the legendary figures of the early years of aviation. When, with Léon Delagrange, he drew the attention of his aviation-minded contemporaries to France's first flying machine, only a few people with inside knowledge knew who were the constructors in the background: two brothers, Gabriel and Charles Voisin, and their engineer Colliex. In a small factory at Billancourt-sur-Seine, set up purely to build aircraft, Farman and Delagrange's flying machines were built.

The manufacture of these machines lay in skilled hands. Some years previously both Farman and his competitor, Delagrange, had carried out practical flying tests, and the Voisin brothers had done much research on air travel. In 1904, for instance, they had designed box kites for Ernest Archdeacon. From this work they gained both theoretical and practical knowledge which helped them in the building of the later Farman and Delagrange machines. Santos-Dumont had followed similar paths. However, the Brazilian, unlike the Voisins, performed his maiden flight without extensive preliminary trials. While a fast motorboat went down the Seine, Charles Voisin sat below the box kite, which, like a modern water ski kite, was lifted up diagonally behind the boat at a height of about 32 ft. In similar experi-

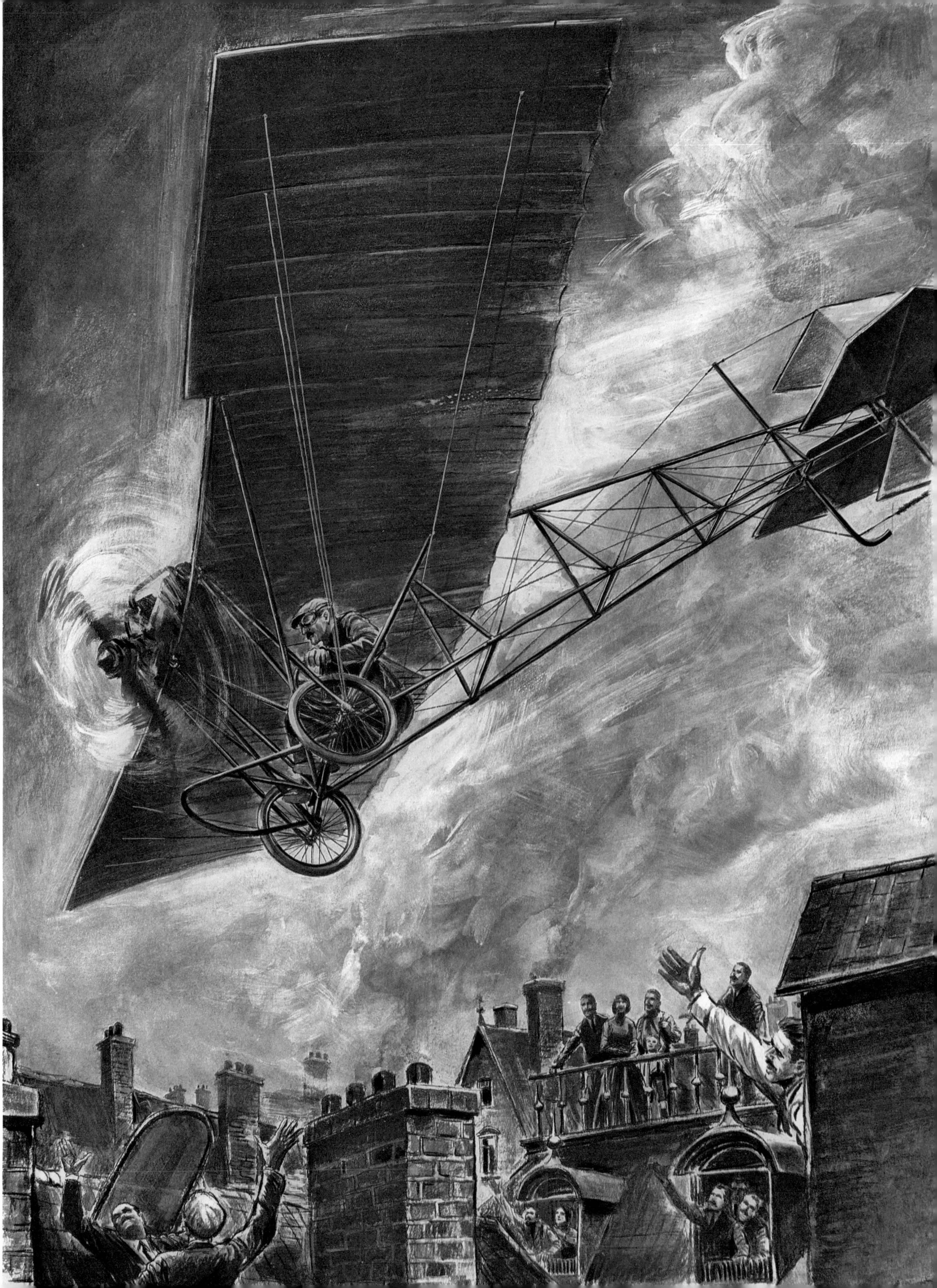

Santos-Dumont No. 20 "Demoiselle" High-Wing Monoplane (1909)

Length . . . . 26 ft. 3 in.
Wingspan . . . . 18 ft. ½ in.
Height . . . . 4 ft. 2 in.
Weight fully loaded . . . . 242 lb.
Engine: 1 water-cooled modified 2-cylinder Dutheil-Chalmers engine (or other engine)
Power: 35 h.p.

1 man crew

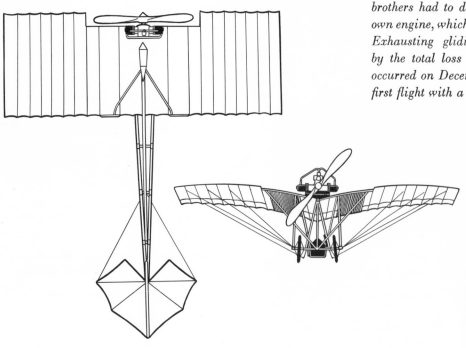

Wilbur Wright was eleven, his brother Orville seven, when their father gave them a toy rotor. The gift left such a lasting impression on the brothers that they devoted their whole life to the problem of flight in machines heavier than air. They worked hard to achieve their ambitions, and the money for their tests, sought in vain elsewhere, they ultimately provided from the proceeds of the small bicycle factory they owned. In 1899, news reached them of Langley's trials with "flying steam engines." Shortly afterwards they became acquainted with Octave Chanute who continued to encourage them in the tests they made on the sand dunes at Kitty Hawk, North Carolina. The Wright brothers had to do everything themselves; they even built their own engine, which drove the airscrew by means of bicycle chains. Exhausting gliding tests were interrupted time and again by the total loss of their glider. Their crowning achievement occurred on December 17, 1903, when Orville Wright made the first flight with a device heavier than air.

Alberto Santos-Dumont, a Brazilian, came to Paris to spend money—not as a playboy, but as an inventor with few interests beyond aviation. In 1909 he exhibited the first version of his No. 20 "Demoiselle." Bamboo, wood and linen were the main components of what was at that time the smallest and lightest aircraft in the world. "Le Petit," as the Parisians called the Brazilian, intended his creation to be a kind of "Everyman's Plane," available for the modest sum of 7,500 francs. It was ultimately placed on the market but was overshadowed by faster aircraft made by manufacturers who proved to be keener businessmen. Santos-Dumont was far more distressed, however, that he had not been the first man to fly—he was three years too late. But on November 12, 1906, he achieved the first flight in Europe with his "box kite," flying over 722 ft. in 21.5 seconds.

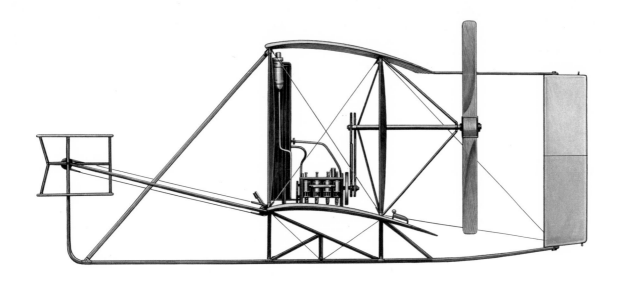

Wright "Flyer" (1903)

Length . . . . 19 ft. 9 in.
Wingspan . . . . 40 ft. 4 in.
Height . . . . 7 ft. 9 in.
Engine: 1 water-cooled 4-cylinder Wright engine

1 man crew

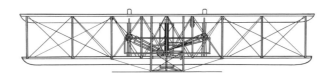

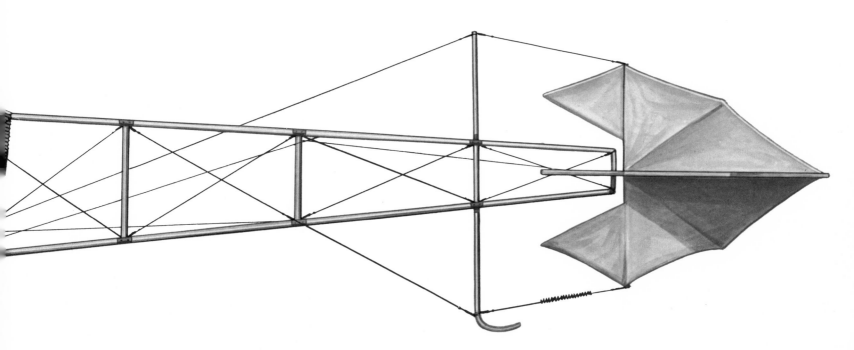

ments, using automobiles as towing vehicles, various Voisin competitors gained painful experience through crashes; even Charles Voisin crashed, but he was fortunate enough to fall more comfortably into water.

Equipped with Voisin flying machines, Farman and Delagrange set about learning to fly. Farman achieved his first leap into the air before Delagrange, not for any technical reasons, but because at an early stage he had made proper arrangements with the French Army High Command. He had, in fact, reached a very simple but important conclusion. Anyone wishing to achieve flight himself, he reasoned, needed a great deal of free space. This space was to be found on the military drill field at Issy-les-Moulineaux (where Canada was later to attempt the first jet start in aviation history). The army allowed Farman to use this training area.

The Voisin flying machines delivered to Delagrange and Farman resembled braced boxes. These biplanes, pushed by their propellers, had wings extending from a central weight-bearing chassis or fuselage. They were of a conventional 1904 design, had a wingspan of 32 ft. 11¾ in., and were powered by a 50 h.p. "Antoinette" engine. The machines quickly aroused interest, and eventually made their way to England. One of Voisin's English customers was J. T. C. Moore-Brabazon, a member of the Royal Aero Club. Moore-Brabazon traveled to Billancourt-sur-Seine, purchased a Voisin airplane, learned to handle it, and brought the "Bird of Passage," as it was christened, by boat to England. There it was soon flying over the Royal Aero Club's aerodrome on the Isle of Sheppey.

Meanwhile, Farman tenaciously and with increasing zeal practised flying over the drill field. Friends, competitors, and committees visited him, until large crowds at Issy-les-Moulineaux became the accepted thing. Mistakes were made by everybody who flew. Even long hops, which no longer followed a ballistic arc, suffered from one shortcoming which was to spur the pioneers' ambition even further: turning in the air remained a far more dangerous maneuver than making a takeoff or landing. So great was the feeling of insecurity about this maneuver that once again Ernest Archdeacon offered a prize to the first man to fly a .62 mile circular course. The sum offered was 50,000 francs. Anyone who flew, thought he could fly, or owned an airplane could compete. The prize, and fame, went to Henry Farman, who on January 13, 1908, succeeded in closing the circle on which the efforts of all airmen had been concentrated. Farman had learned so much so well in France that, with well-founded optimism, he planned to build aircraft himself, and eventually he became a world-famous aircraft manufacturer.

Long after Alberto Santos-Dumont had withdrawn from the scene, the aircraft of Henry Farman ranked among the most successful of the time. Yet earlier the Brazilian had certainly been one of the leaders in the air race, full of energy,

obsessed by his own ideals, and convinced that he was the first successful flier. He had believed fanatically in air travel, but not in the Wright brothers. In 1908, Wilbur Wright appeared in France with his "Wright A," where he immediately demonstrated the vast development of his flying skill. On the racecourse of Hunaudières, near Le Mans, he began what struck Europeans as the first simple demonstration flights. On September 16, 1908, he flew for 39 minutes and 18 seconds at Auvours, and on September 21, 1908, at the same demonstration field, he continued his flight over 41 miles in 1 hour 31 minutes and 25 seconds. As the star turn of his "tour" on December 31, he remained airborne, making turns, for 2 hours and 20 minutes at Auvours.

All Europe's best performances paled against the Wright brothers' flights. At receptions and press conferences Wilbur Wright justifiably boasted, to the great annoyance of the disappointed Santos-Dumont: "The truly operational aircraft was discovered by us—not by Mr. Santos-Dumont!" Little Santos' great dream vanished. He withdrew into his workshop near Saint-Cloud, obsessed now by the thought of aiding other aviators.

Finally, in September 1909, he exhibited to an astonished world the "Demoiselle," which bore no resemblance at all to the "14 bis," the box kite. Santos had built a genuine aircraft, and the British wrote enthusiastically about "the smallest known flying machine in the world." The braced monoplane weighed 258 lb., and its wingspan measured

On December 17, 1903, Orville Wright remained airborne for twelve seconds in a machine constructed by him and his brother, Wilbur. The aviation age which was opened on that day in Kitty Hawk, North Carolina, was soon to progress without limits.

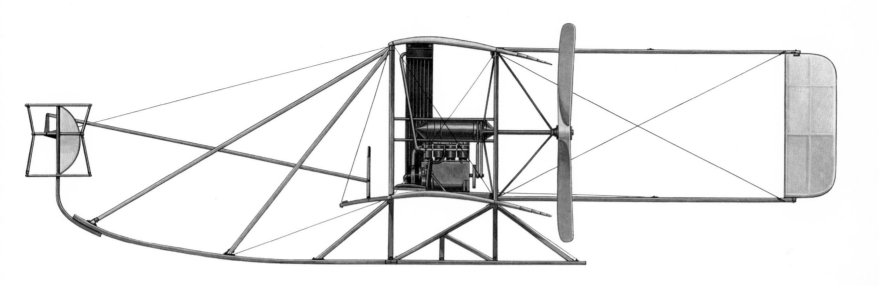

Wright "Flyer" Single-Seater Biplane (1907-09)

Length . . . . 27 ft. 10½ in.
Wingspan . . . . 39 ft. 6 in.
Height . . . . 9 ft. 4 in.
Weight fully loaded . . . . 1,036 lb.
Engine: 1 water-cooled Wright 4-cylinder in-line engine
Power: 30–40 h.p.

1 man crew

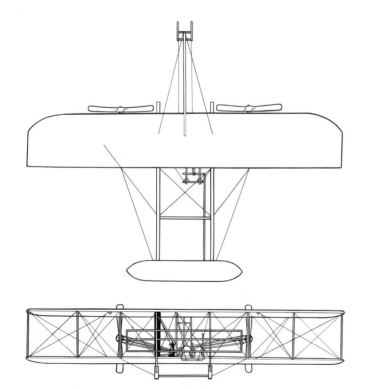

In 1908, the Wright brothers came to Europe for a flight demonstration. At Hunaudières, near Le Mans, they used their improved "Flyer" Model A to set up records which made European pilots tear their hair in envy for months. On September 7, 1908, during a demonstration for the U.S. Army at Fort Myer, Orville Wright, flying in the same model, suffered a severe accident which resulted in aviation's first passenger death—that of Lieutenant Thomas Selfridge. The U.S. Army later purchased a "Flyer" at a price of $25,000 for the Signal Corps. The contract called for a minimum speed of 40 m.p.h. The Wrights delivered a "Flyer" 2.5 m.p.h. faster than this and were paid a bonus of $5,000.

18 ft. ½ in. The Darracq water-cooled 2-cylinder "Antoinette" engine produced 24 h.p. (later 50 h.p.), and the designer had placed it above the front end of his bamboo pole machine. The pilot used his right hand to operate the elevator by a wire rope ending in a lever, and the rudder was operated in a very unusual way: the pilot pressed his back against the right or the left side of a board. During his flights, which again attracted much attention, Santos-Dumont squatted under the wing, completely in the open, between the spoked wheels of the graceful vehicle. This was how he covered the five miles from Saint-Cyr to Bue in about 5 minutes. And he rightly claimed the "world record for the shortest takeoff"— the "Demoiselle" became airborne within 230 ft.

The following year Santos-Dumont unexpectedly and voluntarily gave up his throne. Henry Farman, Gabriel Voisin, Louis Blériot, and Eugène Lefebvre were to carry on, because, the Brazilian said, "aviation no longer needs me." No one succeeded in persuading this self-willed man to alter his decision. He was then only 37. He had money and except for the Wright brothers probably had more experience than anyone else at that time in the new field of flying, which still lacked specialists and in which anyone could become anything or do anything. No one will ever know what really caused Santos-Dumont to bury himself in his country home near Paris. He spent the whole of World War I there, and was to see how the doves of which he had dreamed were transformed into birds of prey.

Santos-Dumont saw airplanes turned into giant birds. He was present at Lindbergh's gigantic reception at the Paris airport, but finally, in 1928, he returned to his Brazilian homeland. And yet there was to be no peace for the pioneer who increasingly sought solitude. A seaplane was named after him and flew alongside his ship to welcome him home, but it crashed into the sea, killing the pilot and all the passengers. Two years later, more than 50 passengers were burned to death in an aircraft, and that was more than Little Santos could bear. He attempted suicide, but friends rescued him just in time.

For every flying accident that occurred Little Santos felt a personal responsibility. He had wanted to teach men to fly, but to him flying now brought forth nothing but evil. Melancholy took hold of a man who should have been free of any cares.

In 1932, when revolution broke out in Brazil, President Vargas launched air attacks on rebels hiding out in São Paulo and in Guaruja near Santos. Alberto Santos-Dumont saw Brazilians dropping bombs on Brazilians, from heavier-than-air flying machines.

Finally, on July 23, 1932, three days after his 59th birthday, the air travel pioneer and romantic technologist put an end to the life which in his view he had devoted to a disastrous development. Alberto Santos-Dumont hanged himself.

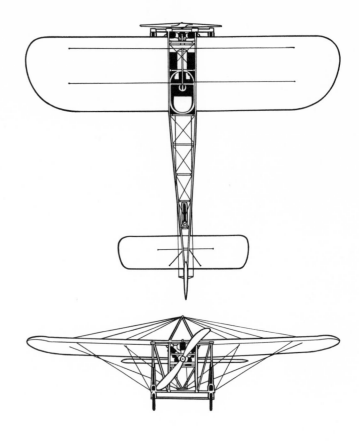

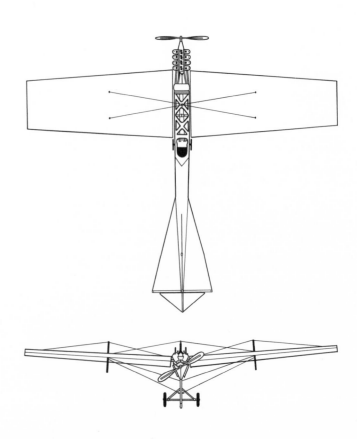

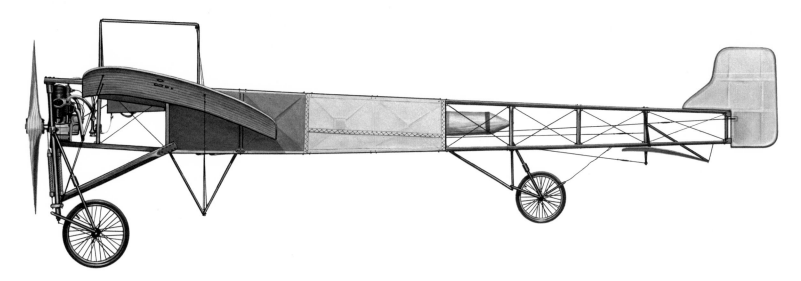

Blériot XI Single-Seater High-Wing Monoplane (1909)

Length . . . . 25 ft.
Wingspan . . . . 25 ft. 7 in.
Weight fully loaded . . . . 507 lb.
Engine: 1 air-cooled Anzani 3-cylinder engine
Power: 22–25 h.p.

1 man crew

The epoch-making machine in which Louis Blériot flew the Channel from Les Baraques, near Calais, to Dover, on July 25, 1909. It now rests in the Musée des Arts et Métiers in Paris. The flight won Blériot a prize of 4,000 francs. It also prompted a British newspaper to remark: "England's isolation is now ended for good and all." Before Blériot received his triumphant welcome in London, he had been subjected to arrest by a customs official immediately upon landing. According to his own statements, the cross-Channel pilot built more than 800 aircraft before 1914, when he took over Deperdussin's factory. Towards the end of World War I, his aircraft factories achieved amazing production figures for that time, eighteen aircraft leaving the assembly lines per day.

Levasseur "Antoinette" Aircraft (1909)

Length . . . . 37 ft.
Wingspan . . . . 46 ft.
Height . . . . 9 ft. 9 in.
Weight fully loaded . . . . 860 lb.
Engine: 1 V 8-cylinder in-line engine
Power: 50 h.p.

1 man crew

Louis Blériot's keenest rival in the competition to be the first pilot to fly from France to England was Hubert Latham. He made several attempts, but each one proved to be unsuccessful because of some small detail. His Levasseur "Antoinette" proved to be one of the best-known aircraft of its day, and it is quite possible that Levasseur machines would have been as popular as Blériot's if luck had been with Latham in his efforts to cross the English Channel. In fact, the "Antoinette" was credited with a better rate of climb than Blériot's craft.

Santos-Dumont 14 bis "Canard" (1906)

Length . . . . 42 ft. 11½ in.
Wingspan . . . . 35 ft. 5 in.
Height . . . . 11 ft. 5¾ in.
Engine: 1 Levassor "Antoinette" engine
Power: 50 h.p.

1 man crew

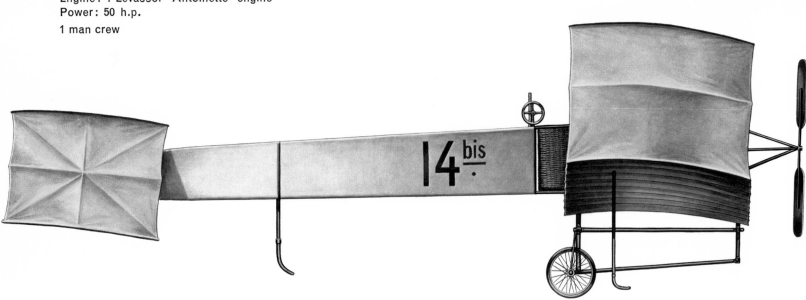

The "Canard" ("Duck") resembled a loose collection of box kites. Alberto Santos-Dumont used this model in his first attempts at flying (on the end of a cable), also for his first jump start, and for the first flight in Europe with an engine-powered heavier-than-air machine. On October 23, 1906, at Saint-Cloud, more than 1,000 spectators witnessed Santos-Dumont's long flight of over 197 ft. Paris, which was so advanced in the early history of European aviation, was pleased to have a new sensation to talk excitedly about. The Brazilian won the cup offered by Monsieur Archdeacon for the first "flight" of 82 ft.

Curtiss (1909-10)

Meanwhile the Wright brothers had many successful competitors in the United States. One of these was Glenn H. Curtiss, who as early as 1909 won the James Gordon Bennett Cup in his Curtiss "Golden Flyer." The following year he considerably improved his "pusher" aircraft.

Henry Farman Light Biplane (1910)

Henry Farman, art student, racing car driver and aircraft manufacturer, designed the first sporting and racing machine. Farman served his apprenticeship with the Voisin Brothers and before World War I he owned the largest aircraft factory in France, to which a flying school was attached.

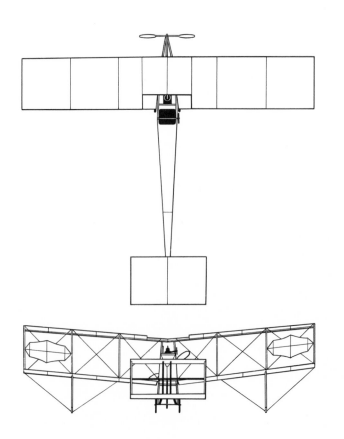

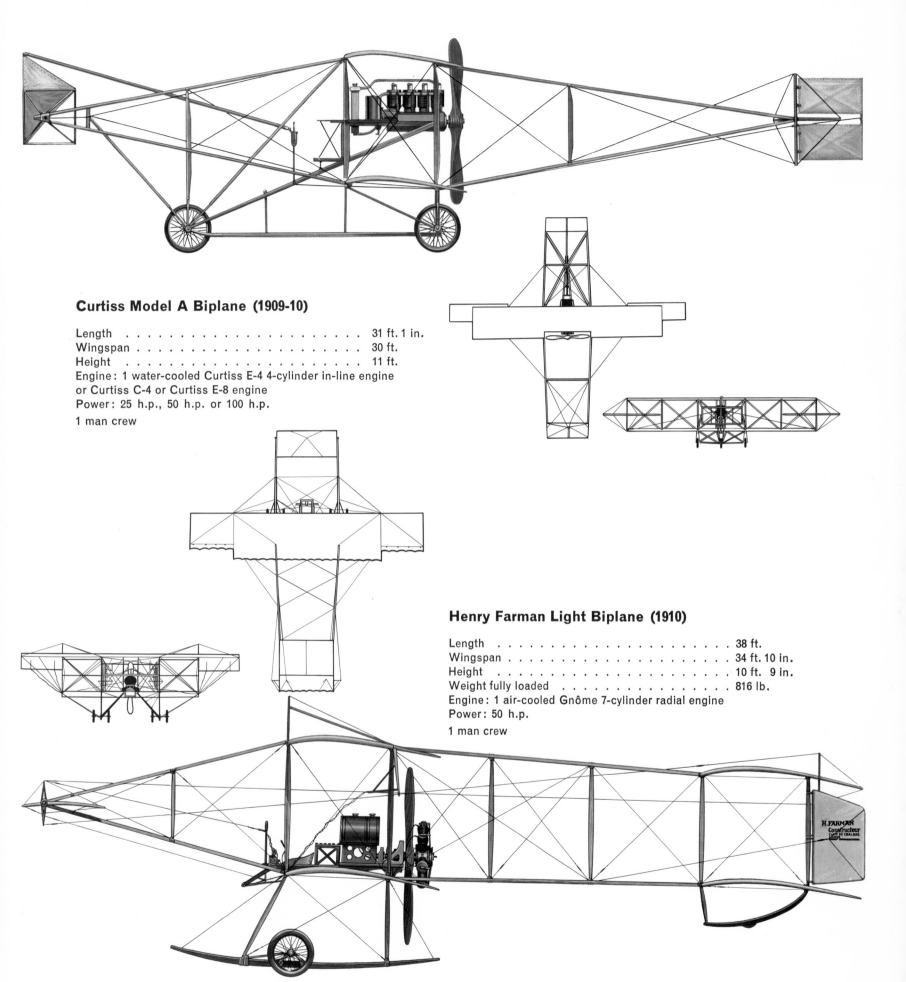

Curtiss Model A Biplane (1909-10)

Length . . . . 31 ft. 1 in.
Wingspan . . . . 30 ft.
Height . . . . 11 ft.
Engine : 1 water-cooled Curtiss E-4 4-cylinder in-line engine
or Curtiss C-4 or Curtiss E-8 engine
Power : 25 h.p., 50 h.p. or 100 h.p.

1 man crew

Henry Farman Light Biplane (1910)

Length . . . . 38 ft.
Wingspan . . . . 34 ft. 10 in.
Height . . . . 10 ft. 9 in.
Weight fully loaded . . . . 816 lb.
Engine : 1 air-cooled Gnôme 7-cylinder radial engine
Power : 50 h.p.

1 man crew

23

Santos-Dumont tested the flight properties of his first airplane, the "14 bis," by suspending the box kite under an airship and taking off with it. Later he stretched a cable and made the first flight in the "14 bis" over rollers. On November 12, 1906, Santos-Dumont, after making numerous trials, hopped 722 ft. over a meadow near Bagatelle to win the Aero Club de France award.

A time of heroes

The stage-coach era of military aviation

The progression from Sputnik to the consideration of orbiting bombs confirms an unfortunate human inclination to inspect any technical innovation for its suitability as a weapon. Man's age-old dream of flying, brought to fruition peacefully by the Wright brothers in 1903 was, in eleven short years, to develop into a nightmare in the skies of Europe. The Kitty Hawk Swallow changed into a bird of prey; the airplane had become a combat weapon. Soon England, then Germany and the other powers at war each had their stars in the form of planes and pilots. Edward Mannock stood out as England's most successful World War I fighter pilot, claiming 73 air victories. His compatriot, William ("Billy") A. Bishop, came in a close second after downing 72 opponents. René Fonck clawed 75 enemy aircraft from the skies for France; Georges Guynemer was honored for 54 victories and Charles Nungesser with 45. Eddie Rickenbacker brought the U.S.A. fame on 26 occasions. Italy's hero of the air, Francesco Baracca, shot down 34 German and Austrian airplanes, and Germany's ace, Baron Manfred von Richthofen, is credited with 80 air victories. Among the machines that made wartime aviation history were the Breguets and Bristols, Fokkers and Farnboroughs, Avros and Albatrosses, Sopwiths, Spads and Nieuports. In today's age of jets and supersonic speeds, the flying crates of World War I have almost been forgotten.

In the beginning, there were reconnaissance planes, and in August 1914, at the outbreak of World War I, England and France together possessed over 1,200 aircraft. Opposing them were 300 German aircraft, with supporting emergency help available from an armada of twelve airships. Initially, the military staffs on both sides showed only limited interest in the use of aircraft. The traditional land and sea forces' mistrust extended even to the pilots, who were still occasionally called "soldiers in neckties."

Conventional thinking dominated all strategy, and aircraft, with average maximum speeds of 74.5 m.p.h., were used principally to keep track of enemy troop movements, to reconnoiter artillery positions and targets, and to undertake the first aerial reconnaissance flights behind enemy lines. This "stage coach age" of military aviation gradually disappeared. New targets arose, and combativity and inventiveness took over; the birds of prey became fully fledged. Battles in the air were, essentially, individual duels from which arose what became proverbial in World War I fighter and combat flying: chivalry.

RECONNAISSANCE PLANES: Many aces of World War I came from the second seat. Eugène Gilbert, Oswald

Boelcke, Hermann Göring, Max Immelmann, Manfred von Richthofen, Eddie Rickenbacker and other great pilots acquired their earliest wartime experiences in the observer seats of two-seater reconnaissance planes.

These men operated cameras and rifles, and in the process they also learned to fly. They and their comrades were the pioneers who, in less than four years, transformed unprotected reconnaissance aircraft into maneuverable single-seater fighters. They were proud of their first steps with flying observer's equipment which, even today, remains essential to all air forces.

Ironically, one of the first planes to make war history was named the "Dove." The plane, designed by Igo Etrich, embodied suggestions from the naturalist Friedrich Ahlborn, and in its day it was considered extremely good-looking. The "Dove" held an altitude record of 21,522 ft., but its 120 h.p. Austro-Daimler in-line engine made it slow. Nevertheless, it achieved military fame by once being instrumental in deciding the fate of a battle.

On August 30, 1914, near Tannenberg, Flight Officer Ernst Canter of the Tactical Flying Squadron Section attached to the von François No. 1 Headquarters Staff climbed into the "Dove" with his observer and flew on a reconnaissance flight in the direction of the enemy. Circling over the Russian lines and harassed by rifle fire, Canter observed that about five miles to the rear the enemy was assembling fresh divisions for an attack. Immediately he turned back through the enemy fire and landed the "Dove" near the German lines to report the situation. Then he took off again and flew to General von François' headquarters. The second-in-command, realizing that without reinforcements he would be in a far from happy situation, urged Canter to request more men from von Hindenburg. The flight officer and his observer climbed back into the cockpit and took off, once again exposed to enemy fire. Instinctively, Canter now used knolls and groups of trees for cover.

Hindenburg had had no idea how close to defeat he was, but after issuing the necessary orders for reinforcements, the day was saved for Germany. "No flier, no Tannenberg!" the Field Marshal later remarked. But soon the machine became outdated as more powerful and faster aircraft equipped with armor were produced.

In France, the aircraft industry concentrated on building older types which had proved their efficiency. These were the lattice-tail, multi-purpose machines. Although this may have been prudent, it was not conducive to progress. Blériot XI-2, Farman MF-7, and Voisin LA S type 5 were the most familiar planes to France's pilots. French designers —and at first English designers too—worked on the principle that all that was needed for flying was a pair of wings, an engine and an undercarriage, with the inevitable tangle of wires. In front of this tangle sat the pilot in a sheet metal bath tub with high sides. Even when the sheet metal bath became more spacious, the crew more numerous and the engines more powerful, the traditional lattice-work structure supporting the tail surfaces was still part of the design.

During the early months of the war, lattice-tail aircraft with pusher propellers were used by England's Flying Corps, and the Vickers FB 5, the R.A.F. 2b and R.A.F. FE 8 flew on countless successful missions until 1917. At the outset of hostilities, however, British engineers had begun to direct their efforts toward producing planes that were suitable as fighters. The reconnaissance aircraft in service were predominantly two-seaters. With them the pusher propeller proved an advantage: it gave the aircraft an unimpeded field of defensive fire ahead.

Germany's aircraft industry soon imposed upon its disorderly variety of designs a fundamental classification system. Planes were distinguished as A, B and C types. Unarmed monoplanes ranked as A types, unarmed biplanes as B types, and then, as the arming of aircraft developed, all reconnaissance planes with one or more seats and machine gun armament were designated as C types. In the meantime, this system did little or nothing to alter the colorful variety of aircraft designs to be seen in the skies.

Albatros B-II came to the fore as a reconnaissance plane and a trainer, and in the winter of 1915, Schubert, the Albatros engineer, produced the streamlined two-seater C-III. This pure reconnaissance plane was equipped with one fixed (later synchronised) machine gun for the pilot and a movable machine gun for the observer; it could also carry a small bomb load. Also appearing on the front were the DFW C-V, AEG C-IV, and LVG C-2. At that time no one in Germany had given the slightest thought to the rationalization of designs in the interests of faster output.

Back in 1910, the chiefs of the Berlin Imperial Staff had considered themselves far-sighted when they made Captain de le Roi responsible for setting up a military flying school. Yet not until October 8, 1916, was all the German flying strength unified as the "German Air Combat Force." Nevertheless, the conservative approach and arrogance of the tradition-steeped military proved a great hindrance to the country's air power. Ironically, the inspection of the flying troops was carried out by the German Railways Directorate under Major Siegert.

Siegert, spurred on by Max Immelmann and Oswald Boelcke, finally agreed to combine individual fighter pilots into units of nine aircraft. This led in 1918 to the fighter squadron composed of four units, but it came too late.

There is one notable point about all the reconnaissance aircraft built during World War I. These were always used as tactical, bomber, and fighter planes, and it is rather unjust that fame usually accompanied the bombers and the fighters.

BOMBERS: When Colonel William Mitchell consolidated his bomber squadrons into the First Brigade in July 1918, he created a strategic arm which 22 years later was to become the famed bomber squadrons of World War II. The American colonel was influenced by his colleague, General Hugh "Boom" Trenchard, whose concept was to transform aircraft into an offensive arm through bomb loads.

"Constant and heavy bomb attacks on the Ruhr area," Trenchard told Mitchell, "must gradually paralyze the Ruhr's industry. That would, however, come about only if everything flying were under a single command—in the long run it's impossible for flying units to remain under Army Command." The General was firmly convinced that the age of the individualist in the air was over.

Colonel Mitchell carried Trenchard's thoughts a stage further: "It should be possible to fly whole infantry divisions across the static trenches from the front to the rear of the enemy and to land them there by parachute," he stated. "Large aircraft could each carry in ten men. Once behind the enemy lines the troops would consolidate and attack. Tactical aircraft would then pin the enemy down until the operation was concluded." The first operation of this kind

Etrich A-II "Taube" ("Dove")
Reconnaissance Aircraft (1914)

Length . . . . 32 ft. 3¾ in.
Wingspan . . . . 47 ft. 1 in.
Height . . . . 10 ft. 4 in.
Weight fully loaded . . . . 2,094 lb.
Engine: 1 water-cooled Austro-Daimler 6-cylinder in-line engine
Power: 120 h.p.

1–2 man crew

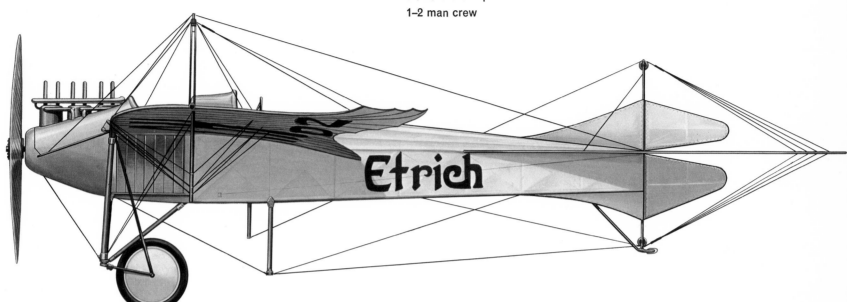

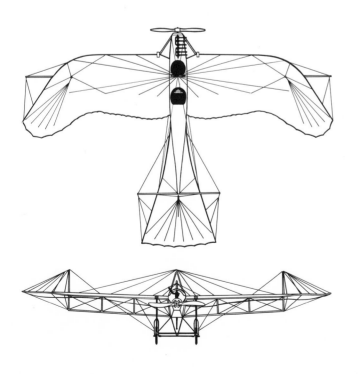

Like the Wright brothers and a large number of other contemporary aviation enthusiasts, the Austrian, Igo Etrich, took his lead from Otto Lilienthal, and made his first experiments with gliding wings. Then a Hamburg professor, Friedrich Ahlborn, drew his attention to the flight properties and shape of the Zanonia palm seed. In 1909 Etrich added altitude and lateral controls and, in 1913, the two-seater "Dove" was in reconnaissance service for the German army. It was considered by many to be the most stylish design of its day compared with the lattice-work tail structure of French, English and American planes. In 1910, the manufacturing rights were acquired by Edmund Rumpler, who dispensed with the name of Etrich. Hellmuth Hirth and Gunther Plüschow ("The Tsind-tau Fliers") first made their names as pilots with a "Dove."

was planned for the winter of 1919, but by then the war was over. Its end had also delayed the birth of the paratroops.

Large aircraft, conceived by U.S. strategists as troop carriers, played only a limited experimental part as bombers. The bombers which Mitchell wished to unify as strategic air fleets were already firmly established parts of all air forces at the time he reached his conclusions. As in the case of the fighter and the reconnaissance plane, the bomber had developed from the unpretentious all-purpose aircraft of the war's early days. The slow, two-seater reconnaissance planes had to rely on the men's use of hand grenades or stones. Later in the war, on July 13, 1917, Germany's "England Squadron," commanded by Captain Brandenburg, made a daylight raid on London in large twin-engined aircraft, the Kaiser and his warlords' opposition to bomb-launching airships having been disregarded.

Before airplanes had achieved their later maturity in World War I, military powered balloons had been designed to carry bombs. This was described in detail by First Lieutenant Hermann Hoernes, editor of the three-volume "Aviation Book," published in 1912.

"As with torpedoes in the Navy," the book states, "the Army's heavy artillery will at some future date extend its powers of destruction through air torpedoes launched downwards from flying vehicles. War waged in this way will be more humane than it is today, because in fact only the enemy's means of resistance will be destroyed, whereas one virtually unavoidable side-effect of an artillery bombardment from the surrounding country is the unintentional destruction of other buildings.

"Suitable means of destruction to be dropped from an airborne vehicle are the most powerful explosives, inflammable materials and any noxious chemical substances such as make any continued human presence in the premises impossible, and render unusable any foodstuffs or forage coming in contact with them. On technical aeronautical grounds, the amount of weapons carried by the vehicles will be strictly limited.

"The following technical requirements must be met if the airship is to perform its duties:

a) it must be able to travel at a height to protect it as far as possible from anti-aircraft fire;

b) it must be able to drop a volume of weapons sufficient to achieve its objective;

c) it must further have sufficient ballast available to ensure a safe return and a safe landing.

"The ballast available to a combat airship must therefore be divided up as follows: *combat ballast* to drop onto the target, *ballast* to be dropped so as to reach a safe altitude at takeoff, *maneuvering ballast* for the journey out and back, and *landing ballast*. The number of explosives to be dropped in order to achieve a destructive effect only experience will show.

"Dropping its weapons will cause the airship to rise; the exact height of the rise can easily be determined from the law of ballast effects. For dropping high explosive charges, the larger and heavier airship is better than the smaller and lighter one, because of the relatively smaller upward change in its center of gravity position. It must be affirmed that shells will very accurately hit their targets if correctly handled."

The Austrian lieutenant's theories that war conducted in this way was more humane may or may not have been taken as gospel when airships from the Zeppelin and Schütte-Lanz factories flew across the Channel to launch bombs on England. In any case, these raids, the first to produce a London blackout, did not, any more than the far more disastrous ones in World War II, diminish the British people's morale in the slightest; on the contrary, by arousing their anger the attacks merely strengthened Britain's will to win.

Captain Peter Strasser, Commander of Germany's England Airship Department, was at first convinced of his fleet's strategic importance. He did not accept Hoernes' views and believed that greater advantages would accrue from reconnaissance flights and long-range naval reconnaissances of up to 24 hours' duration. But in the end he admitted that the Austrian had a point, and in August 1915, the raids on London started—always conducted by groups of airships at night and always at new moon, so that the English soon knew exactly when to expect them.

In his book "The History of Flight," Arthur Gordon noted that the most successful German airship commander was Heinrich Mathy, who flew 120 missions, thirteen of which were attacks on England. In his LZ 13 he appeared over London on September 8, 1915, and dropped about two tons of bombs. It was the heaviest attack of the war and, according to German claims, caused fires and destruction amounting to £500,000. During a later raid on October 1, 1916, Mathy was killed.

After 1917 airship attacks became gradually less frequent, despite the resistance of the Kaiser, who wished them to cease entirely. Then on August 5, 1918, the famous airship leader Strasser crashed with his flagship LZ 70, and any further attempt at using airships as bombers was abandoned. Thus a short and uneven chapter in the history of aviation was closed.

Airships had little effect upon the art of war, except for some progress in the field of bomb development. Actually, there was only a short step in development between the two 4 lb. bombs which were dropped by hand on the outskirts of Paris on August 13, 1914, and the 660 lb. bombs which were released mechanically from bomb racks toward the end of the war. Similarly brief was the stage between the first British Vickers FB 5 lattice-tailed planes dating from

German Flight Officer Ernst Canter saved the day for von Hindenburg on August 30, 1914. Canter and his observer, Lieutenant Mertens, flew the Etrich "Dove" through enemy fire and returned to report the troop movements of the Russians. This enabled Field Marshal von Hindenburg to change his plans —and ultimately to win the Battle of Tannenberg.

Albatros B-I Reconnaissance Aircraft (1914-16)

Length . . . . 25 ft. 6 in.
Wingspan . . . . 42 ft. 6 in.
Height . . . . 10 ft. 4 in.
Weight fully loaded . . . . 1,874 lb.
Engine : 1 water-cooled Hiero 6-cylinder engine or Mercedes engine
Power : 145 h.p. or 120 h.p.

2 man crew

The Albatros B-1 was the first product of the "Österreichische Albatros-Werke," an Austrian subsidiary of the German firm of the same name. The prototype closely followed the German original—the B-2—the major differences between the two versions being that the Austrian Albatros had slightly cambered wings and was generally fitted with engines of Austrian manufacture. Later on, Professor Richard Knoller designed further wings which allegedly gave the craft better aerodynamic qualities. From 1915 onwards, the B-1 was equipped with a machine gun for the observer, making it very similar to the German Albatros C-1. The Austrian Albatros was used by the pilots of the Imperial and Royal Austro-Hungarian tactical air squadrons on the various Balkan fronts.

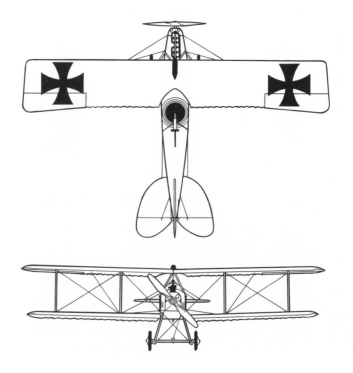

30

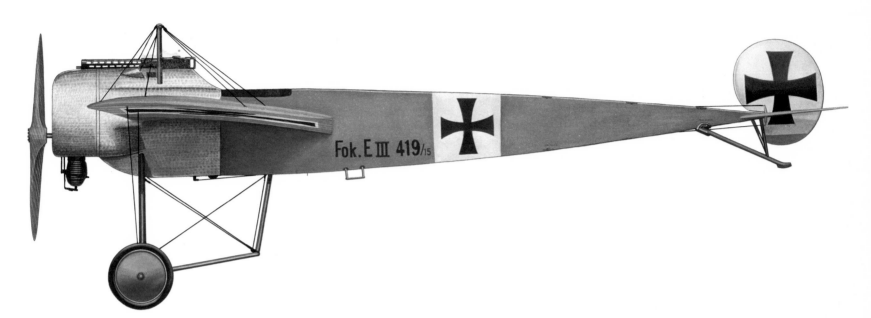

Fokker E-III (M 14) Fighter Monoplane (1915-16)

Length . . . . 22 ft. 7⅓ in.
Wingspan . . . . 31 ft. 3 in.
Height . . . . 7 ft. 10½ in.
Weight fully loaded . . . . 1,345 lb.
Engine: 1 air-cooled Oberursel U 1 rotary engine (standard)
Power: 100 h.p.

1 man crew

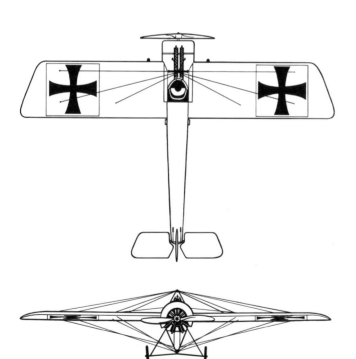

In August 1915, the Fokker E-III began to support and complement the E-I and E-II versions on the German Western Front, and later it replaced them. This single-seater fighter, equipped with one or two fixed Spandau machine guns synchronized to fire through the propeller blades, proved the best of the three E models. Some 500 of these planes were built. Allegedly, Morane-Saulnier contributed indirectly to this aircraft. Fokker and his construction chief, Kreutzer, designed the prototype of the E models, the M 5, from the Morane-Saulnier H monoplane. British test pilots, however, made an interesting discovery, when on April 8, 1916, an undamaged Fokker E-III made an emergency landing behind their lines. When tested, its highest speed was 6.2 m.p.h. less than had been assessed.

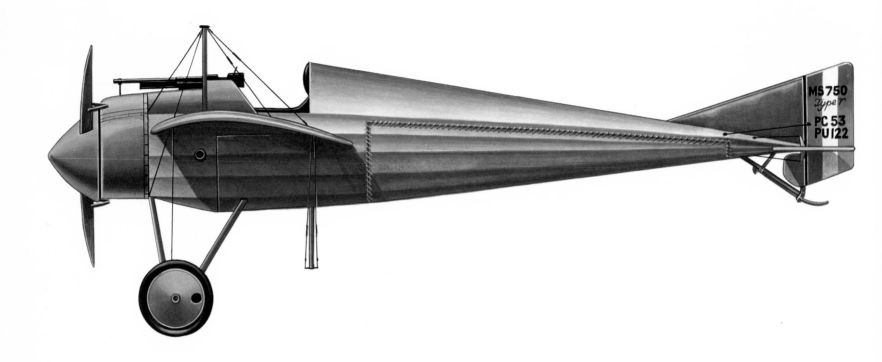

Morane-Saulnier N Fighter Monoplane (1915-16)

Length . . . . 21 ft. 11½ in.
Wingspan . . . . 27 ft. 3   in.
Height . . . . 8 ft. 2   in.
Weight fully loaded . . . . 970 lb.
Engine: 1 air-cooled Le Rhône rotary engine
Power: 110 h.p.

1 man crew

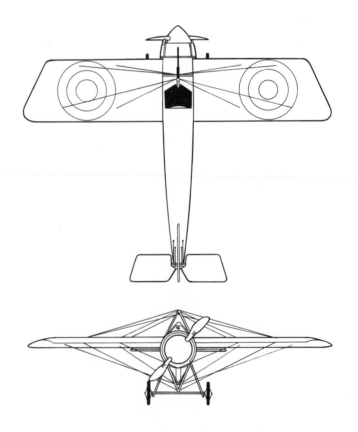

In 1914, Captain de Vergnettes, the commander of the French squadron M.S. 23, made a wise decision. He sent Roland Garros to Villacoublay where he designed a new single-seater fighter with Saulnier. In March 1915, Garros brought Morane-Saulnier's N model to the front. It carried unusual armament; its fixed Hotchkiss machine gun fired, without synchronization, through the propeller blades, and the airscrew was covered with steel bullet deflectors. There was considerable skepticism at first, but Garros provided the most effective argument when, in April 1915, flying in his Morane-Saulnier N, he shot down an enemy plane. Both the British Royal Flying Corps and the Russian 19th Air Squadron were equipped with Morane-Saulnier monoplane fighters.

1915 and such giants as the Handley-Page 0/400 with twin engines, or the four-engined Sikorsky "Murumetz." Since war, like necessity, appears to be the mother of invention, the potential operational uses of aircraft, their further development and the vigorous drive for their improvement can also be said to have been subject to this same law.

Despite the high hopes of military leaders in all the countries at war, the effectiveness of the bombers used so far had been disappointing. Designs conceived before the war, such as Hirth's 1913 six-engined transatlantic aircraft, were either never completed or had proved unsatisfactory. The failings observed in the process of developing individual reconnaissance aircraft applied equally to bombers: there was no design rationalization. In Germany, all too often bribery won preference for one bomber design over a second and perhaps better one. More than a thousand different bomber projects were thought out and developed for widely differing purposes by the various powers at war. Particularly notable were Britain's legendary Handley-Page 0/400 and Germany's giant VGO I-RML.1 machines. The latter, stated British historian G.W. Haddow, were "the biggest ever to have attacked England—and that applies to both World Wars."

It was rather a rash undertaking, some eleven years after the Wright brothers' first powered flight, for the Germans to attempt to build aircraft with three or four engines and with a wingspan of up to 138 ft. 5 in. The origin of these Staaken designs, executed by the Versuchsbau GmbH. Gotha-Ost, actually went back to pre-war days. As early as the summer of 1913, Robert Bosch, an electricity magnate, had provided Hellmuth Hirth and Gustav Klein with the financial backing to build a transatlantic aircraft. The greatest obstacle to the scheme was the unreliability of the engines that were then available, a weakness which was to affect the fullest utilization of large-scale aircraft until long after the war.

The outbreak of hostilities in 1914 had put an end to the well-advanced plans of Hirth and Klein, but Count Zeppelin took a fresh look at the fliers' scheme. As a result the count began plans for a mammoth plane which could drop a 1,000 lb. bomb on London's docks. This, he thought hopefully, would destroy all the ships lying at anchor there. Meanwhile, the German Naval High Command had managed to get its large finger into Count Zeppelin's pie, and all the factory owner's plans were countermanded. It was Zeppelin's close friend and military opponent, Admiral von Tirpitz, Head of the Imperial Fleet, who had clamped down on the count's project. However, this merely prompted Zeppelin, together with Hirth, Robert Bosch and his director, Klein, to reassess the validity of their concepts for large aircraft. Finally, the aviation chief and the Navy Shipbuilding Department opposed the Ministry of War, and Bosch and Zeppelin founded the Versuchsbau GmbH. Gotha-Ost.

Despite all the obstacles the Ministry of War placed in the way, the team carried out its planning agreement by December 1914. The team included such men as Alexander Baumann, Hellmuth Hirth, Claudius Dornier and Dr. Adolph Rohrbach. They had worked so fast that when they were ready for the Maybach engines these were nowhere in sight. The VGO I's design and construction turned into an out-and-out competition between the men in Gotha-Ost and Friedrichshafen, who were convinced that their ideas were right, and the opposing Prussian military administrators in Berlin.

The latter tried to hinder the conclusion of the project further by ordering the removal from the factory of all workers in uniform. This had only a temporary effect, and on April 11, 1915, the VGO I-RML. 1, piloted by Hellmuth Hirth, triumphantly took off on its maiden flight.

The crew consisted of two pilots in a huge open cockpit, a commander, simultaneously acting as navigator, and three flight mechanics—one for each engine. Communication between the men proved tricky. The crew worked with bell signals (developed for later versions into a kind of mechanical telegraph) or held up slates on which orders were chalked. Hirth preferred to speak with his hands. The engine arrangement was a combination of the two systems known at the time: a tractor propeller at the front tip of the fuselage, and two pusher propellers to the left and right behind the wings.

The design of the first VGO's forward center of gravity and cellular construction introduced something new: the undercarriage consisted of two twin wheels on both the left- and right-hand sides. These were attached to the engine gondolas by tubular struts, while two parallel wheels in front of them made up the nose undercarriage. A tail skid aided stability at takeoff and landing; and when the plane was on the ground, the unsupported tail protruded in the air. Later Staaken versions changed back from a nose to a tail wheel. (In the Second World War, Hitler declared the nose wheel an "American invention," forbade its use, and thus for years mass production of the first jet fighters, which were also planned for a nose wheel, was delayed.) The main source of worry in the first large-sized German aircraft was the engines. They derived from successful airship types, but suffered from extreme overheating at takeoff when under full load. The designers were finally obliged to use less powerful but more reliable engines.

On June 6, 1915, the VGO I took off on its first long-distance flight from Gotha to Friedrichshafen, where it was to be equipped with new engines. Six months later, on December 15, despite these new engines the aircraft failed to reach its destination. The giant plane, with Hirth commanding and Hans Vollmöller and Willi Mann as pilots, ran into a snowstorm over the Thuringian Forest. A leak in the oil system put both outer engines out of action: the 240 h.p. of the remaining engine was not enough to keep the

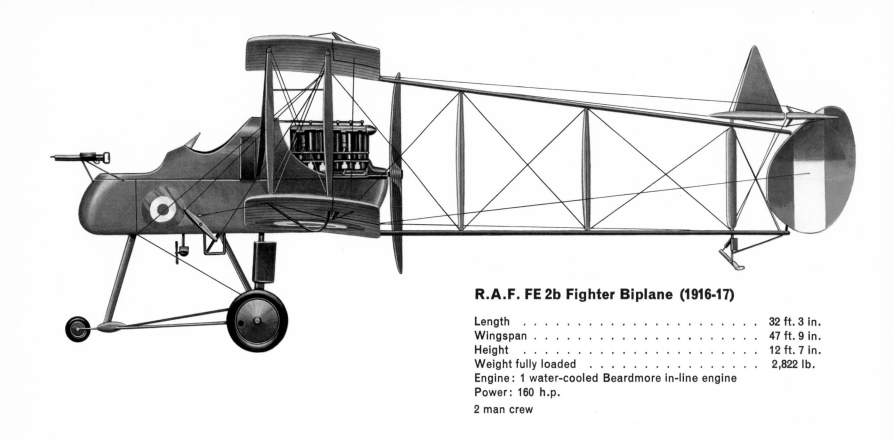

R.A.F. FE 2b Fighter Biplane (1916-17)

Length . . . . 32 ft. 3 in.
Wingspan . . . . 47 ft. 9 in.
Height . . . . 12 ft. 7 in.
Weight fully loaded . . . . 2,822 lb.
Engine: 1 water-cooled Beardmore in-line engine
Power: 160 h.p.

2 man crew

De Havilland DH 2 Fighter Biplane (1915-17)

Length . . . . 25 ft. 2½ in.
Wingspan . . . . 28 ft. 3 in.
Height . . . . 9 ft. 6½ in.
Weight fully loaded . . . . 1,433 lb.
Engine: 1 air-cooled Gnôme-Monosoupape (single-valve) radial
engine
Power: 100 h.p.

1 man crew

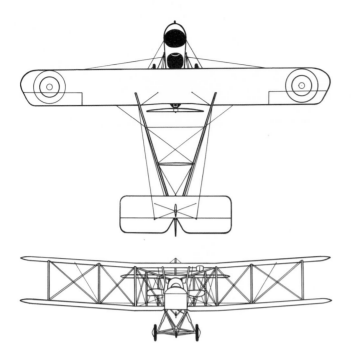

At the outbreak of World War I, the Royal Flying Corps ordered a total of twelve R.A.F. FE 2b aircraft. All saw front line service from early in 1916 until the autumn of 1917. In all, 2,190 of them were built. Events proved that the FE 2b, despite its pusher propeller, was superior to the German Fokker monoplanes. Its top speed of 91 m.p.h. made it appreciably faster than the Fokker.

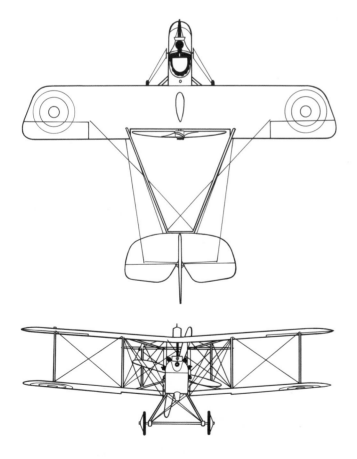

The first prototype of the De Havilland DH 2 reached the front on July 26, 1915, and immediately ran out of luck. On August 9, the aircraft, piloted by Captain R. Maxwell-Pike, disappeared behind the German lines. The pilot had been wounded and the DH 2 was in German hands. Right up to the end of the war experiments were made with various engines, and for a short time, DH 2's were used experimentally against Zeppelins. Though its fame was short-lived, it was still in service until 1918.

At the end of 1915, the German Fokker E-III with its synchronized machine guns competed favorably with the British De
Havilland DH 2. During World War I, the reconnaissance plane
developed into a weapon for attack and its pilots into heroes.

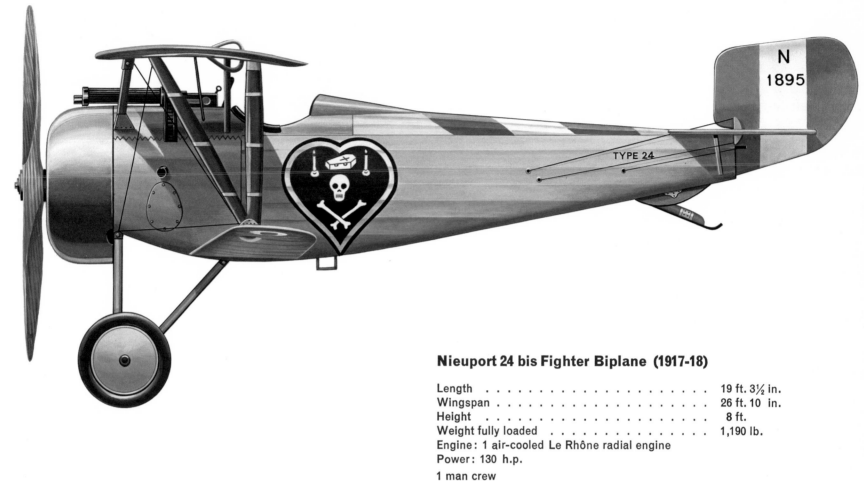

Nieuport 24 bis Fighter Biplane (1917-18)

Length . . . . 19 ft. 3½ in.
Wingspan . . . . 26 ft. 10 in.
Height . . . . 8 ft.
Weight fully loaded . . . . 1,190 lb.
Engine: 1 air-cooled Le Rhône radial engine
Power: 130 h.p.

1 man crew

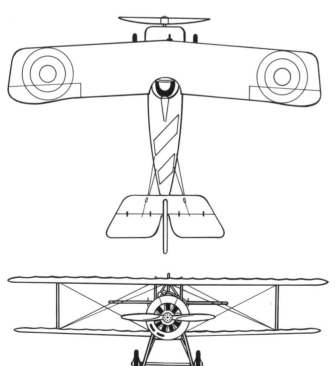

The 24 bis proved to be a very popular aircraft. When it was replaced by the technically superior Spad, many French fighter pilots stuck firmly to their Nieuports. One of them was France's fighter ace, Charles Nungesser, who won the majority of his 45 air victories with a 24 bis. In fact, this aircraft had such a reputation for safety, that as late as November 1917, the U.S. Air Force ordered 140 of them from the "Société des Etablissements Nieuport" at Issy-les-Moulineaux, in order to be put to use as trainers.

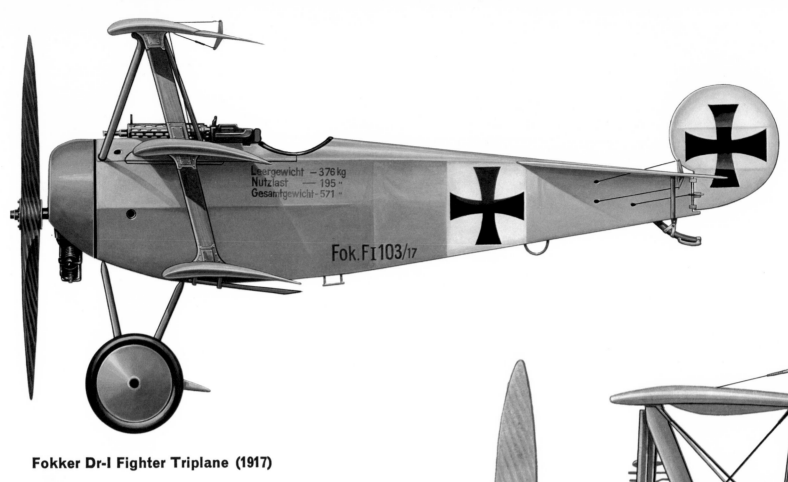

Fokker Dr-I Fighter Triplane (1917)

Length . . . . 18 ft. 11⅛ in.
Wingspan . . . . 23 ft. 7 in.
Height . . . . 9 ft. 8½ in.
Weight fully loaded . . . . 1,279 lb.
Engine: 1 air-cooled Le Rhône rotary engine (longer version with Oberursel UR III engine)
Power: 110 h.p.

1 man crew

When the British Sopwith "Camel" and the French Spad S 7 threatened to win air superiority on the Western Front, the German High Command came up with a new Fokker aircraft— the triplane Dr-I. In developing it, Fokker and his construction chief, Reinhold Platz, had deliberately sacrificed maneuverability and power of climb for higher speed. The "ugly duckling" proved itself in the Jasta Fighter Squadron of "Red Baron" Manfred von Richthofen. In 21 days they shot down 22 enemy aircraft. The Dr-I had made a breakthrough.

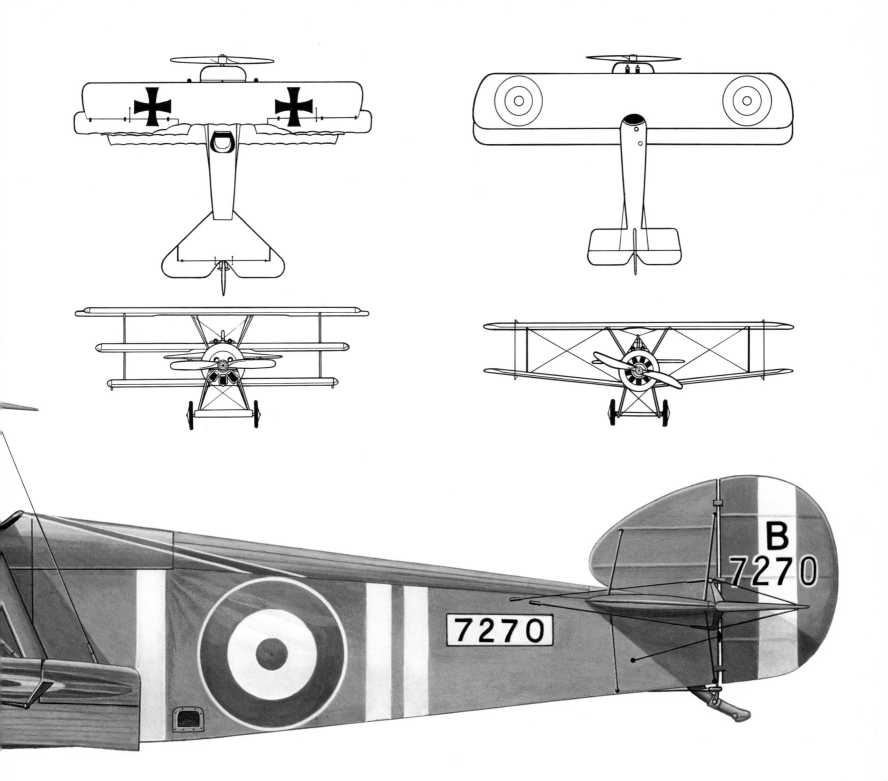

Sopwith F 1 "Camel" Fighter Biplane (1917-18)

Length . . . . 18 ft. 9 in.
Wingspan. . . . . 28 ft.
Height . . . . 8 ft. 6⅓ in.
Weight fully loaded . . . . 1,455 lb.
Engine: 1 air-cooled Clerget radial engine (or other engines)
Power: 130 h.p.

1 man crew

The Sopwith "Pup" was to have 5,490 modified and considerably improved successors. The legendary F 1 "Camel" got its nickname from the hump on the nose in which twin machine guns were mounted. In the hands of experienced pilots, the "Camel" gave superior maneuverability and fighting power, but beginners tended to overturn the aircraft which possessed some longitudinal instability. The Sopwith "Camel" which, incidentally, was designed as the world's first carrier-based aircraft, was regarded as the Allies' most successful achievement.

20,992 lb. plane airborne in the storm. The pilots managed to land the plane in a clearing without harm to the crew, but with the total loss of the plane.

There were other accidents: during a takeoff at Schneidemühl one plane encountered heavy gusts of wind and somersaulted; another machine wrecked its undercarriage when landing at Königsberg; and on March 10, 1917, the last VGO I version (later re-named the RML.1) was destroyed at Staaken. On that day Hans Vollmöller was first pilot, Curt Kuring copilot, and the plane was commanded by Gustav Klein. They made a perfect takeoff; the aircraft rose easily and began to circle round the airfield, when suddenly there was an explosion. Parts of the port engine spun to the ground and the airscrew stopped. The pilots attempted to correct the list to the left by use of the controls; the plane responded, righted itself and appeared about to land parallel with the main hangar. Kuring then realized that a defect in the control system (noticed and reported by him three days earlier) had not been corrected. The rudder jammed, and the lateral controls' cables running outside along the fuselage no longer responded.

Vollmöller stopped the other two engines and the plane made a sharp right turn. Kuring released his safety belt and in a flash had climbed beneath the cockpit to free the jammed cables. But he was too late: the VGO I crashed into the main hangar door. Vollmöller was killed instantaneously, and Klein died a few hours later. Kuring survived and recovered sufficiently from a fractured skull to rejoin his Naval Fighter Squadron later on.

Count Zeppelin died two days before the loss of his VGO I. Thus within three days German aviation had lost three of its leading men.

Other designers and pilots continued with the task. Siemens-Schuckert had an R-VIII designed with six engines and a wingspan of 157 ft. 5¾ in. It was intended that the aircraft would become a milestone in history, but it never flew. The Russian genius, Sikorsky, renowned later for his Pacific Clipper and helicopter designs in America, built 80 four-engined bombers which saw successful service between 1915 and 1917. As late as 1920, Staaken produced the E 4/20, a four-engined high-wing monoplane in which Kuring achieved a maximum speed of nearly 140 m.p.h., a figure which at that time was astonishing for a machine of the kind.

The end of the war brought an end to Germany's aerial developments for many years. While for a long time the Ministry of War in Berlin had opposed a heavy bomber—just as Hitler was later to reject a new jet fighter in favor of lightning bombers—the British Admiralty proved far more receptive to experiments.

In 1915, plans were being made in England for operational bombing warfare. The Short factories at Belfast were assigned the production of a suitable combat bomber, and they came through with 83 machines bearing their name. "Short" aircraft were powered by Rolls-Royce "Eagle" V engines giving 250 h.p.; the wingspan measured 83 ft., the length was 45 ft. and the height 15 ft. The maximum speed (78 m.p.h.) and the rate of climb (6,500 ft. in 21.5 minutes) were considered unsatisfactory; furthermore the bomb load of 926 lb. was light. One strategic bomber unit, set up in the spring of 1916, was equipped with "Shorts" toward the end of that year. In 1917 they were replaced by the fabulous Handley-Page 0/400's.

The Handley-Page was an excellent bomber. Although only 80 of these machines were produced, less than the "Shorts," the 0/400 won itself a place of honor in the history of aviation. The biplane was powered by two 250 h.p. Rolls-Royce V engines, its wingspan was 100 ft., its length 62 ft. 9 in. and its height 22 ft. At low altitudes the Handley-Page 0/400 had a maximum speed of 100 m.p.h., and its range exceeded 745 miles. A four man crew sat in the cockpit, and for protection they were provided with four or five movable Lewis guns. The bomb load was 1,984 lb.

Disarmament at the end of the war saw the end of the Handley-Page 0/400 as well as many other designs. However, Britain, France, the United States, Italy and Switzerland continued to pursue aircraft ideas brought forth by the war, and they also began designing larger planes for peacetime use.

Today's giants, the U.S.A.F. strato-bombers and the projected supersonic passenger airliners, have a substantial ancestry.

FIGHTER PLANES: Total war in the air came with the fighter planes. Combat troops took a dim view of being watched as if on G.H.Q. maps, and soon fighter cover was employed to protect reconnaissance planes. Previously, a low-flying aircraft had often been hit by well-aimed machine gun bursts, or even by a good shot from a quick rifle marksman.

The excessive lengths to which the protective measure of fighter cover could be carried is exemplified by a British R.A.F. BE-2, which on February 7, 1916, was accompanied by no less than twelve fighters while on a reconnaissance flight.

By February 1916, the idea of the merely protective role of the single- or two-seater escort gave way to a new concept of the accompanying fighter. As an attacking combat weapon, the fighter became king of all aircraft. The days when pilots shot at each other with pistols or when their

A British Royal Air Force SE 5a in a dogfight with a German Fokker Dr-I triplane. The era of chivalry with its so-called "Knights of the Air" began in World War I.

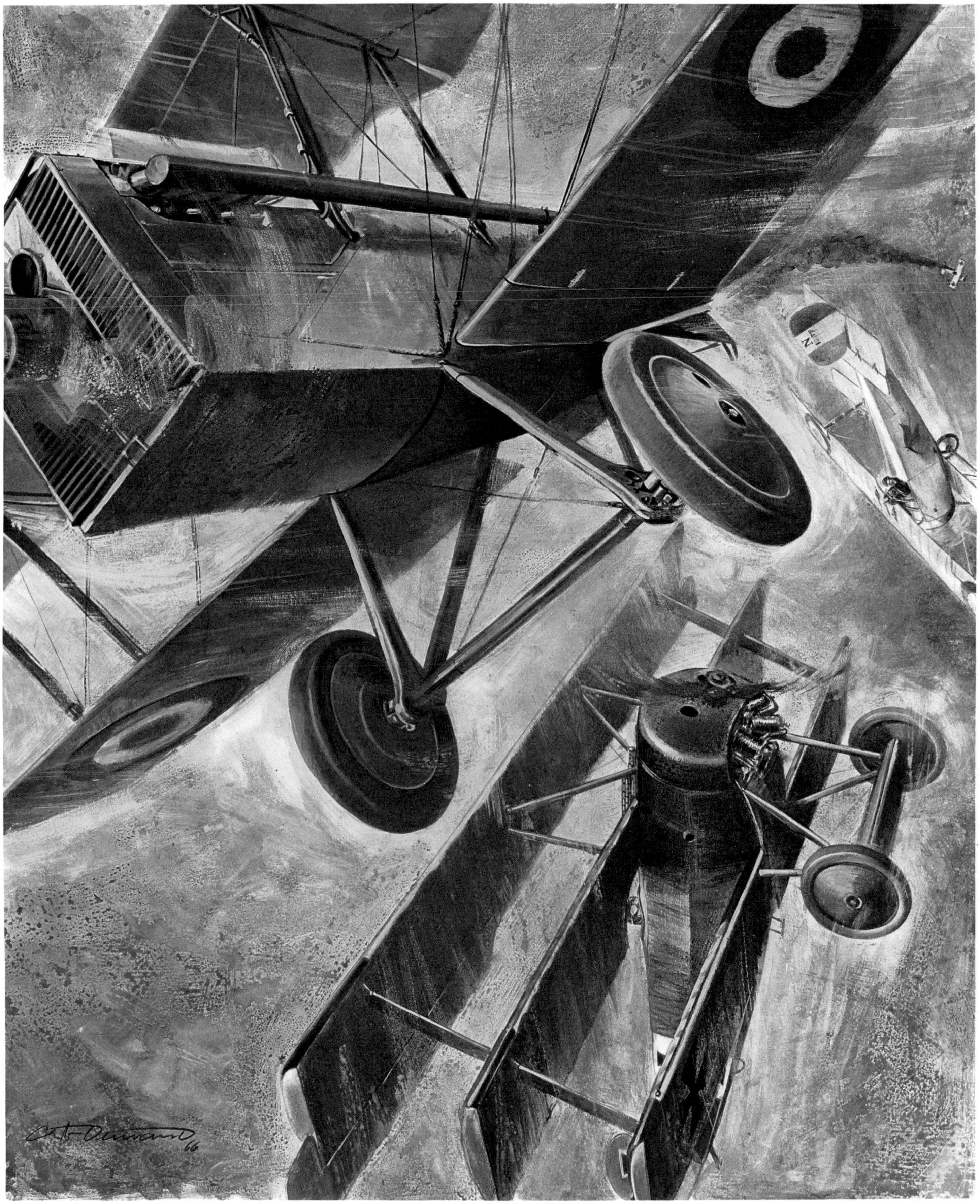

Albatros D-Va Fighter Biplane (1917-18)

Length . . . . 24 ft.   5/8 in.
Wingspan . . . . 29 ft. 8¼ in.
Height . . . . 8 ft. 10¼ in.
Weight fully loaded . . . . 2,072 lb.
Engine : 1 water-cooled Mercedes D IIIa in-line engine
Power : 180 h.p.

1 man crew

This fast and maneuverable aircraft was built in vast numbers, and was in service from June 1917, until the end of World War I. It was an advanced design, but the biplane's lower wings had a tendency to snap, particularly in dive attacks.

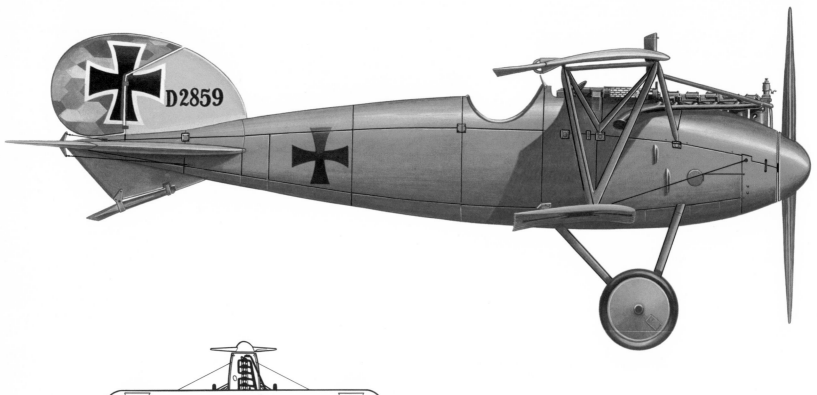

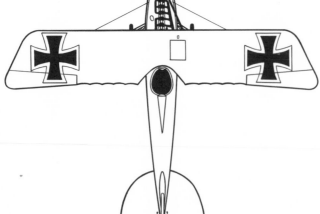

R.A.F. SE 5a (1917-18)

The reputation as the most successful British fighter plane in World War I was shared about equally by the Sopwith "Camel" and the R.A.F. SE 5a. The British Royal Aircraft Factory built 5,205 craft of this type. Britain's ace, Captain W. A. Bishop, was particularly successful in piloting the machine.

Curtiss JN-4D "Jenny" (1917-18)

This was the American counterpart of the British Avro 504K, designed by B. Douglas Thomas. It was manufactured by Curtiss in the United States. By the end of World War I, some 9,000 of these planes had been built, and many were used afterwards as trainers. The "barnstormer" American pilots who maintained public interest in air travel after the war by aerobatic displays and spectacular transport flights, liked to fly in the "Jenny." One of the "barnstormers" was Charles Lindbergh, who was to make aviation history some few years later.

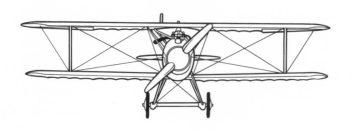

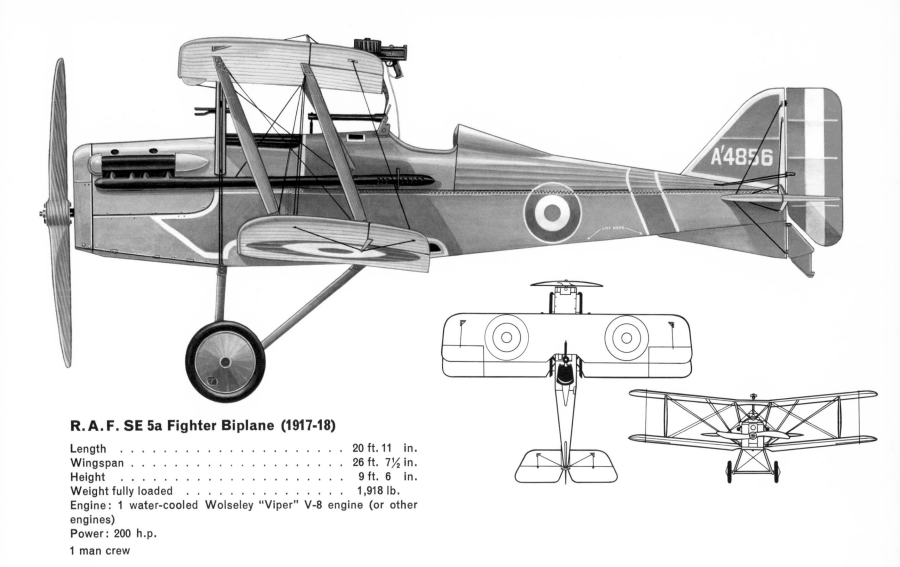

R.A.F. SE 5a Fighter Biplane (1917-18)

Length . . . . 20 ft. 11 in.
Wingspan . . . . 26 ft. 7½ in.
Height . . . . 9 ft. 6 in.
Weight fully loaded . . . . 1,918 lb.
Engine: 1 water-cooled Wolseley "Viper" V-8 engine (or other engines)
Power: 200 h.p.

1 man crew

Curtiss JN-4D "Jenny" Trainer and Reconnaissance Biplane (1917-18)

Length . . . . 27 ft. 4 in.
Wingspan . . . . 43 ft. 7⅜ in.
Height . . . . 9 ft. 6½ in.
Weight fully loaded . . . . 1,896 lb.
Engine: 1 water-cooled Curtiss OX-5 V-8 in-line engine
Power: 90 h.p.

2 man crew

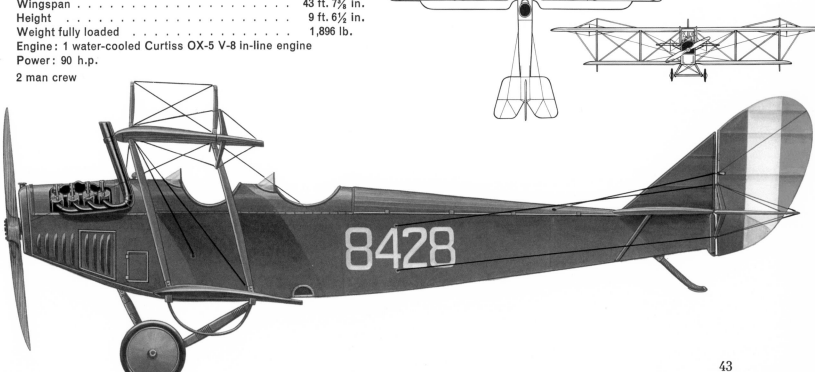

Fokker D-VII Fighter Biplane (1918)

Length . . . . 22 ft. 11⅝ in.
Wingspan . . . . 29 ft. 3½ in.
Height . . . . 9 ft. 2¼ in.
Weight fully loaded . . . . 1,984 lb.
Engine: 1 water-cooled BMW-III 6-cylinder in-line engine (or Austro-Daimler)
Power: 185 (210) h.p.

1 man crew

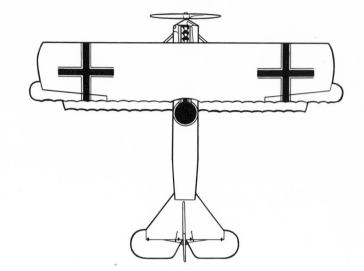

Fokker's toughest combat plane continued to worry the Allies even after the war. The terms for reparations of German war material mentioned the D-VII by name. Of 200 aircraft to be handed over to the United States, 114 had to be of the D-VII type. The new fighters came into service in May 1918, and were feared for their particular maneuverability and their ability to stand up to the most trying flying conditions. German pilots perfected their tactics of climbing steeply and attacking from below, and, on operations, the D-VII's proved remarkably adaptable. With his new Fokker fighter, Ernst Udet maintained his reputation as an ace "Pour-le-Mérite" flier. He gave expression to his well-known lightheartedness by decorating the side of his plane's fuselage with the nickname of Lo, his girlfriend at the time. On the elevator he painted the mysterious motto: "But never you." This aircraft was tailor-made for Udet, who, apparently, could do almost anything with it. In the 1920's the flier turned his exceptional skill into good business by becoming one of the cleverest acrobatic fliers. His most hair-raising trick was picking up a handkerchief with a thorn attached to his plane's wing. Fokker's good business had come much earlier when he negotiated with the Air Forces Inspectorate a fixed price of 25,000 gold marks for each D-VII unit.

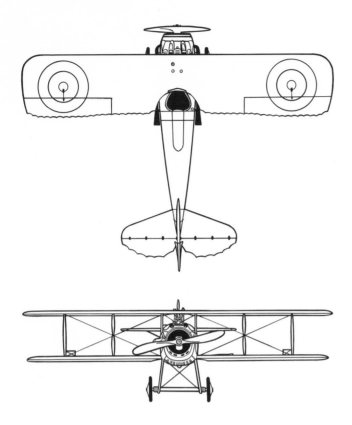

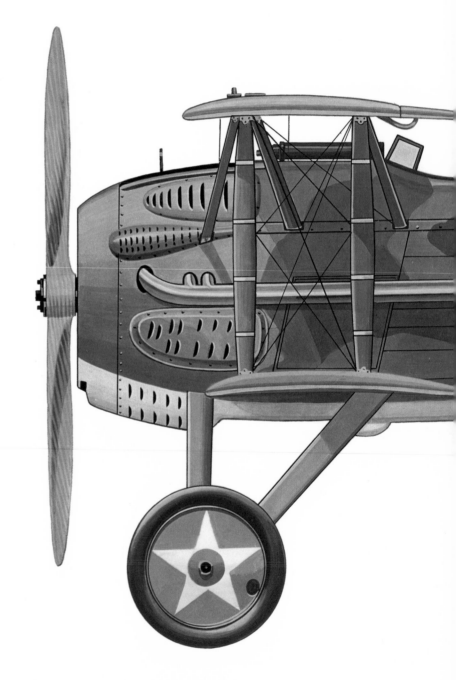

Spad S 13 Fighter Biplane (1917-18)

Length . . . . 20 ft. 8 in.
Wingspan . . . . 26 ft. 11 in.
Height . . . . 7 ft. 11 in.
Weight fully loaded . . . . 1,808 lb.
Engine: 1 Hispano-Suiza 8BA V-8 engine (1917); Hispano-Suiza 8BEc V-8 engine (1918)
Power: 220 h.p. or 235 h.p.

1 man crew

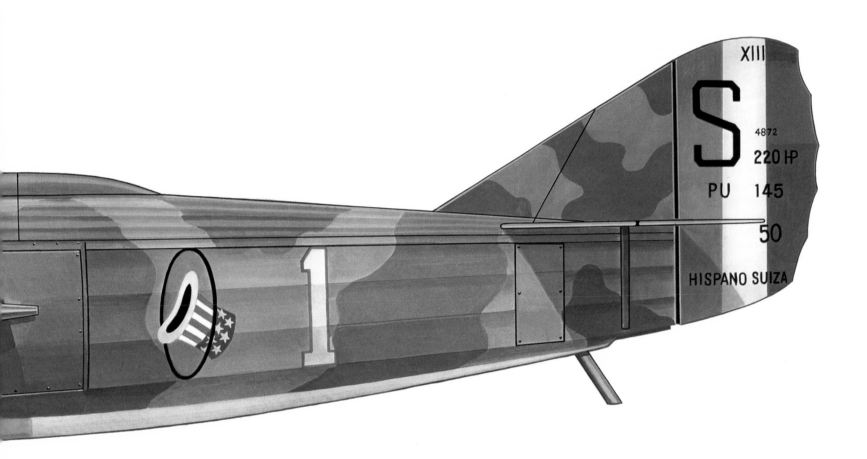

The Spad S 13 came from a firm with a long tradition: S.P.A.D. ("Société pour Aviation et ses Dérivés"). This factory, owned by Armand Deperdussin, held all the absolute speed records in 1912 and 1913. The aircraft, produced between 1914 and 1916, after the take-over of the business by Louis Blériot, were not exceptionally successful. But in the summer of 1916 the picture changed completely, and the Spad S 13 rapidly became one of the Allies' outstanding aircraft. What it lacked in maneuverability it more than made up for in speed. Its maximum of 142 m.p.h. was produced by a 220 h.p. Hispano-Suiza engine. Eddie Rickenbacker, whose 26 victories made him America's most successful pilot in World War I, was one of the best known S 13 aces.

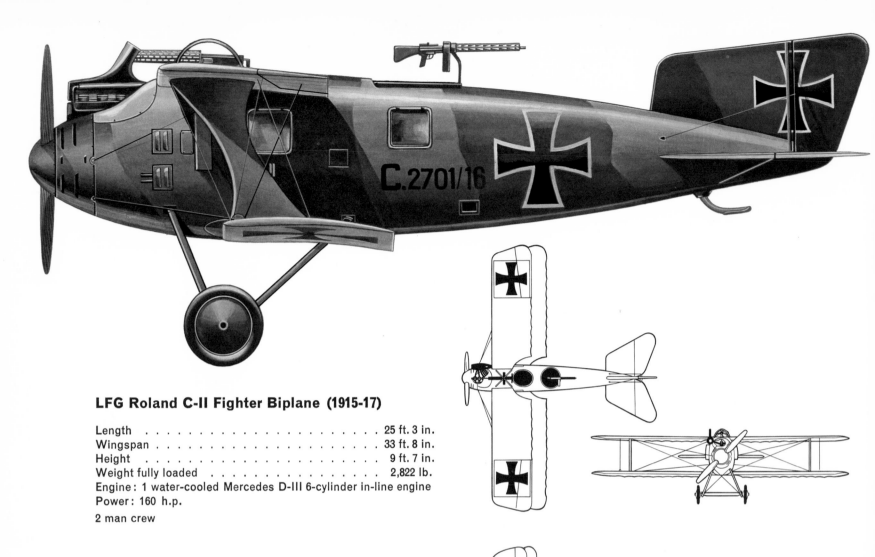

LFG Roland C-II Fighter Biplane (1915-17)

Length . . . . 25 ft. 3 in.
Wingspan . . . . 33 ft. 8 in.
Height . . . . 9 ft. 7 in.
Weight fully loaded . . . . 2,822 lb.
Engine: 1 water-cooled Mercedes D-III 6-cylinder in-line engine
Power: 160 h.p.

2 man crew

Bristol F.2B Biplane Fighter (1917-18)

Length . . . . 25 ft. 10 in.
Wingspan . . . . 39 ft. 3 in.
Height . . . . 9 ft. 9 in.
Weight fully loaded . . . . 2,800 lb.
Engine: 1 water-cooled Rolls-Royce "Falcon" III in-line engine
Power: 275 h.p.

2 man crew

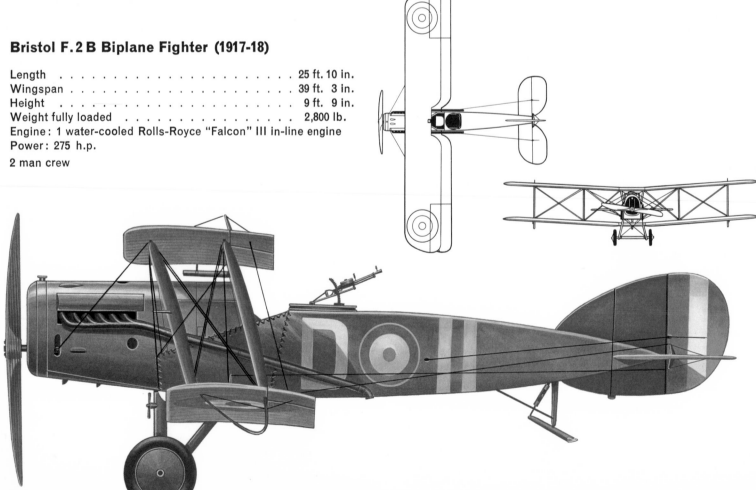

observers in the second seat aimed at their foes with rifles, had passed. The early arguments between officers on flying duties as to whether honor and good manners would allow the sword to be drawn struck front line fliers as a corny joke.

The machine gun, which in all air-minded countries had for years been subjected to endless tests as armament for planes, now turned the planes themselves into weapons. But before a satisfactory answer could be found to the best way of mounting the guns, many difficulties had to be overcome.

Back in 1911, Major Brooke-Popham had experimented in England with machine guns as aircraft arms, and in Germany August Euler had also carried out armament tests. Both men had failed. Tests were also made in other countries, and useless designs kept being turned out until finally the reconnaissance plane became a fighter by any means available.

Once, when the English pilot Lieutenant L. A. Strange was flying a French Farman MF 7, he remembered a two-seater Vickers with a pusher propeller which, with a Maxim machine gun at the tip of the fuselage, had been exhibited at the 1913 Paris Air Exhibition. In do-it-yourself style, Strange mounted a Lewis gun on the nose of his own pusher propeller biplane, and on August 22, 1914, he took a shot at his first German plane. The speed of the Farman was too slow, and the enemy got away. After returning to base, Strange was reprimanded by his superior: "In future, Lieutenant," he was told, "leave these arms to the infantry where they rightly belong!"

Yet pusher propeller aircraft proved well suited for one or two machine guns to be mounted. The guns, operated by the pilot and the observer, were generally on a swivel and offered a field of fire in virtually all horizontal directions. However, fighter pilots and designers soon gave tractor propellers preference because of their better performance. In such decisions, aerodynamic calculations usually played a very minor part; more important was intuition, naked-eye measurements and flair. The tractor propeller had one fatal disadvantage, however; bullets passing through it would break it to bits, causing the aircraft to crash or at least to make an emergency landing.

Meanwhile, the French aircraft industrialist Raymond Saulnier had done intensive research into ways of synchronizing machine guns. The ammunition of the Hotchkiss machine gun with which he was working was so unreliable that it completely eliminated any practical advance. Saulnier fitted the blades of his airscrews with steel bullet deflectors. However, even when this device enabled French pilot Raymond Garros to shoot down three enemy planes in as many weeks during April 1915, the inventor was not assured that his answer was the last word in ballistics wisdom.

Then Anthony Fokker, a young Dutch pilot, outstanding air ace and one of the best-known aircraft manufacturers of his day, was talked into designing a synchronized machine gun. Within a day or two, Fokker and his technicians came up with an ingenious system: they connected the machine gun to the engine's crankshaft by means of an arrangement of tappets similar to the valve controls on an Otto engine. The crankshaft thus directly fired the machine gun when no propeller blade was in front of its mouth. German pilots grew enthusiastic about the new weapon, but the advantage they had gained over the enemy was short-lived. When fog forced a German fighter to land behind enemy lines in April 1916, the synchronization system was discovered and copied by the Allies.

Further progress was made by a Rumanian, George Constantinescu, who designed and built a hydraulic system in which a cam on the airscrew shaft actuated a piston. This piston compressed a fluid which, when released by a valve synchronized with the position of the propeller, fired the machine gun. A lever on the joy stick brought the device into play. Sopwith "Camels" were the first aircraft to be equipped with this new system, and British Royal Flying Corps pilots found it so successful that in 1917 more than 6,000 of these machine gun controls, and in 1918 more than 20,000, were built and mounted into aircraft.

No longer did pilots fire from rifles screwed into position, even though as late as July 1915, Captain Lance Hawker of the Royal Flying Corps, while flying a Bristol "Scout," succeeded in shooting down a German two-seater in this manner. Nor, as an alternative, was it necessary to attempt the Russian roulette of shooting at the enemy through the propeller. The French fighter ace Roland Garros, among others, used to employ this technique.

Aircraft and their armament were now well matched. Any technical advantage or design superiority gained by either side was short-lived, and the "fighter plane" became identified with the fighter pilot. His courage, his skill and that of his opponent were hotly contested in the battles of the air.

Great importance was attached to the pilot's skill. The instruments of a World War I aircraft were limited to an engine rotational speed indicator, fuel gauge, compass and map table, together with a pair of binoculars. Link trainers for blind flying were still unknown, and good weather for flying was essential. Nevertheless, weather forecasts were often unreliable, and fog or cloud banks made life hard for these daring young men in their flying crates.

"One peculiarity which caused a lot of trouble both to fliers who had overcome their fear of cloud flying and to the manufacturers of aircraft and aircraft compasses," wrote Hellmuth Hirth in 1914, "is the rotation of the aircraft's compass in cloud or, in flying jargon, the compass going mad. After many experiments I have been unable to determine the reason. A long time ago I observed that whenever I ran into clouds my compass began to rotate. The fact is it is not the compass but the aircraft that rotates. The reason for this is that the engine rotating to the right provides the aircraft with an impulse to turn to the left. This in turn arises from the torque produced by a plane engine of at least 100 h.p. With the earth in sight, the aircraft, if left to itself, will make a slight turn to the left.

"Naturally aircraft manufacturers have to allow for this, and in some models the tendency to turn is compensated for, to some extent, by appropriate design. The simplest remedy for the tendency to turn left is to warp the left wing more strongly than the right. Without the torque to the left the aircraft would seek to make a slight turn to the right with the greater warp of the left wing. This tendency and the torque arising from the motor now cancel each other out.

"In clouds the torque is far more powerful because of the heavy water-laden air, so you have to trim sharply to the right in order to be able to fly straight ahead. I have frequently tested this out. I flew into low hanging clouds and left the controls to themselves. When I came out of the clouds on the other side I repeated the experiment and had to exert quite a strong pressure with my right leg on the controls to make the aircraft pass through in a straight line. During the first experiment my compass began to rotate the moment I entered the clouds. When I kept the controls sufficiently hard to the right that the compass remained firmly on course, I remained on a straight course throughout the flight.

"I made a very interesting flight in my biplane over the Berlin-Munich route, which many years earlier I had covered in the opposite direction. Between Leipzig and Dresden, or about half way, low hanging clouds stretched out so far that after about a further 18 miles I decided to fly over the clouds. They hung so low that I was afraid I would not escape the approaching mountains near Probstzella.

"With my 6-cylinder Benz engine I could easily have risked making good any unevenness on the ground, but the mountains hidden in the clouds made me feel it was foolhardy to drive straight through them. They were about 2,500 ft. thick, and for ten minutes I flew through fog. I had to press my foot down so hard on the controls that I soon got cramp-like feelings. In the cold weather and the moist atmosphere I had the greatest difficulty in keeping constant mastery of the controls.

"At long last I got above the clouds. It was shortly before twelve noon so I took the opportunity of checking my compass by the sun. I flew straight into the sun and saw that I was five degrees off course in the north-south direction. I got back onto my compass course, which ran almost due south, and flew on over a brilliantly lighted sea of cloud. The cloud horizon which at first was sharply defined became increasingly hazy the further south I flew. After half an hour I was covered with such a layer of mist that I could only glimpse the sun in one or two places. Finally the horizon

completely disappeared, the upper layer of cloud coalesced with the lower, and I had the feeling of hanging suspended in a poorly lighted frosted glass ball of gigantic size. Yet this strange appearance of the atmosphere did not worry me much. The light I found very unpleasant, so unpleasant that I was sometimes dazzled and had to close my eyes. I also felt extremely tired. Whenever I opened my eyes I was again dazzled and could not see anything at all, because unfortunately I had not brought my sunglasses with me.

"Finally I lost all sensation of above and below. I kept track of the altitude from the revolution counter of my engine, which was running smoothly, so I didn't vary too much up and down. I kept the wings level after saying to myself it isn't easy to know which way you're being pushed because the seats are very well upholstered. I took out my watch and secured the chain to my joy stick so that I had a pendulum. Things now went rather better and I attempted, as far as was possible, to keep the watch chain parallel with the stick. I succeeded for several hours. At last I'd had enough of flying under these conditions, but could not bring myself to cut out the engine and fly under the clouds.

"On three occasions I decided to continue below the clouds, but each time a very strong feeling kept me from doing so. It was not until I saw that I had already spent three and a half hours above the clouds that I had the uneasy feeling it was time to stop the engine and dive right down into the clouds. I left them 1,300 ft. above the ground. I sensed strongly that this was the right time, and, in fact, there was Munich just ahead of me. This presentiment confirmed for me once more that a sense of direction can be innate. Once again instinct had not let me down."

In the early days of air warfare the situations and counter measures for unusual flying conditions were not appreciably different from those encountered by Hirth. With no less primitively equipped weapons of war—which all aircraft still were in World War I—the combat pilot on both sides had to grapple with the elements as well as with an equally determined opponent.

Among the German World War I fighter pilots whose names have come down through history are Max Immelmann, Oswald Boelcke, Hermann Göring, and Manfred von Richthofen. The French nation worshiped René Fonck and Charles Nungesser; in 1916 Georges Guynemer became a popular hero and Roland Garros is remembered as a reckless combat pilot.

Winning air victories for the British Royal Flying Corps were Lieutenant "Billy" Bishop (among Britain's most decorated wartime pilots), Captain Albert Ball, whose French fighter pilot friends called him the "Guynemer of England," and William Sholto Douglas, who won several decorations in 1915 and became Marshal of the Royal Air Force in the Second World War. The great American air hero of World

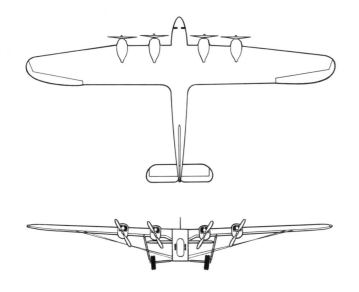

British aviation historians described the four-engined Staaken as "visible proof of the progress made by German makers during the war years, in the design and building of large all-metal aircraft." Alfred Colsmann, the Zeppelin director, made heavy demands on these aircraft. He insisted, before planning started, that the large plane must be able, in an emergency, to fly safely on two engines with a full load. One of Count Zeppelin's ideas was used in making the aircraft as light as possible; it was clad in aluminum. Originally, the Staaken was intended to provide regular services over the Friedrichshafen-Berlin route. The Inter-allied Control Commission suspected the aircraft to be a new bomber, and the pioneering Staaken E 4/20 was broken up.

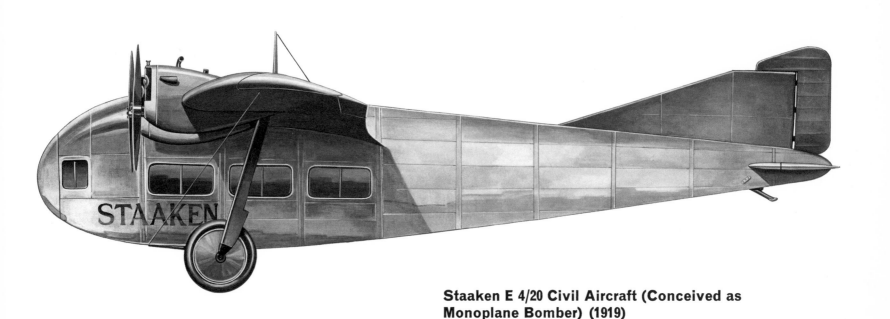

Staaken E 4/20 Civil Aircraft (Conceived as Monoplane Bomber) (1919)

Length . . . . 54 ft. 1 in.
Wingspan. . . . . 101 ft. 8 in.
Height . . . . 17 ft. ⅔ in.
Weight fully loaded . . . . 18,742 lb.
Engines: 4 water-cooled Maybach Mb.IV.a in-line engines
Power: 245 h.p. each

2 man crew — 12 passengers

Breguet 14 B 2 Reconnaissance and Bomber Biplane (1917-18)

Length	29 ft. 6¼ in.
Wingspan	47 ft. 1 in.
Height	10 ft. 10 in.
Weight fully loaded	3,880 lb.

Engine : 1 water-cooled Renault 12-Fcx V engine (or other engines)
Power : 300 h.p.

2 man crew

The Breguet 14 B 2 differs from the 14 A 2 only in weight and type of engine.

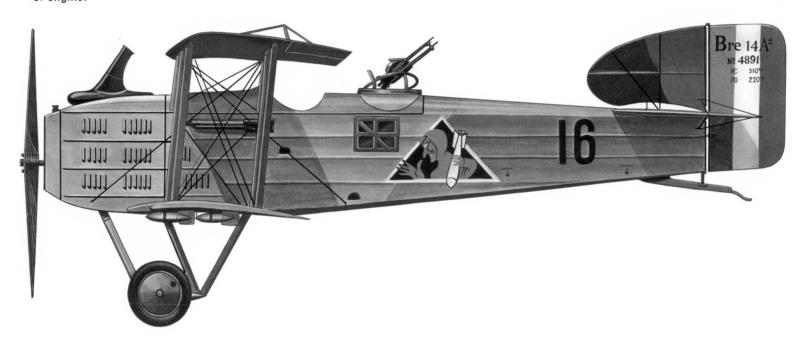

Aesthetic design was never a hallmark of Louis Breguet's aircraft, yet long life and excellent flight qualities fully made up for its shortcomings in style. This bomber was produced in great numbers even after World War I (a total of 8,000 were built), and it was on active service from March 1917, until the end of hostilities. On several occasions the Breguet 14 B 2 made front page news. It won its manufacturer the "Croix de Guerre" as a pilot, and in November 1918, a Breguet 14 carried the German Major von Geyer from Tergnier to Spa for the armistice negotiations. The aircraft enjoyed popularity in the armed services of foreign countries. It flew in the air force units of Brazil, China, Czechoslovakia, Denmark, Finland, Greece, Japan, Poland, Portugal, Siam, and Spain, and was well known in all the French colonies. Even Vietnam was familiar with the Breguet 14, for a small number were said to have been assembled in the workshops of Hanoi and Saigon.

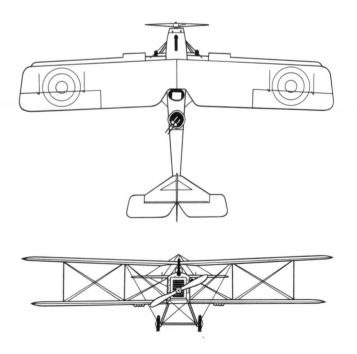

52

War I was Eddie Rickenbacker; Italy's was Francesco Baracca, and Russia's was Alexander Kasakov.

Not only the men but also their aircraft became famous. France produced the Caudron G-III, the Nieuport 17, the Breguet 14, and the Spad S 13, a design particularly favored by United States pilots. The Nieuport 17, flown by the air ace Albert Ball, marked a particularly significant stage in development.

In 1918 an important role was played by the JN-4D, designed by America's Glenn H. Curtiss. The "Jenny," as it was called, was already a veteran when the U.S. Army Air Service's 148th Squadron used it at Dunkirk, and it continued to give excellent service as a trainer for many years after World War II. It had also been used with telling effect before the United States entered the war.

In 1915 and 1916 Britain's Royal Flying Corps brought into service a two-seater biplane with a lattice-tail and a pusher propeller: the Vickers FB 5. This fighter rapidly gained popularity among the allied pilots and soldiers under its nickname "Gun Bus." The observer and air gunner, who also operated the Lewis gun, sat forward in the split cockpit. Behind him sat the pilot, and, behind him, was the 100 h.p.

The Vickers FB 5 "Gun Bus" enjoyed great popularity with the Allies in 1915 and 1916. But this two-seater double-decker also had its weaknesses: its Gnôme engine was considered unreliable. Nevertheless, solid construction and good properties made this lattice-tail "Gun Bus" a force to be reckoned with.

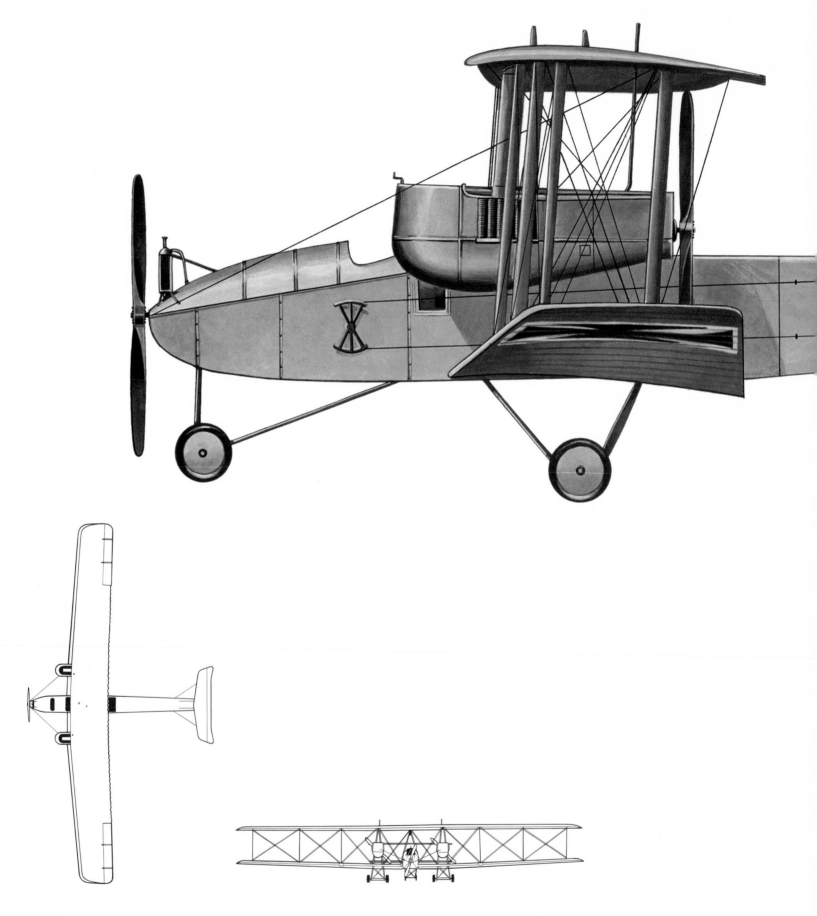

VGO I-RML.1 Bomber Biplane (1915-18)

Length	. . . .	78 ft. 9 in.
Wingspan	. . . .	138 ft. 5½ in.
Height	. . . .	21 ft. 7½ in.
Weight fully loaded	. . . .	20,992 lb.

Engines : 3 water-cooled Maybach-HS in-line engines
Power : 240 h.p. each

6 man crew

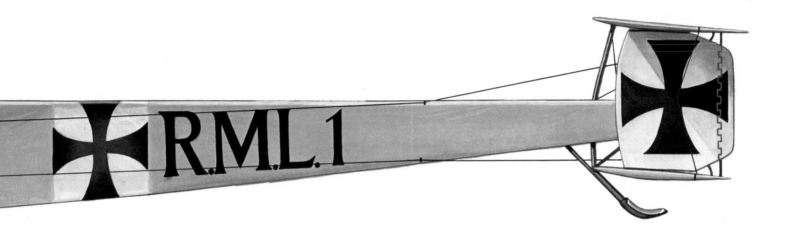

The planning of these "giant aircraft" bombers was the result of Count Zeppelin's persistence. The first VGO model's center of gravity and cellular construction produced the novelty of two parallel nose wheels. The crew consisted of a pilot and copilot, a commander who also acted as navigator, and three flight engineers—one for each of the two pusher propellers, and the third for the tractor propeller in the nose. After many difficulties during trials, a VGO III made its first operational flight on August 15, 1916. Shortly afterwards, on September 1, 1916, this VGO III developed engine trouble and had to make an emergency landing. The aircraft was supposed to be rebuilt at Staaken, but the persistent engine troubles could not be rectified in a new version. The giant aircraft finished up ingloriously after Hans Vollmöller and Gustav Klein, the test pilot and construction chief appointed by Count Zeppelin, had paid for a mechanical defect with their lives—on March 10, 1917.

The developments and tests of large aircraft claimed the lives
of many pilots. Hans Vollmöller and Gustav Klein crashed and
died in this VGO I-RML.1 after a test flight on March 10, 1917.

"The ban or even limit on aerial combat led to forceful discussion," reported the Viennese professor Dr. Hans Sperl in 1912, following the Madrid Congress of the Institute of International Law. Two British lawyers had, together with a Belgian, protested against the use of aircraft as weapons. "Westlake and Holland and the Belgian, Alberic Rolin," continued Dr. Sperl, "were eager for a complete interdiction of every form of aerial fighting; opposing them, however, were the French under Monsieur Fauchille." Congress members compromised by agreeing to restrict aerial combat to "vertical flying methods": exchange of fire was to be permitted only between aircraft and ground forces. Dr. Sperl recognized the futility of this half measure and declared that either total permission or total prohibition should be enforced, and that "any life respecting human being or progressive politician could only give his support to the latter." The German lawyer Ludwig von Bar's view that aerial combat was morally condemnable, found no substantial support. Three years later the nations were at war, and doubts of "moral condemnation" were cast aside. The first tentative shots exchanged between airplanes escalated to air chases, air combat and bombing warfare. Only one single stipulation in the international code of aerial rights, prepared from May 31 to June 2, 1911, in Paris, could be applied to disputes on aerial combat. Participating nations unanimously agreed that "every aircraft must bear an identifying insignia of nationality." Thus (right), insignias already helped in World War I to distinguish friend from foe. Left row, from top to bottom: Germany 1914–15; Germany 1915–17: Germany 1917–18; Germany 1918; Turkey 1915–18; Bulgaria 1914–18. The emblems of the Royal Austro-Hungarian Empire were the same as the German. Right row, from top to bottom: Great Britain; France; the United States of America; Italy; Belgium; Russia.

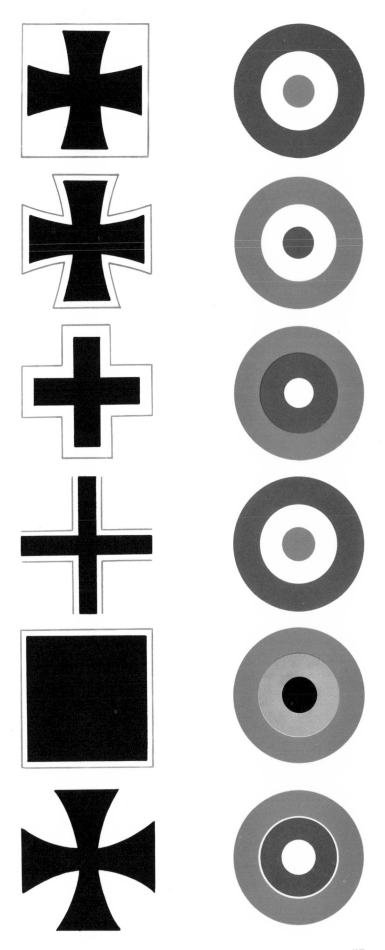

Gnôme single-valve engine which drove the pusher propeller. The "Gun-Bus" had a flying ceiling of 1,500 ft., and a maximum speed of 70 m.p.h. Its wingspan measured 36 ft. 6 in. The plane was 27 ft. 2 in. long and 11 ft. 6 in. high.

On February 5, 1915, the Royal Flying Corps' 5th Squadron took delivery of its "Gun Bus," and German fighters tried to keep well out of its way. Squadrons 2, 5, 11, 16 and 18 swore by their Vickers FB 5, which was officially described and used both as a fighter and a reconnaissance plane.

In Germany the line of development ran from the Fokker E-III through the Dr-I up to the young designer's D-VII, and the streamlined Albatros D-III.

World War I fighter pilots held a special place among the fighting units. They regarded themselves, rightly so, as out-and-out aviation pioneers. They were combatants, but had no protective screens, and, once in the air, they depended solely upon their individual decisions. During aerial combat neither direct nor indirect orders could be given a pilot by a superior officer. Even in unit formation, these men were essentially alone with their opponents.

It was quite remarkable, although fully understandable, that chivalry should have played such an important part among the pilots of these nations at war. They became, as it were, knights of the air. It was quite common for a pilot who had shot down an opponent, either above or behind his own lines, to drop his victim's personal belongings and a photograph of his grave onto his airfield base. Survivors' biographies give countless examples of friendly post-war meetings between former foes. Although they shot at each other, they felt themselves members of the youngest and most exclusive warriors' order.

William E. Barrett wrote: "James Norman Hall, probably the only pilot in the war to have fought under three flags (Britain, France and the U.S.A.) hailed from Colfax, Iowa. When, on May 7, 1918, Hall was shot down by a German Albatros pilot—and came out of it with only a broken nose—the German took photos of him after his capture, and Hall was given prints. Souvenir photos such as these were common mementos of air fighting." In the photograph Hall with his nose bandaged is seen sitting at the back of an ambulance holding a dachshund in his arm.

The group of World War I air force veterans has all but gone. One of them who might speak for all, no matter on which side their allegiance lay, remembers the years 1914 to 1918 when "heaven was hot."

"Even in those days," said the veteran, "we employed tactics which were still up-to-date in World War II. In the early years we often flew to within inches of our opponents and only fired when virtually nothing could miss. Feints, attacks out of clouds, out of the sun or from behind it; all types of acrobatics were everyday things. One day I was out with two comrades—it was now or never. After about half an hour the man on my right sighted an enemy aircraft far behind us, far behind our lines. It could only be an enemy, as no other aircraft from our squadron had taken off. We reached agreement by hand signs. The two of them were to fly on: I was to take care of the silver dot. I started off by climbing to 9,800 ft. The other aircraft continued to make wide circles. Anyhow, it struck me that he hadn't seen me yet. I kept close to the supposed enemy and kept on flying in such a way that I was constantly hidden by small clouds.

"I now climbed in a tight spiral for about another 650 ft. right into the middle of the soup. Then I dived, flying blind in the direction of the enemy plane. When I came through the bottom of the cloud, he was just turning for home. Fortunately I was still high enough above him, so I made a tight right turn to get behind him—that was a half roll—then I opened fire. I didn't hit him. He pancaked and then took evasive action. It is possible that he had to go home because his fuel was running out. At any rate he didn't show any great eagerness for a fight.

"But he had guts. He flew so low that I thought he must crash into the shot-up stumps of trees. But he evaded them as nimbly as a hare.

"Meanwhile he was going a little more slowly than I was. That got him a burst into the upper right half of his wing. Another burst went into his elevator and diagonally through the fuselage. The pilot himself I didn't hit, that I know. But his controls must have been damaged. He hit the ground at a flat angle and finished up with his undercarriage on the edge of a shell crater, then overturned several times. I can't imagine any pilot surviving that. With mixed feelings, but pride predominating, I turned back to our airfield. It was my fifth air victory."

No matter whether a pilot had five air victories or 80, whether he was a fighter, bomber or reconnaissance plane pilot, it all depended on the man, what experiences as an aviation pioneer World War I brought him. It meant frenzy and triumph, danger and adventure. That was the feeling of having helped to open up new territory, the borders of which had been crossed by the Wright brothers a bare decade before organized military aviation started.

In 1908 Orville Wright had convincingly demonstrated to Washington military chiefs at Fort Myer, Virginia, the practical advantages of aircraft. Then and again in 1917 he repeated his basic ideal: "When my brother and I built and flew the first powered aircraft, we imagined we were giving the world an invention which would prevent all future wars!"

He had concluded that if men had a bird's eye view of the world, everybody would know exactly what everyone else was up to and warfare would become senseless. But then someone came up with the idea of armored reconnaissance planes, and put an end to his optimism.

VICKERS FB 27 "VIMY"

A check from Churchill

The first non-stop transatlantic crossing from west to east

On June 14 and 15, 1919, Captain John Alcock and Lieutenant Arthur Whitten-Brown crossed the Atlantic in seventeen hours from Newfoundland to Ireland. Bad weather, including fog, the icing up of controls and engines made the risks even greater. The 350 h.p. Rolls-Royce engines, which had been transferred from a World War I bomber to the Vickers "Vimy," lifted the biplane to a height of 5,000 ft. in fifteen minutes. Today the biplane's power plants and size—43 ft. 8 in long with a wingspan of 67 ft.— make it seem more like a toy than a craft capable of flying the Atlantic. Yet Alcock and Brown attempted the feat, and they succeeded. The £10,000 prize offered by the newspaper proprietor, Lord Northcliffe, repaid their efforts and brought them world fame. The check was handed to them by Winston Churchill, who was then Britain's Secretary of State.

John Alcock and Arthur Whitten-Brown pushed their way through an excited crowd which had gathered at the entrance of the London Royal Aero Club. Alcock carried a small linen bag in his hand, and after greeting General Holden, Vice-President of the Club, he handed over the bundle of 197 letters that Dr. Robinson, Postmaster in Newfoundland, had entrusted to the fliers. These were then rushed to the nearest post office, where they were franked and forwarded (airmail stamps not yet having been invented).

The letters had made the long journey from Lester's Field near St. John's, Newfoundland, to London in record time. At Lester's Field, Alcock and Brown had climbed into their "Vimy" flying crate to prove, as Alcock put it, that "there are possibilities of flying non-stop from the New World to the Old." Like Köhl, Fitzmaurice, and von Hünefeld, who were to fly in the opposite direction nine years later, Alcock and Brown had wanted to take off on a Friday the 13th. But the two Englishmen actually set out in their converted World War I Vickers bomber on June 14.

After three weeks of exhaustive preparation, they had finally made their start. Some of their efforts had been spent in attempting to find a smoother takeoff point than Lester's Field, but after a week of combing the rough terrain, they gave up the search.

The sky was overcast, even though the latest meteorological report from United States Lieutenant Clements had forecast good weather conditions. It was 1:40 p.m. as the "Vimy," with the throttle wide open, and both engines at full power, taxied over Lester's Field's bumpy ground. Alcock

headed his aircraft into the west wind. "Depressingly slowly the 'Vimy' taxied toward a dark pine forest at the end of the airfield," Brown reported. "The echo of the roaring motors must have struck quite hard against the hills around St. John's. Almost at the last second Alcock gained height. We were only inches above the top of the trees." Alcock's recollections were rather more brief: "At 1:45 p.m. we were airborne," he said.

1,890 nautical miles of open sea and sixteen hours of flying time lay ahead of the Englishmen who, only fifteen and a half years after the Wright brothers powered flight, had set off on what turned out to be one of the most breathtaking flights in the history of aviation. The sirens of vessels in St. John's Harbor blew a final farewell as the "Vimy" passed overhead at a height of 1,083 ft. Alcock turned the aircraft eastwards, in the direction of Ireland. The biplane gained height, and the coast of Newfoundland was left behind. The altimeter soon read 1,300 ft.

For four hours, the "Vimy" flew peacefully in the open sky, and the difficult takeoff was forgotten. For Alcock and Brown it was just one more of the 1,001 takeoffs they had made as Flying Corps pilots. Already anticipating his arrival in England, Brown remarked, "Great Scott, what a banquet we'll have in London. Roast duck, I can just imagine it, green peas..."

Few people were even aware of Alcock and Brown's plans. England was enjoying her first post-war summer, and the newspapers were filled with reports of Germany's reaction to President Wilson's Fourteen-Point program. Special editions also carried stories of Bela Kun's revolution in Hungary and the Allies' successes against the Bolsheviks on the Archangel Front. However, there was a five-line story on the back page of one newspaper which mentioned the preparations being made for the "Vimy" in Newfoundland. But no one paid much attention to it.

As the "Vimy" flew over the Atlantic, the conversation of the two men seated in the open cockpit turned to the friends who had helped them at Lester's Field: Bob Lyon, Maxwell Muller, Montague and Harry Couch. And they recalled the various attempts that others had made to cross the waste of water between the old and new worlds. Five years earlier a British company, Martin and Handasyde Ltd., had set about building a transatlantic aircraft. The scheme had been financed by Edgar MacKay. As with the "White Bird," in which Nungesser and Coli later undertook their ill-fated attempt to fly the Atlantic, the undercarriage of the aircraft was to be released shortly after takeoff. The fuselage was built like a boat. Misfortune seemed to hang over the undertaking. Shortly before the aircraft's completion, Gustav Hamel, the appointed pilot, failed to return from a routine flight in his Morane-Saulnier over the English Channel.

Alcock and Brown's ambition was to fly the Atlantic non-stop. Although they would not be the first to make the crossing, they aimed at being the first to do so without intermediate stops.

Four weeks earlier, three American Curtiss flying boats had taken off for a west-east flight over the Atlantic, but none of them had accomplished a direct flight. Glenn H. Curtiss, the American air pioneer in the early days of flying, had interested Rodman Wanamaker in financing the project, and J. C. Porte, a former British lieutenant, had helped him with the preparations. In his book "Atlantic Wings, the Conquest of the North Atlantic by Airplane," Kenneth McDonough described the Curtiss flying boats' adventure. On May 8, 1919, three boats, the NC-1, NC-3, and NC-4, commanded respectively by Lieutenant Commander P.N.L. Bellinger, Commander J. H. Towers, and Lieutenant Commander A. C. Read, took off from Far Rockaway Station, Long Island, New York, on the 1,000 mile flight to Trepassey Bay. A fourth aircraft, NC-2, was withdrawn. Commander Towers' copilot was Lieutenant Commander Byrd, who, after many months' preparatory work, still hoped to obtain permission to make a further flight to Europe and thus fulfill his most sincere wish.

On the way to Newfoundland the three aircraft encountered bad weather. NC-4 developed engine trouble and was forced to make an emergency landing on water about a hundred miles from Chatham, Massachusetts. Read was forced to limp to the coast on his two remaining engines. This took NC-4 the rest of the day and the whole night. Meanwhile, the other two flying boats reached Halifax, Nova

Curtiss NC-4 Atlantic Flying Boat (1919)

Length . . . . 68 ft. 5 in.
Wingspan . . . . 125 ft. 11½ in.
Height . . . . 24 ft. 4 in.
Weight fully loaded . . . . 28,003 lb.
Engines : 4 Packard "Liberty" engines (3 tractor screws, 1 pusher airscrew)
Power : 400 h.p. each
5 man crew

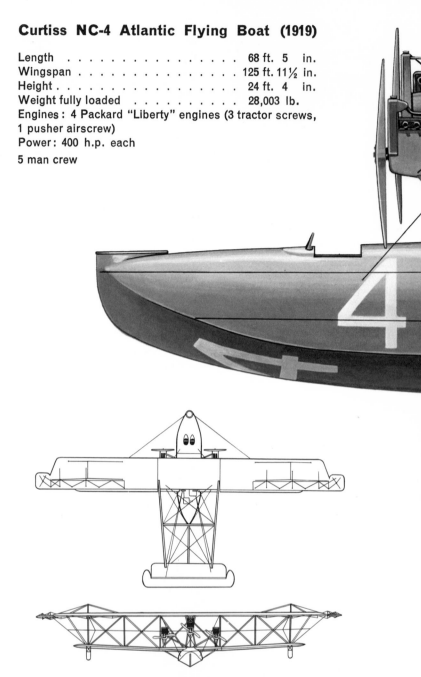

In 1919, Glenn H. Curtiss planned to cross the Atlantic for the United States Navy Department with four NC (Navy Curtiss) flying boats. Three of these took off from Jamaica Bay on May 8, 1919 amid tremendous publicity and excitement. The event got the biggest headlines in the American press since the Armistice. The fourth craft, flying boat NC-2, had already been withdrawn, but the three sister ships made a good start. However, NC-1 and NC-3 had to give up en route, the former never reaching the Azores and the latter landing on the water before Ponta Delgada. The NC-4, after breaking its journey at the Azores, took off again and reached Lisbon safely. Flying time for the 2,400 miles was 25 hours, 1 minute. Curtiss' careful plans for the first Atlantic crossing had ended in a triumph.

60

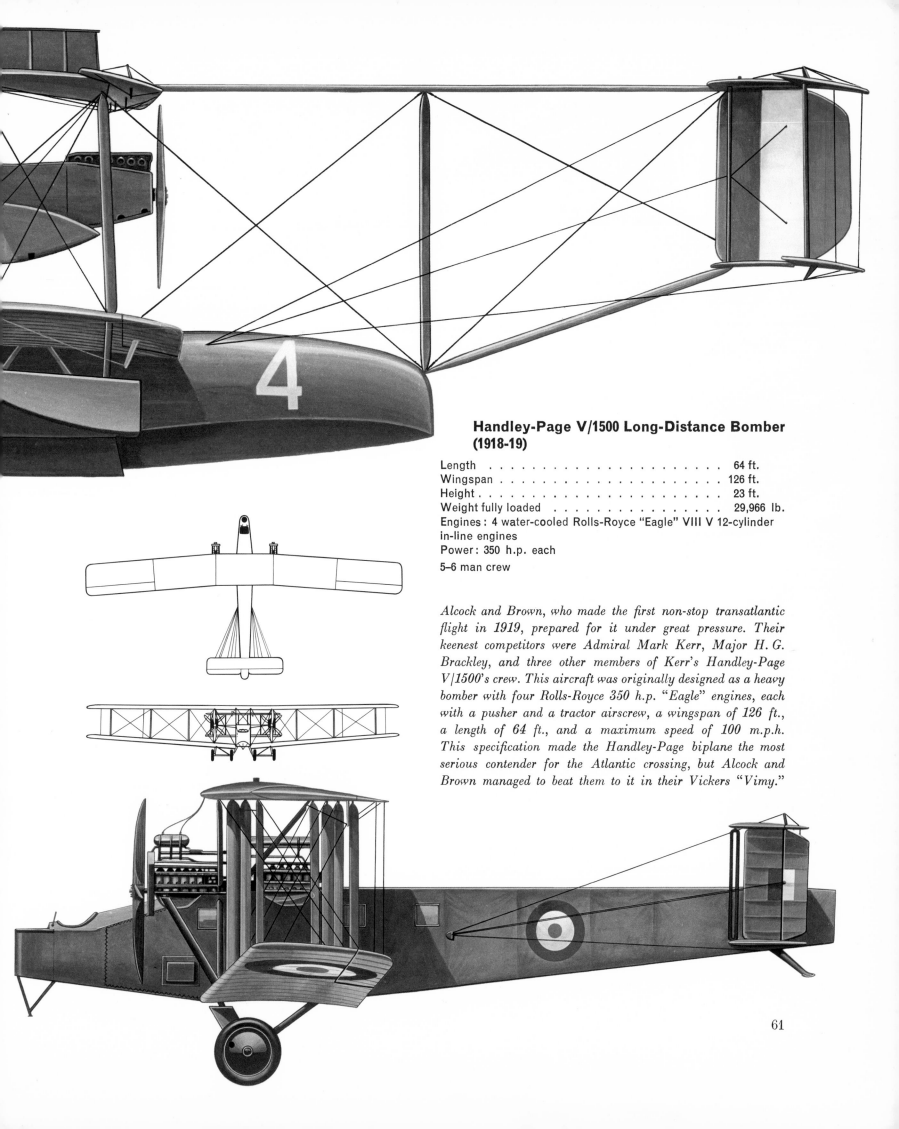

Handley-Page V/1500 Long-Distance Bomber (1918-19)

Length . . . . 64 ft.
Wingspan . . . . 126 ft.
Height . . . . 23 ft.
Weight fully loaded . . . . 29,966 lb.
Engines: 4 water-cooled Rolls-Royce "Eagle" VIII V 12-cylinder in-line engines
Power: 350 h.p. each
5–6 man crew

Alcock and Brown, who made the first non-stop transatlantic flight in 1919, prepared for it under great pressure. Their keenest competitors were Admiral Mark Kerr, Major H. G. Brackley, and three other members of Kerr's Handley-Page V/1500's crew. This aircraft was originally designed as a heavy bomber with four Rolls-Royce 350 h.p. "Eagle" engines, each with a pusher and a tractor airscrew, a wingspan of 126 ft., a length of 64 ft., and a maximum speed of 100 m.p.h. This specification made the Handley-Page biplane the most serious contender for the Atlantic crossing, but Alcock and Brown managed to beat them to it in their Vickers "Vimy."

The American Curtiss flying boat NC-4 made the first Atlantic crossing in 1919. The pioneer flight was carried out in stages: from Jamaica Bay over the Azores to Lisbon's harbor.

Scotia, in nineteen hours, and took off again the following day en route to Trepassey. On May 16, 1919, Commander Towers ordered his flying boats to head for the Azores.

"In the early morning hours of May 17," McDonough writes, "the NC-4 navigator sighted from 3,600 ft. the southernmost point of Flores Island, the most westerly island of the Azores. The course was set to Ponta Delgada in São Miguel. Fog, however, forced Read to land at Fayal after a flight of 1,380 miles. Three days later the NC-4 continued its flight to Ponta Delgada, where it was held up for an entire week until a change in weather enabled its commander to take off for the second part of the trip."

On May 27 Read and his NC-4 crew flew the remaining 925 miles from Ponta Delgada to Lisbon in 9 hours 43 minutes. Lieutenant Commander Read, Lieutenants E. Stone, W. Hinton, and J. W. Breese, together with Ensign H. C. Rodd and Chief Engineering Petty Officer E. S. Rhoads were the first—with an intermediate stop—to have flown from the American continent to Europe. And they were, in fact, the only ones of the Curtiss air fleet to reach the appointed goal. NC-1 had to make an emergency landing on the water 100 miles west of the Azores. NC-3 had to make a similar landing—and was obliged to make for Ponta Delgada under its own power on the sea.

Alcock and Brown were familiar with all the known attempts at Atlantic crossings, both the successes and the failures. They had no illusions at all about the dangers they were running. Any of the disasters that had overtaken their predecessors they knew could also befall them. They had made very careful preparations, just as their competitors had done, and luck proved to be on their side.

They recalled that as recently as May 18 Raynham and Morgan had attempted a non-stop west-east flight from Newfoundland in a Martinsyde "Raymor." At the moment of takeoff the aircraft crashed, and it was pure chance that the pilots were rescued from the wreckage.

A second attempt was made on the same day, May 18, 1919. Kenneth Mackenzie-Grieve and Harry G. Hawker climbed into their Sopwith "Atlantic," and headed for Ireland. The flight started off smoothly at a height of about 13,000 ft., then Hawker noticed that the temperature of the water in the cooling system was rising alarmingly. Hawker used his throttle to make the "Atlantic" lose altitude; the cooling water temperature fell correspondingly. But when he tried to regain altitude the temperature rose once more. Mackenzie-Grieve also drew the pilot's attention to the failing oil pressure. To make matters worse, a powerful north wind was carrying the aircraft about 150 miles south of the planned course. The engine now started to run irregularly, and sometimes it cut out completely. For two and a half hours Hawker and Mackenzie-Grieve circled over a rough sea in loops which they tried to carry further eastwards. At last

they sighted a Danish ship, the "Mary." Hawker flew round it while Mackenzie-Grieve let off rockets to draw the attention of the crew. Then Hawker brought the "Atlantic" down on the water as carefully as he could, directly in the ship's course. Before the two pilots could launch their emergency dinghy the "Atlantic" had sunk. The fliers' drenched flying suits made swimming difficult, but they kept afloat until a lifeboat from the "Mary" picked them up. The only relic of the Sopwith "Atlantic" which survives today is the undercarriage, which was jettisoned after takeoff. A fisherman found it awash in the sea. Today it is a showpiece in a museum at St. John's.

When the news of Hawker and Mackenzie-Grieve's rescue reached Newfoundland, Alcock and Brown had not even received their "Vimy." Now two competitors were out of the race and, according to McDonough, "The only other serious rivals, the Handley-Page team in 'Harbour Grace,' gave no visible signs of an earlier takeoff." Meanwhile, the two Englishmen were on their way to Europe: 26 year-old Alcock, who had learnt to fly as early as 1912, and 32 year-old Whitten-Brown, who made his name in aerial reconnaissance in World War I.

An essential requisite for men engaged in such an undertaking is mutual respect, and Alcock and Brown knew that they could, without question, rely upon each other. Their ambition to cross the Atlantic had made their friendship close at the outset. Earlier, during an interview for a job at Vickers, Brown had spoken at length about the problems of navigation over the Atlantic, and Alcock, whose plans by then were already far advanced, was short of a navigator. Now the navigator sat beside him, equally committed to the adventure, and performing his duties with the expertise Alcock required and expected of him.

At 5 p.m. fog banks suddenly appeared on the horizon, stretching without a break from north to south. "We've got no choice," Alcock said. "We've got to go in!" Brown made another calculation of their position and recorded the wind speed as zero. The "Vimy" disappeared into the fog. It was so thick that neither man could make out the blades of the airscrews. Even the comforting roar of the Rolls-Royce "Eagle" engines was muffled, and Alcock and Brown continued to fly virtually soundless and blind.

Time went slowly. Brown glanced at his wristwatch. It was six o'clock. "Won't this ruddy fog ever end?" he grumbled. Instead of replying, Alcock slowly took the "Vimy" higher, hoping to find good visibility above the fog bank. Before dark Brown might once more be able to take his position by the sun; but after nightfall it was questionable whether the stars would be bright enough to guide the fliers reliably on their course.

Suddenly a terrifying noise broke the silence; the right-hand engine sounded like a machine gun blazing. The two

Vickers "Vimy" Transatlantic Aircraft (1919)

Length	43 ft. 6½ in.
Wingspan	69 ft. 7 in.
Height	15 ft. 5 in.
Weight fully loaded	13,290 lb.

Engines : 2 water-cooled Rolls-Royce "Eagle" VIII-V 12-cylinder engines

Power: 350 h.p. each

2 man crew

The "Vimy" was a rush development by Vickers. It took the manufacturers only four months to design, build and test the machine. The model was not ready in time to see action at the front, but remained in service with the Royal Flying Corps for several years after World War I. Without John Alcock and Arthur Whitten-Brown's historic first non-stop Atlantic flight in it the Vickers "Vimy" would probably have sunk into oblivion as an "also ran." Alcock had learnt from Harry G. Hawker's bad luck; his engine cooling water came to the boil and forced him down into the open sea. Alcock boiled the cooling water and filtered it before pouring it into the radiators. He and Brown also filled up the "Vimy" tanks with fuel filtered through chamois leather.

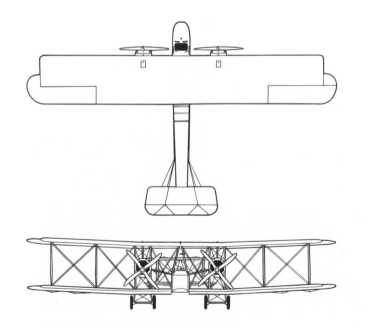

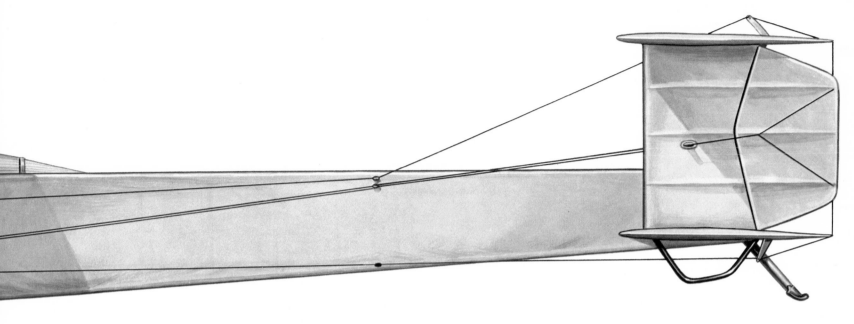

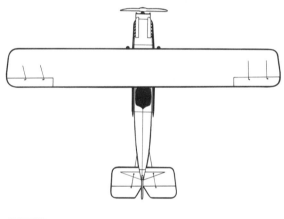

Sopwith "Atlantic" Transatlantic Aircraft (1919)

Length . . . . 31 ft. 6 in.
Wingspan . . . . 46 ft. 6 in.
Height . . . . 11 ft. 1 in.
Weight fully loaded . . . . 6,129 lb.
Engine: 1 water-cooled Rolls-Royce "Eagle" VIII V 12-cylinder
engine
Power: 350 h.p.

2 man crew

Lord Northcliffe's prize had also attracted Kenneth Mackenzie-Grieve and Harry G. Hawker. On May 18, 1919—well ahead of all their competitors—they took off from Newfoundland in their Sopwith "Atlantic." Five hours after takeoff they had their first trouble with too high temperatures in the cooling water. They struggled on anxiously for a few more hours and were then forced to make an emergency landing on the water. The two fliers were picked up by the Danish vessel "Mary."

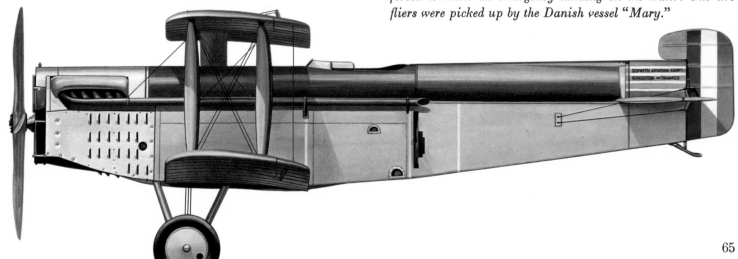

men were scared stiff. The exhaust pipe of the cylinder facing inwards had split, and the engine was shooting naked flames into the slip-stream. Alcock and Brown remained helpless as the metal turned red hot, melted away and finally started striking the controls in white-hot globules.

On top of this nerve-shattering clatter, a further discomfort developed. The heating in the men's leather flying suits stopped working. The batteries had run out. "We froze like young puppies," Alcock said later, "and in the narrow cockpit we had no room to move about. At any rate," he added somewhat ruefully, "Brown did manage to get some movement later..."

Flying above the fog brought them no luck. They had barely broken through the upper level of the bank when they discovered clouds above them, and not a sign of the hoped-for sun. And directly ahead lay mountains of cloud which were too near to be avoided. The "Vimy" plunged straight into them, and was thrown like a leaf. The experience that today's supersonic pilots, astronauts and acrobatic and fighter pilots with their advanced equipment and controls barely notice represented severe physical discomfort to Alcock and Brown: the up and down of their stomachs caused by the plane's bucking response to controls and gusts of wind. Again and again they had the feeling that the "Vimy" stood motionless before plunging down.

Alcock, who had been pressed down into his seat by the violent movement of the plane, glanced at the altimeter. The reading was 4,000 ft. The pointer began to jump about as the instrument recorded 3,200 ft., then 2,900 and down to 1,000 ft. The plane was descending in a spiral. But it occurred to neither pilot nor navigator that their end might have come. Their one thought, according to Alcock, was "However shall we get back on our original course and avoid being lost in the endless waste of the Atlantic?"

The altimeter, at that moment the most important instrument, showed 100 ft. Their chances of survival narrowed, when suddenly, at a mere 65 ft. above the waves, Alcock managed miraculously to regain control of the "Vimy." The weather had begun to change. When Brown was later asked how he and his captain reacted to their worst ordeal, he replied, "We grinned!"

Alcock had opened the throttle to the full. He swung the plane through 180° onto its old course, pulled back the joy stick and climbed slowly to a height of 7,200 ft. There was now more to it than just grinning: both men suddenly realized that they felt very hungry. Alcock made his feelings known by pointing his left hand at his mouth while he closed and opened it. Brown got the message. He reached behind him for their frugal meal of sandwiches which had been prepared for them by Miss Agnes Dooley at St. John's. They had also brought some whisky on board as well as a bottle of beer which they emptied and finally threw overboard.

The long-distance flight routine continued. Checks were made regularly on the revolution rate of both engines, on the cooling system temperature, on the oil pressure, and on the fuel consumption as they switched from an empty tank to the next full one. This gave Brown a task for which he was thankful: it made him warm. Before the tanks which directly fed the engines were empty, they had to be refilled by vigorous pumping from the main tank in the fuselage.

All these experiences and five hours of flying were behind them when they again saw the sun. It was now directly behind them. Brown knelt on his seat, grasped the sextant and calculated their position. It was a small triumph for them that they were only a few miles south of their planned route. Then once again they were swallowed up by cloud. They continued to fly with no visibility, chilled and deafened by the noise of the right-hand engine, until 9 p.m.

Then Brown wrote on a page in the log book: "Can you get above the clouds by 9:30? We need stars as soon as possible." He held up the scribbled lines and focused a pocket flashlight on the page. Alcock nodded his head rather indecisively. They were now flying at 5,400 ft., and climbed even higher, but found no way through the cloud.

Midnight came and went. It was now June 15, but there was no relief for the fliers. At 12:05 a.m. Brown wrote to Alcock: "Must see stars now." Their altitude was 6,500 ft. and they were surrounded by clouds and darkness. The only illumination was the green glow of the control panel lighting and the bursts of flame from the starboard engine. Alcock pulled the joy stick back lightly and opened the throttle. The clouds went on without end.

At 12:15 a.m. Alcock dug his fingers into Brown's shoulder, and pointed above his head. There was the moon, Vega, the Pole Star! Like a shot Brown was up on his seat, operating the sextant with his numbed fingers. In the frozen cockpit, Brown placed the open log book on his knee, spread out the navigation tables on the right-hand side, held them with his elbow and calculated the "Vimy's" position by the dim light of the flashlight which he held in his left hand.

At 12:25 a.m. their position was 50° 7' latitude north, 31° longitude west. They were already nearly half way across, but were still flying a little too far to the south. Brown made further calculations. They had already flown 850 nautical miles, which meant that about 1,000 more still lay ahead. Their average speed had been 106 knots.

At 12:30 a.m. the two optimists enjoyed some more sandwiches and coffee. Brown laced his coffee with whisky. "I looked towards Brown, and saw that he was singing," Alcock said, "but I couldn't understand a word." Brown's song about the swallow that flies so high and the river that never dries up was lost on the wind.

Meanwhile, in the newsroom of London's "Daily Mail" discussions about the "Vimy" and its crew were gloomy. A

A stiff leg, caused by a war wound, failed to keep Arthur Whitten-Brown from climbing out on the wings of the Vickers "Vimy" high above the waves during the first non-stop flight from America to Europe. Halfway across the Atlantic, icing of the engines had threatened disaster, and Brown's life depended on the skill and composure of pilot John Alcock. The two Englishmen landed in Ireland on June 15, 1919.

cable from St. John's had announced the takeoff; since then there had been no news either from Newfoundland or from the fliers. The newspaper staff knew that the "Vimy" carried a radio transmitter, but after three hours' flight it had gone dead, a fact neither Alcock nor Brown knew at the time. If all went well, the competitors for the £10,000 prize should reach the Irish coast at 9 a.m., but there was no sign of life from the "Vimy." Dispatches piled up on the news editor's table, but not one of them was from Alcock and Brown.

At 3 a.m. the fliers thought they saw the first signs of dawn. Suddenly they also saw something else: a new mountain of cumulus cloud ahead, again too close to circumvent. A sudden turbulence seized the machine and flung it out of control. Alcock and Brown felt themselves being pressed down into their seats. They were drenched by rain, which turned into hail. The swirling journey went on and on. At 90 knots the speedometer jammed. Alcock struggled to regain control and ended up more by luck than by good judgment in the safety of a nose dive. He cut off the gas and relied heavily on his experience as a night bomber pilot. The plane plummeted from 4,000 ft. to 100 ft. and, just above the surface of the water, Alcock gained control of the "Vimy." For a fraction of a second he could not believe his eyes—he saw the sea lying vertically, and then with a quick automatic reflex action he straightened out the "Vimy" and opened the throttles to the full.

"The salty taste we noted later on our tongues was foam," Alcock reported. "In any case the altimeter wasn't working at that low height and I think that we were not more than 16 to 20 ft. above the water." Brown's only comment was: "I kept thinking about Lieutenant Clement's weather report." Specifically, he had failed to forecast the snowstorm into which they had flown immediately after their recent narrow escape.

Like a shroud, snow covered the wings, fuselage, the struts, even the engines. Ice formed on the engine parts and Alcock needed all his strength to move the rudder. Unless something drastic was done, the men knew that the engine would stop and all the controls would go out of action. Once again, at an altitude of 8,500 ft., the non-stop fliers fought their way forward. Snow piled up in the cockpit, and both men crouched behind the windshield for protection from the icy wind. Snow on the carburetor air filters made both the engines run irregularly. Brown knelt on his seat and took off his goggles so that he could see more clearly. Ice now began to form on the engine intake connection; at the same time a layer of it was spreading over the inspection windows through which the fuel supply could be observed.

As far as Brown was concerned, the only possible way of avoiding a crash was to make a trip out onto the wings. He grabbed a knife and swung his legs out onto the nose. Seeing what he had in mind, Alcock stood up from his seat and tried to hold his companion back. Brown jerked himself free, and, in the blinding snow, he wriggled forward from strut to strut and from cable to cable, holding on with one hand. His left leg caused him difficulty because it was still stiff from wounds he had received in the war.

The limping lieutenant gradually removed the ice from the inlet connections and cautiously cleaned the inspection window of the fuel intake. The slip-stream tugged at him, and frost nibbled at the flesh on his hands. Brown cleared the air filters of snow—then he had to go back again, back and over the nose to the other wing and the other engine.

Meanwhile, Alcock had more than enough to do to keep the plane as steady as he could—flying at 8,000 ft. over the Atlantic in a snowstorm! One false move and Brown would have been plunged to his death, and his own number would undoubtedly have been up soon afterwards.

With astonishing bravery, Brown repeated his acrobatics, not once, but four times. Not a single step or a single movement of the hand was free from risk.

At 6:20 as day broke, the lateral controls were not operating. They too had iced up. An hour later the "Vimy" was flying approximately 3,800 ft. higher (at 11,800 ft.) when the sun appeared. For the last time the navigator stripped the gloves from his aching fingers and took up the sextant. His calculations showed that they were still on course. But it was obvious that the plane had to be lowered into warmer air if the elevator and other controls were to be prevented from freezing. Alcock moved the joy stick forward; the plane descended and was engulfed in cloud. Again the fliers had no visibility.

Icing presented a problem for which, in those days, there was virtually no practical answer. Even during this latest descent of the "Vimy" there was a distinct danger of the elevator's icing up. They were now only 30 minutes away from their longed-for goal. Alcock kept his eyes glued to the altimeter as the plane descended from 9,800 ft. to 6,800 ft. With the reduced throttle settings, the cutout engines were running perceptibly quieter. Then at 3,200 ft. Brown suddenly shouted: "It's melting! The ice is breaking up!"

Both men were soon sitting in a puddle; in the cockpit, too, the snow was melting. At 1,000 ft. above the ominously rough ocean, Alcock re-opened the throttles, and the engines responded; both ran smoothly. Twenty minutes later the men were triumphant: they had sighted land. Brown searched on his map. It was not Galway, for which they had been heading, yet Brown knew that the land must be Ireland. Then he saw the top of Connemara, identified the town of Clifden, and scribbled his observations into the log book which he held up for Alcock to read.

After flying toward the small town at a low height, Alcock circled over the streets and looked for an outlying meadow on which to land. He made a slow curve, found nothing suitable, then headed towards the Clifden radio-station and circled round it. Beyond the transmitter's tower he noticed an invitingly green meadow. The men in the transmitter building waved and gesticulated in vain. Below the deceptive green covering lay the extremely dangerous swamp, Derrygimla Moor. Alcock thought that the people in the tower were waving a welcome, and he brought the "Vimy" down—into the swamp. The plane ploughed a short, deep four-track furrow and buried its nose far into the mud. After 1,890 miles and 15 hours 57 minutes of flying time the heroes had landed in a bog. They had to remain seated, held fast by their safety belts.

The men who had watched the "Vimy" land rushed toward the plane, jumping from one grass tuft to another through the swamp. A man by the name of Taylor was the first to reach the fliers and he asked breathlessly:

"Anybody hurt?"

"No."

"Where are you from?"

"America."

The news of the adventure spread like wildfire, and there followed for Captain John Alcock and Lieutenant Arthur Whitten-Brown a hectic round of greetings, receptions, speeches, galas, and banquets. Brown made his shortest speech in Clifford Street, London. When he appeared with Alcock on the Aero Club balcony he stopped the cheering and said: "No speech now. You wanted us. Here we are!" At the banquet which followed the officers were greeted with an unforgettable menu unlikely to be found anywhere else. It consisted of: Oeufs Pochés Alcock, Suprême de Sole à la Brown, Poulet de Printemps à la Vickers Vimy, Salade Clifden, Surprise Britannia, Gâteau Grand Succès.

After the fliers received Lord Northcliffe's £10,000 prize from Winston Churchill, they insisted that the Vickers and Rolls-Royce mechanics who had helped them should receive a £2,000 share of it.

Official recognition of their pioneering achievement came a few days later from King George V. Captain Alcock and Lieutenant Whitten-Brown were received at Buckingham Palace. They left the Palace as Sir John and Sir Arthur.

On June 14, 1919, at 1:45 p.m., pilot John Alcock and navigator Arthur Whitten-Brown took off from Lester's Field, Newfoundland. After a difficult start in their over-laden Vickers "Vimy," the two fliers set off in the direction of Europe on a daring nonstop flight that was to make history.

Five years after the successful Curtiss flight, the United States, spurred by the flying achievements of lone British pilots, launched a large-scale project. Four twin-float seaplanes derived from the Douglas DT-1 and DT-2 "Torpedo Seaplanes" called "World Cruisers" and named "Seattle", "Boston", "Chicago," and "New Orleans," were to fly around the world. On April 6, 1924, they took off from Seattle. After encountering every kind of hardship, three of the planes reached Calcutta, where the floats were exchanged for wheels. The "World Cruisers" then flew via India, Persia, Asia Minor and the Balkans to France. From Paris they continued their flight to Croydon. Fog and cloud banks nearly brought the round-the-world flight to disaster over the North Atlantic. Finally two of the planes reached their home base at Seattle. The fliers took a host of records with them; they had covered some 28,000 miles in 175 days and 371 flying hours at an average speed of 74.5 m.p.h.

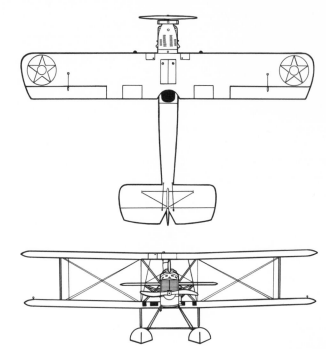

Douglas DWC/DOS/0-5 "World Cruiser"
Long-Distance Seaplane (1924)

Length . . . . 35 ft. 2½ in.
Wingspan . . . . 50 ft.
Weight fully loaded . . . . 8,797 lb.
Engine: 1 water-cooled "Liberty" V 12-cylinder engine
Power: 400-420 h.p.

2 man crew

Columbus 1928

The first non-stop transatlantic crossing from east to west

Prior to 1910, Professor Hugo Junkers made his living from the manufacture of heating appliances. Then, at the age of 51, he revealed his secret hobby, aviation, and published his "Nurflügel-Patent." The manufacturer, born on February 3, 1859, at Rheydt on the left bank of the Lower Rhine, thus added an aviation research center to his bath water heater factory at Dessau. The year after World War I broke out, on December 12, 1915, the Junkers Ju-1, with its metal cantilever wings, made its maiden flight amid the general suspicion and alarm of the Allies. By 1918, Junkers, in collaboration with Fokker, had built nearly 400 military aircraft, but from then on he devoted himself solely to passenger aircraft. From the Junkers F "Anneliese," designed in November, 1918, the F-13 was developed, the first Junkers all-metal low-wing monoplane. This passenger aircraft had four seats in an enclosed cabin. The "Junkers-Flugzeugwerke" was launched in June 1919, and the "Junkers Luftverkehrs A.G." in 1924. By 1925 some 178 Junkers machines had carried about 100,000 people over a total distance of 3,000,000 miles. That year the German Government used devious financial means to deprive Junkers of the ownership of his plant, and in 1934 the Nazis took it over completely. A year later, on his 76th birthday, the shy pioneer died. Nevertheless, his reputation continued to be linked with the output of the Junkers factory. His name was also associated with the sensational first east-west crossing of the Atlantic by Hermann Köhl, James Fitzmaurice, and Baron Günther von Hünefeld, who flew in a Junkers W-33 from Ireland to Labrador on April 12 and 13, 1928.

This great achievement began through the dismissal of Köhl from the newly formed "Deutsche Lufthansa," where he had been head of the Night Flight Department. The company was less interested in its staff, sporting records, and personal achievements than in profit from passengers, and when it heard of Captain Köhl's plans it fired him. Flying the Atlantic was, admittedly, a spectacular adventure, but adventure was not what Lufthansa was after. It just wanted to extend its passenger network.

Köhl had already flown as far as Baldonnel Aerodrome near Dublin with his wealthy "passenger," the aviation enthusiast Baron Günther von Hünefeld, and a mechanic named Spindler, and it was there that Köhl received news of his dismissal. The letter which relieved him of his duties was backed up by press releases in which Lufthansa officially dissociated itself from its night flight manager. Köhl's reaction was mild: "If I don't make it over there, I shan't need another job," he commented pertinently. "If I do make it, I shan't need to worry about one."

In Dublin, Colonel James Fitzmaurice, a commander in the Eire Air Force, joined the Köhl-Hünefeld team. Fitzmaurice was an experienced pilot and eager to take part in the adventure. Meanwhile, Spindler was sent back home. Köhl remained captain of the plane, Fitzmaurice acted as copilot, and Hünefeld, who had contributed a considerable amount of money to the venture, acted as interpreter to the two pilots. This trio planned a more northerly route than the one Lindbergh had taken in the opposite direction.

Many prophesied disaster. It was pointed out that on August 14, 1927, the "Bremen's" sister aircraft "Europa" had hardly left the German mainland when it ran into bad weather over the North Sea and had to turn back. Soon afterward, Köhl and Lohse, piloting the "Bremen," had to turn around and return in exactly the same way, because strong head winds had caused fuel consumption far beyond the calculated limits. Experts were unanimous in saying that an east-west flight would prove incomparably harder than Lindbergh's west-east flight, as the head winds would considerably increase the flying time. But the main argument against the planned venture was the unhappy experiment of the previous year. On May 8, 1927, the World War I fighter pilot Charles Nungesser, with his copilot François Coli, had set out to cross the Atlantic for the glory of France. They took off from Le Bourget airport for New York in their

Levasseur aircraft, "l'Oiseau Blanc," and were never seen again. All these objections had finally decided Lufthansa from permitting any such attempts to be made in its name.

But Köhl was tenacious, and Baron von Hünefeld, although in poor health, supported him fully. Fitzmaurice was eager to fly for the name of his Irish homeland, as well as to satisfy his taste for adventure. Furthermore, the three men had good grounds for believing in the reliability of their Junkers Ju W-33. Since 1919, when John Alcock and Arthur Brown had crossed from Newfoundland to Ireland in their Vickers "Vimy," great technical progress had been achieved in aircraft production, and the W-33 held several long-distance and endurance records. The low-wing monoplane, with fuselage and wings built of a light metal framework with corrugated sheet metal skin, had a wingspan of 58 ft. 3 in., a length of 34 ft. 9½ in., and stood 10 ft. 5 in. high. Junkers built 199 of these aircraft. The standard power unit, a 310 h.p. Junkers L-5 in-line 6-cylinder engine, was replaced by a 350 h.p. model. Nevertheless, because of the additional weight from the reserve fuel tanks, the W-33's average cruising speed of 100 m.p.h. now became the maximum speed. The postal and freighter version of the W-33 had a range of 620 miles. Köhl, Fitzmaurice, and Hünefeld would have to cover more than three times this distance in the "Bremen," in their resolute bid to cross the Atlantic.

At 5:23 a.m. on April 12, 1928, the "Bremen's" single engine was started. Köhl let it warm up for fifteen minutes; then he closed the cabin and pushed the throttle forward to the full. It was 5:38 when the overweighted craft began to move hesitantly forward. The fuselage and wing tanks contained 440 gallons of fuel. The W-33's normal flying weight of 5,512 lb. had been considerably exceeded.

In his book "Bremsklötze weg!" Köhl described the hazardous takeoff. The grass runway was bumpy and muddy. "I could feel the wheels sinking deep into the moist ground and it almost looked as if the feeble engine with its mere 350 h.p. would fail to drag the four tons behind it up the slope. What was quite certain was that we were not getting the essential increase in speed.

"Two ambulances suddenly darted out from behind the hangars. If we crashed at takeoff, they would be ready to drag us from the wreckage of our aircraft. We started to race the ambulances up the slope. At the time it almost looked to me as if they would reach America before we did. The top of the airfield ran quite smoothly. Now we began to win the race. The last third sloped gently downward. I hoped that here we would make up the speed we had not initially reached, since we needed to achieve 75 m.p.h. in order to leave the ground and our speed indicator was already hovering round 68 m.p.h. I felt triumph in my grasp when Fitz suddenly shouted something in my ear. The next moment I saw him snatch the elevator control.

"A sheep had walked from the right, straight onto the runway. Fitz had noticed it and at the very last minute got the aircraft higher, but it lacked sufficient speed and stalled, and because of the undercarriage suspension bumped several times along the ground. I thought it was all over and that we would certainly crash.

"Ahead of us the exhaust pipe was red hot and spewing flames, behind us 440 gallons of fuel were stored. If a spark brought the two of them together, we were done for. I wondered if it might not be better to switch off the ignition.

"Then the propeller would stop. We couldn't have that! So I left the ignition on and kept the plane very steady. Ahead of us lay a further 1,300 ft. of flat meadowland. At this point we should have been proudly airborne. We taxied for a further 800 ft., then I felt from the controls that the aircraft wanted to leave the ground. About 500 ft. ahead rose an embankment 13 ft. high with tall trees on top. We then did the only thing that we could: we held the plane to the ground to give it more speed and only at the very last second immediately before the obstacle did we give it height.

"The plane soared up, the undercarriage whipping through the tops of the trees. Later the machine stalled heavily more than once but remained airborne. Takeoff had been satisfactorily completed, as things worked out, but we were heading straight for a mountain. To the left, to the right, and ahead, its sides rose more speedily than we could climb. Only on the right behind us stretched a flat valley.

"I didn't think it possible that an aircraft so heavily loaded, at such a low height and slow speed, could undertake a turn to the right. But as the wheels were almost touching the ground we had to take this final risk. We started to make the turn. The right wing dipped low; it skimmed the grass surface, struck a hedge, but thanks to the aircraft's excellent aerodynamic qualities we got it through, had the valley ahead and passed straight on. Immediately afterward the 'Bremen' was traveling at 75 m.p.h., and 90 seconds later was flying at 500 ft. We were off to a successful start." The pilots quietly brought the aircraft higher; then "we made the final adjustments and set our course for America."

At 7:30 a.m. the "Bremen" was sighted for the last time from Ireland. Köhl, Fitzmaurice, and Hünefeld flew over Clifden, where Alcock and Brown had landed from America nine years before. From this point on the trio was wrapped in silence—of necessity, since the radio had been sacrificed in favor of additional fuel.

The weather was relatively good at the start. The first few hours went by without difficulty. Köhl and Fitzmaurice relied on the Air Ministry weather report which had been worked out right up to one final question mark—the fog bank near Newfoundland, which was virtually incalculable. The pilots worked in turn in three-hour shifts. Hünefeld plotted the course by compass, kept the log book, and trans-

Savoia Marchetti S-55 "Santa Maria" Transatlantic Flying Boat (1927)

Length	54 ft. 2 in.
Wingspan	78 ft. 9 in.
Height	16 ft. 5 in.
Weight fully loaded	14,619 lb.

Engines: 2 water-cooled Isotta-Fraschini "Asso" 12-cylinder in-line engines

Power: 525 h.p. each

3 man crew

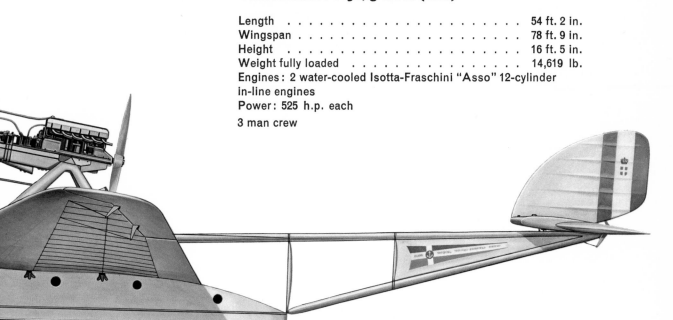

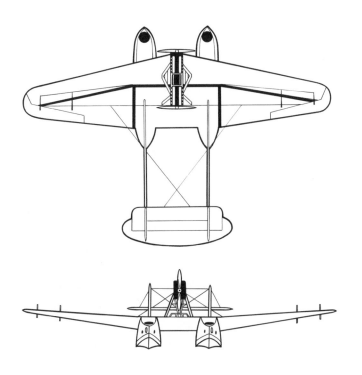

The S-55's manufacturer, Marchetti of the "Società Idrovolanti Alta Italia," designed it in two versions, as both a military and a civil flying boat. The Italian had original ideas. He located the cockpit in the mid-section of the thick broad wing. In addition he equipped the "Santa Maria" with a seawater distiller, fishing equipment, and a safety raft for emergency use. The Savoia-Marchetti S-55 became famous in the history of flight over the South Atlantic. Marquis Francesco de Pinedo, who in 1925 had flown from Rome to Tokyo, was also to fly for Mussolini in the "Santa Maria" with Captain Carlo del Prete as copilot, and with one mechanic. On February 13, 1927, de Pinedo flew via Morocco and Dakar to Pernambuco, Brazil, which he reached on February 24. Later, the "Santa Maria" took off for the West Indies, Cuba and New Orleans. Then after flying all around the United States, de Pinedo finally started from Arizona to San Diego, when fuel on the water burst into flames and the "Santa Maria" was destroyed by fire. The crew members were saved and Mussolini spoke of "anti-fascist sabotage." He sent the "Santa Maria II" to New York, and de Pinedo flew home in it from the Azores on May 23, 1927—the day when all the world was congratulating Lindbergh.

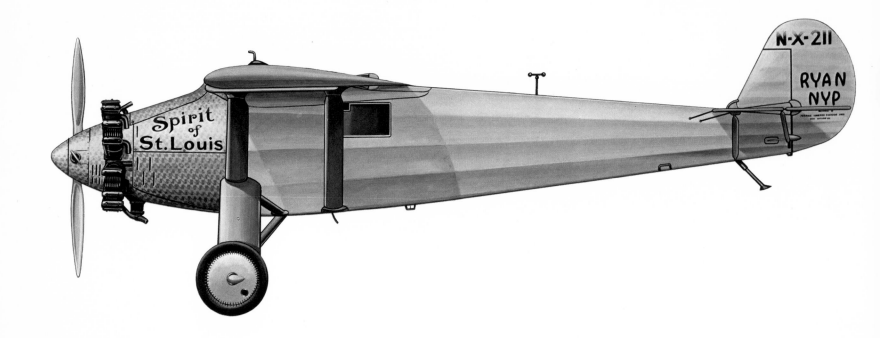

Ryan "NYP" "Spirit of St. Louis" Transatlantic Aircraft (1927)

Length . . . . 27 ft. 8 in.
Wingspan . . . . 46 ft.
Height . . . . 9 ft. 10 in.
Weight fully loaded . . . . 5,071 lb.
Engine: 1 air-cooled Wright "Whirlwind" J-5C 9-cylinder radial
engine
Power: 220 h.p.

1 man crew

Three "unknowns" became victors in the struggle to win the Orteig Prize for the first non-stop flight across the Atlantic, from New York to Paris. They were the Ryan Company of San Diego, which built the "Spirit of St. Louis" in the record time of 60 days; the small aircraft company's construction chief, 28 year-old Donald A. Hall, who designed the aircraft; and the 25 year-old mail pilot, Charles A. Lindbergh. Their famous competitor, the conqueror of the North Pole, Richard E. Byrd, made available to Lindbergh an extended runway on Roosevelt Field, and the young pilot, seizing his chance, took off at 7:52 a.m. on May 20, 1927, on his flight to Paris, and into history. At 22:24 hours on May 21, after a lonely flight of 33½ hours over 3,610 miles, Lindbergh landed at Le Bourget. Immediately his name became a symbol of heroism, and the "Spirit of St. Louis" a byword.

Bellanca W.B.2 "Columbia" Transatlantic Aircraft (1927)

Length	27 ft.
Wingspan	46 ft. 4 in.
Height	8 ft. 5½ in.
Weight fully loaded	5,402 lb.

Engine: 1 air-cooled Wright "Whirlwind" J-5 9-cylinder radial engine

Power: 200 h.p.

2 man crew

For 51 hours, 11 minutes and 14 seconds Clarence D. Chamberlin and Bert Acosta circled over Long Island, New York, setting a world record in their "Columbia." They had attained two objectives. A best performance for continuous flight without refueling, and assurance that their Bellanca W.B.2 could make a non-stop flight from New York to Berlin. In the end, Chamberlin made his transatlantic flight with Charles A. Levine, Bert Acosta having by then joined with Richard Byrd. Chamberlin and Levine took off for Berlin on June 4, 1927, and they landed at Eisleben two days later. An error in navigation had caused them to fly past the German capital. After a short interlude involving refueling, getting directions, and struggling with language difficulties, they flew on for Berlin but landed at Kottbus where the mayor provided them with a new propeller which got them, finally, to their goal.

lated. "In the daytime we flew by the sun and at night we navigated by the stars," Köhl wrote. He hit upon the idea of smoke bombs. "Every four hours we dropped a smoke bomb, and circled the spot from which the smoke rose. Then with our help Hünefeld worked out the direction and the speed of the wind." It was as simple as that. Fortunately their average height was often no more than 115 ft.

As night approached on April 13, the instrument-board lighting went out, and, except for the stars which could be seen from time to time through breaks in the clouds, they were left flying blind. When ordered to do so, Hünefeld aimed

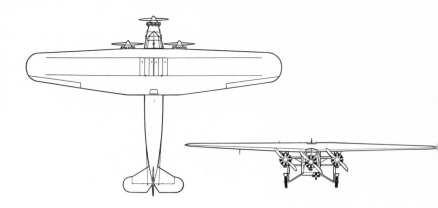

The public was getting restless, and Fokker himself was out of sorts. Yet Richard Byrd, Bert Acosta, Bernt Balchen, and George O. Noville refused to give up their preparations for a non-stop flight to Europe. They planned with foresight and care, but not until they were airborne did it become clear that Acosta had no blind flying experience. From then on Balchen flew by instruments, and Acosta by sight. They piloted the Fokker C-2 "America" right to Paris, where they were clearly heard over Le Bourget, but because of fog they flew back over the open sea. After cruising around they landed on the water just off the coast near Ver-sur-Mer in the Department of Calvados. The men had taken off from New York on June 29, 1927, and on July 1 they "ditched" in sight of France.

Fokker C-2 "America" Transatlantic Aircraft (1927)

Length . . . . 48 ft. 7⅓ in.
Wingspan . . . . 71 ft. 2½ in.
Height . . . . 12 ft. ½ in.
Weight fully loaded . . . . 7,409 lb.
Engines: 3 air-cooled Wright R-730 9-cylinder radial engines
Power: 220 h.p. each

3 man crew

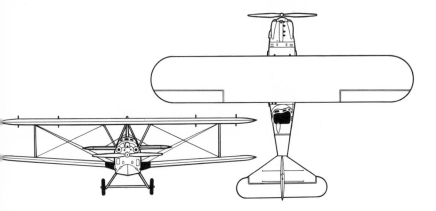

the rays of a pocket flashlight at the most important instruments. Then there was an alarming smell of fuel. The fuel pipe had broken, and fuel was leaking into the cockpit! Köhl reported the dramatic seconds which followed: "Fitzmaurice took the flashlight from Hünefeld and crawled back to the point where the pipe came out of the fuel tanks. We had no dividing wall between the tanks and the pilot's cabin. The pipe ran along the floor and that's where the leak was. Fitzmaurice found and repaired it with insulating tape, I believe. It all took place very quickly. The engine didn't even begin to miss."

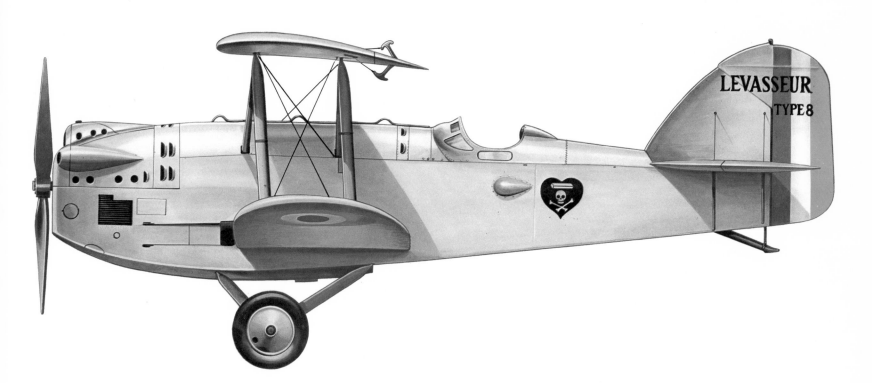

Levasseur PL-8 "L'Oiseau Blanc" ("White Bird") Transatlantic Aircraft (1927)

Length	32 ft.
Wingspan	48 ft.
Height	13 ft.
Weight fully loaded	10,936 lb.

Engine: 1 water-cooled Lorraine-Dietrich 12-cylinder "W" engine
Power: 450 h.p.

2 man crew

On May 8, 1927, the French fliers, Charles Nungesser and François Coli, set off from Le Bourget near Paris on a nonstop flight to America. Shortly after takeoff, Nungesser jettisoned the Levasseur PL-8's undercarriage, and a few hours later he and his copilot were seen over Ireland—for the last time. A report of their arrival in New York set the French buzzing with excitement. But their joy turned to sorrow when they learned that the report had been false and all hope of finding the two men alive gradually faded. Nungesser and Coli were never found; they and their "White Bird" had disappeared for all time.

Then at daybreak the compass went inexplicably out of action, and, without a radio, there was no remaining instrument by which they could guide their flight. New York must lie 1,000 miles to the south. They had enough fuel for that distance, but it was now impossible to determine their exact position. There was nothing else for it: "We'll keep on flying till we reach land," Köhl said.

He and Hünefeld had in the meantime decided to work in single-hour shifts. Finally they were flying over land, but they failed to see it. Thick layers of clouds concealed the fact that the plane had carried them north-westward and that they had flown over the north-eastern coast of Newfoundland. They could only guess at how much fuel remained, but after 36 hours of flying they knew the fuselage and wing tanks must be low. They decided to risk landing.

Köhl, who had just taken over from the Irish pilot, brought the aircraft lower. Suddenly he spotted a ship trapped in the ice near the coastline. As he brought the aircraft lower still, three pairs of eyes sought a flat surface that could serve as a landing place. What they had taken for an ice-bound ship turned out to be a lighthouse. There was no sign of a good surface—only blocks of ice, snow drifts, and frozen land. Köhl then began the most successful emergency landing of his career. He made for the frozen surface of a pond. With as much care as if dealing with a raw egg, he brought the "Bremen" down on the ice. A few yards further on the undercarriage crashed against a block of ice. The aircraft almost somersaulted, and one propeller blade was broken. Nevertheless, after a historic flight lasting 36 hours and 2 minutes, Köhl, Fitzmaurice, and Hünefeld had landed safely on Greenly Island off the coast of Labrador.

Attempts to get the aircraft airworthy again were unsuccessful, and the three men went by dog sleigh to the nearest settlement, Long Point. It was from here that the world heard the great news.

But there was a tragic sequel. It cost the life of the aviation pioneer, Floyd Bennett. He had been Byrd's pilot on the 1926 North Pole flight and in 1927 had himself crossed the Atlantic in a three-engined Fokker from America to France. He heard about the "Bremen's" crew and their accident on landing. Bennett was suffering from influenza, but he set out at once to pick up Köhl, Fitzmaurice, and Hünefeld, only to die en route from inflammation of the lungs. This shadow darkened the great achievement, but not for long. President Coolidge awarded Hermann Köhl the highest American aviation award, England welcomed the trio as guests of honor, and Germany gave them a royal welcome.

Meanwhile, Lufthansa sent its warmest congratulations to "its Hermann Köhl." It made him, the summarily dismissed employee, a notable offer, inviting him to become one of the four directors of the aviation company.

Hermann Köhl rejected the offer.

This low-winged monoplane was the first aircraft to cross the North Atlantic non-stop from east to west. Unlike Alcock and Brown, who were the first to span the ocean from west to east, Köhl, Fitzmaurice and von Hünefeld had the comfort of a plane with an enclosed cockpit. Furthermore, the Junkers L5 engine was well proven, and between 1926 and 1929, the Ju W-33 aircraft had set seventeen records, including the best performances for endurance and altitude. At about 5 a.m. on April 12, as the "Bremen" was due to take off from Baldonnel Airport in Ireland, the fliers got a great send-off, including the blessings of the President of the Irish Free State. An Irish Air Force biplane accompanied the "Bremen" as far as the coast, then for the next 36 ½ hours the fliers encountered the appalling weather conditions that had been forecast. Köhl, Fitzmaurice and von Hünefeld did not bring the "Bremen" down in New York, but on April 13, 1928, they made a skillful crash landing on ice in Newfoundland, and were able to telegraph from Point Amour that they had succeeded in making the first non-stop Atlantic flight from east to west.

Junkers Ju W-33 "Bremen" Transatlantic Aircraft (1928)

Length . . . . 34 ft. 9 ½ in.
Wingspan. . . . . 58 ft. 3 in.
Height . . . . 10 ft. 5 in.
Weight fully loaded . . . . 5,512 lb.
Transatlantic version . . . . 8,820 lb.
Engine: 1 water-cooled Junkers L5 6-cylinder in-line engine
Power: 350 h.p. (modified)
3 man crew

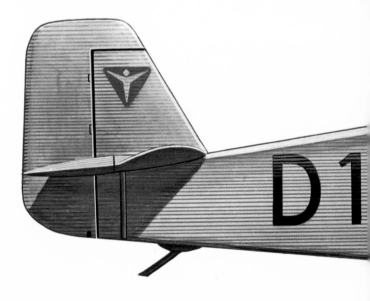

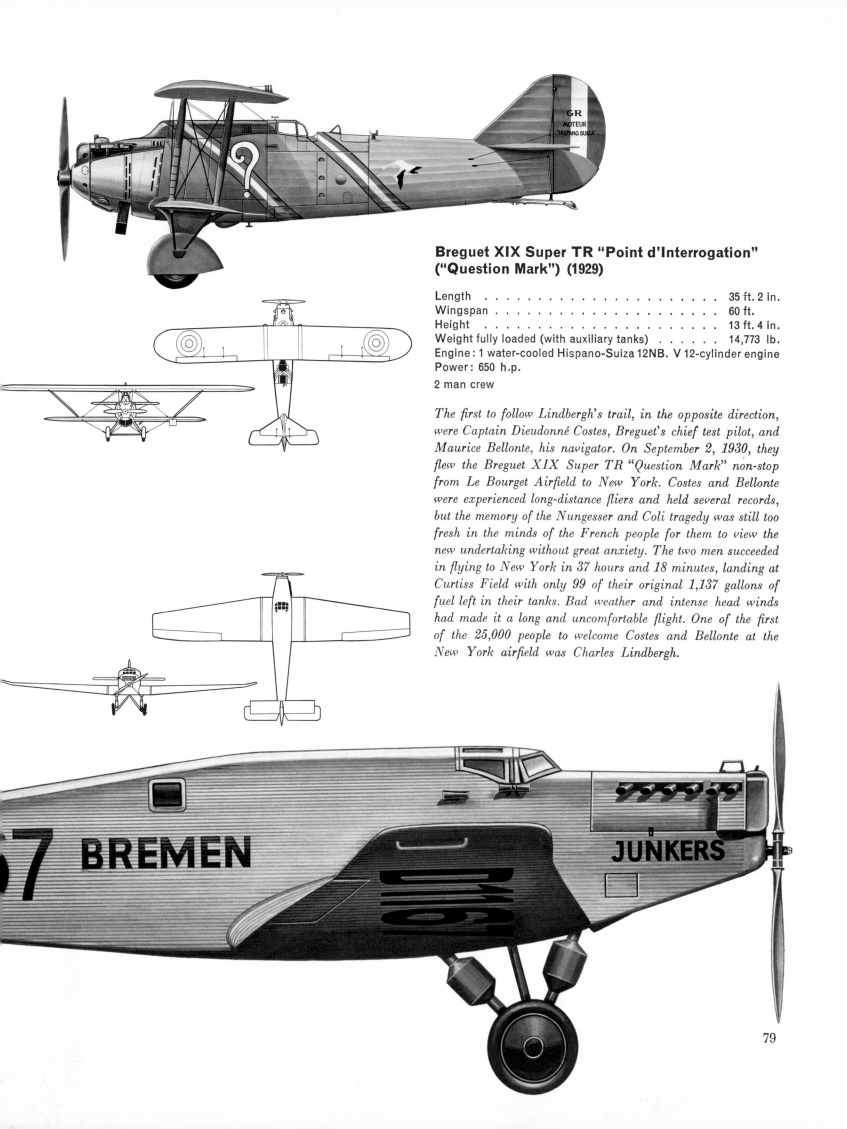

Breguet XIX Super TR "Point d'Interrogation" ("Question Mark") (1929)

Length . . . . 35 ft. 2 in.
Wingspan . . . . 60 ft.
Height . . . . 13 ft. 4 in.
Weight fully loaded (with auxiliary tanks) . . . . . . 14,773 lb.
Engine: 1 water-cooled Hispano-Suiza 12NB. V 12-cylinder engine
Power: 650 h.p.

2 man crew

The first to follow Lindbergh's trail, in the opposite direction, were Captain Dieudonné Costes, Breguet's chief test pilot, and Maurice Bellonte, his navigator. On September 2, 1930, they flew the Breguet XIX Super TR "Question Mark" non-stop from Le Bourget Airfield to New York. Costes and Bellonte were experienced long-distance fliers and held several records, but the memory of the Nungesser and Coli tragedy was still too fresh in the minds of the French people for them to view the new undertaking without great anxiety. The two men succeeded in flying to New York in 37 hours and 18 minutes, landing at Curtiss Field with only 99 of their original 1,137 gallons of fuel left in their tanks. Bad weather and intense head winds had made it a long and uncomfortable flight. One of the first of the 25,000 people to welcome Costes and Bellonte at the New York airfield was Charles Lindbergh.

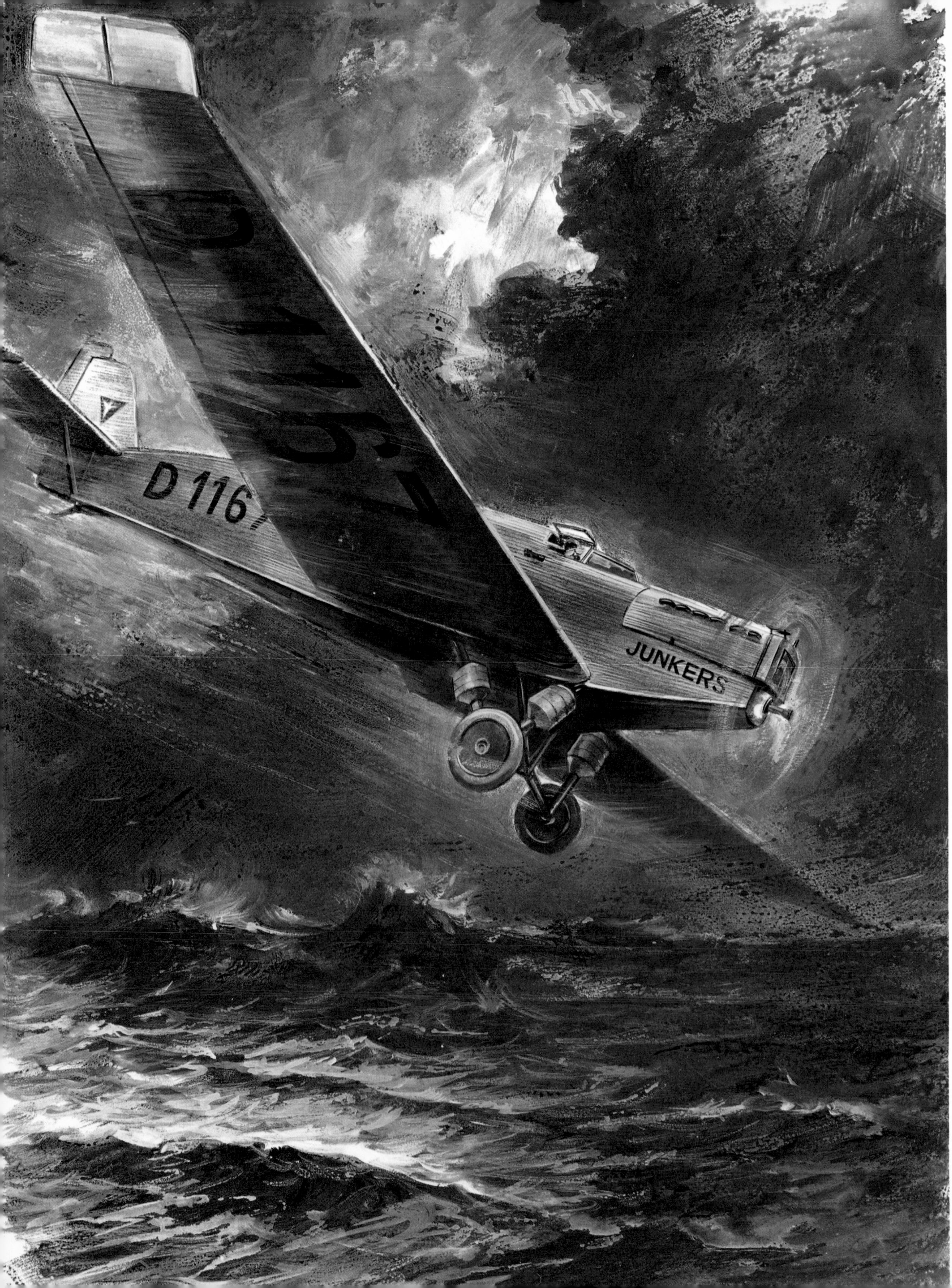
D 116
JUNKERS

Köhl, Fitzmaurice and Hünefeld made the first east to west non-stop flight over the North Atlantic in 1928. They flew in a Junkers Ju W-33, and landed off the coast of Labrador on April 13.

In 1927, the Frenchmen Nungesser and Coli took off from Paris in a Levasseur PL-8 for New York, but they never arrived. No trace of the fliers or their "White Bird" was ever found.

Duel among nations

The Schneider Cup

Aerial races and other competitive events became important incentives for the construction of more technically advanced aircraft, especially during the pioneer years between 1903 and 1939. Altitude records, climbing contests, long-distance records, endurance flights, stunt flying, and transport of heavy cargo continually stimulated aviation research. Speed races, which gave the greatest impulse to technical progress over the years, were the most spectacular. America had her Pulitzer races; Britain's pilots competed for the coveted "King's Cup," flew their own "Aerial Derby" as early as 1913, and staged long-distance races from England to Australia (the "MacRobertson Trophy") or to South Africa. Top French aviators competed for the "Coupe Deutsch de la Meurthe," and other nations constantly stove for new records in all events and classes. The "Schneider Prize," an international race for sea-planes, was one of the biggest shows of all. In 1931 an English Supermarine won the trophy for the third time running. Italy remained frustrated, but then went all out to break the world's absolute speed record, finally succeeding on October 23, 1934.

The "B. Z. am Mittag" published a report on September 30, 1927, on the "Schneider Prize" competition in Venice. Its author was Walter Kleffel, reporter for Berlin's Ullstein Publishers. A few days later, the journalist was invited by the British Ministry of Aviation to come to London; Kleffel had written a sensational report with detailed technical data on England's winning Supermarine machine. The British suspected a leak in their security system. But they didn't learn until much later that it had been Director Weiller of the French Gnôme-Rhône aircraft engine factory who had slipped Kleffel the information. Motivated by Gallic national pride and indignation, the French had given the plans of the English plane to a German; France's machine had not been finished in time for the event. In the Schneider Cup for the world's fastest aircraft—as so often happens in sports—prestige and vanity had exchanged roles with fairness and sportsmanship to the disadvantage of the latter.

Aviation enthusiast and Mülhausen industrial magnate Jacques Schneider founded the prize for the speediest of the speedy in 1913. The race was to take place annually and be open to all air-minded countries, and its aim was to promote the design of seaplanes, since Schneider attached great importance to this branch of flying. Seaplane racing began three years after Curtiss made the first takeoff from water in 1910. The first Schneider Cup race took place in

Monte Carlo on April 6, 1913, and a Morane-Saulnier, two Nieuports and a Deperdussin qualified out of 24 entries.

The show was exciting. Marcel Prévost started in his Deperdussin, Garros in the Morane-Saulnier, Espanet and Weymann flew Nieuports. Garros was the first to drop out; Espanet was forced down a little later because of damage to the fuel system. The race became a duel between Prévost and Weymann, over 174 miles in 28 laps. Weymann had already taken the lead by the fourth lap, but was forced to give up soon after because of engine trouble. The first Schneider Cup ended in a breeze-in for Prévost at an average speed of 46 m.p.h. (Prévost would have made better time if he had not had to repeat half a lap, after he had already landed, due to a timekeeper's error of not stopping the clock.)

Nevertheless, the first running of the Schneider Cup was considered a great success, and rightly so. For unlike other aerial races the pilots did not start in groups like racing cars, but took off singly at intervals, flying against the clock. The conditions of the contest also added to its difficulties; the winner's time had to be at least 5 miles an hour faster than that of the previous year to be acknowledged as a new record. Moreover, the pilots had to be masters of their art. Each lap had to be flown with precision and uniformity without losing a single foot of altitude or flying too far out from the check points on a single turn. This precision provided constant publicity for the event, which drew thousands of enthusiastic spectators year after year until it abruptly dropped into oblivion.

In addition, the racing committee set down strict regulations. Art for art's sake was out; the machines had to prove they were true seaplanes in every situation even before the event itself took place. The qualifying tests followed a complicated pattern. Every machine had to:

- move over the water in rough seas beyond the starting line under its own power;
- start and land after executing a loop;
- move on the water under its own power at a minimum velocity of twelve m.p.h. over a half-mile stretch between buoys;
- repeat the above-mentioned procedure;
- then start and land once again.

The machine also had to stay anchored for six hours to demonstrate its buoyancy and to prove that it remained seaworthy even while moored.

Prévost's success in the first Schneider Cup race particularly encouraged French pilots. No less than eight were entered the following year. But an Englishman won the contest: C. H. Pixton with his Sopwith "Tabloid" almost doubled Prévost's earlier speed. From that day onward England's pilots were determined to dominate the future scene. Apart from one French, two American, and three Italian victories, they succeeded as follows:

1913 *Winner:* Marcel Prévost, *France*
Machine: Deperdussin
Average speed.: 45.75 m.p.h.
Place: Monaco

1914 *Winner:* C. H. Pixton, *England*
Machine: Sopwith "Tabloid"
Average speed: 86.75 m.p.h.
Place: Monaco

1919 All machines eliminated; Italy's Savoia disqualified after ten laps at an average speed of 124.5 m.p.h.
Place: Bournemouth, England

1920 *Winner:* Luigi Bologna, *Italy*
Machine: Savoia S-12
Average speed: 107.20 m.p.h.
Place: Venice

1921 *Winner:* Lt. Briganti, *Italy*
Machine: Macchi M-7
Average speed: 117.85 m.p.h.
Place: Venice

1922 *Winner:* H. C. Baird, *England*
Machine: Supermarine "Sea Lion" III
Average speed: 145.70 m.p.h.
Place: Naples

1923 *Winner:* D. Rittenhouse, *U.S.A.*
Machine: Curtiss CR-3 Navy
Average speed: 177.38 m.p.h.
Place: Cowes, England

1925 *Winner:* James Doolittle, *U.S.A.*
Machine: Curtiss CR-3 Army
Average speed: 232.57 m.p.h.
Place: Baltimore, U.S.A.

1926 *Winner:* di Bernardi, *Italy*
Machine: Macchi M-39
Average speed: 246.49 m.p.h.
Place: Hampton Roads, U.S.A.

1927 *Winner:* S. N. Webster, *England*
Machine: Supermarine S-5
Average speed: 281.65 m.p.h.
Place: Venice

1929 *Winner:* Flt. Off. Waghorn, *England*
Machine: Supermarine S-6
Average speed: 328.63 m.p.h.
Place: Cowes, England

Britain's Supermarine machines remained uncontested victors of the Schneider Cup for seaplanes for three years running. In 1929 it was Flight Officer Waghorn who won the trophy in his Supermarine S-6, at Cowes, at an average speed of 328.63 m.p.h.

1931 *Winner:* J. H. Boothman, *England*
Machine: Supermarine S-6B
Average speed: 340.10 m.p.h.
Place: Lee on Solent, England

Italy's fliers, spurred on by their spirited pioneer, Marshal Balbo, never got over England's victories in 1927, 1929, and 1931, which retired the cup permanently to the British Isles. The Italians were to watch the last race on September 13, 1931, from the sidelines. Two of their aces for the Schneider Cup race, Monti and Bellini, crashed during test flights and were killed; the new Macchi never emerged from the testing stage. Other nations were no less plagued by misfortune. France had to withdraw her entry after one of the pilots crashed and both Nieuport machines failed to be ready in time. The United States could not enter because of lack of a suitable aircraft, and even England lost another pilot. The British Ministry of Aviation advised against taking part in the race; nevertheless, a Lady Houston donated £500,000 from her personal fortune to promote England's glory. Such a sporting gesture should not go unheeded, the aviators decided. Hence a two-man race: two Supermarines, two pilots, of whom Lieutenant Boothman won.

Between the first Schneider Cup competition in 1913 and the last classic machine to owe its existence to the race, the MC-72, lay a difference of nearly 400 m.p.h. in speed and indisputable advances in design. But the technical know-how gained by the designers during the planning and construction of the Schneider Cup aircraft was limited to the exclusive field of high-powered machines with pontoons. Another disadvantage also appeared. It soon became apparent that twelve months was entirely too short a time to design new models that always had to be faster than their predecessors. The period was too brief to enable more powerful engines to be developed and tested. There was seldom enough money, for the sums required to keep the participating aircraft competitive grew constantly — a phenomenon that appears to be inseparable from motorized racing. Thus the competitors decided to hold the race every other year, with one condition still unchanged: the event would take place in the country that had won the cup last.

Like automotive developments, airplanes kept pace with the demand for speed and more speed. When Orville Wright flew the first heavier-than-air machine on December 17, 1903, his brother Wilbur was able to trot alongside. In 1926, 23 years later, Italy's Major Bernardi attained a speed of 246 m.p.h. with his Macchi M-39, winning the Schneider Cup for Italy. His special Fiat engine, a genuine Italian "Macchina Nervosa," developed over 800 h.p.

One year later, Lieutenant S. N. Webster of England won the coveted trophy over the waters of the Adriatic with his

Deperdussin (1913)

On December 5, at an Aero Club de France banquet to award the Gordon Bennett Prize, Jacques Schneider, son of a prosperous industrialist, announced that he was founding a new contest: an annual race for seaplanes with a prize of £1,000 and a trophy for the winner. On April 6, 1913, Marcel Prévost, the French Deperdussin pilot, became the first to be inscribed on the Schneider Cup's list of winners. As early as 1912, French designer Bechereau had drawn up the basic plans of the externally braced Deperdussin monoplane, with which Prévost won the Gordon Bennett Cup race from September 27 to 29, 1913. The plane was distinguished by an aerodynamic styling so far ahead of its time that the United States, Great Britain and Germany withdrew their entries from the Gordon Bennett race. The superiority demonstrated by the Deperdussin seaplane in winning the Cup doubtless contributed to their decisions.

Sopwith "Tabloid" (1914)

The English Sopwith "Tabloid" won pilot Howard Pixton the Schneider Cup in 1914; it also influenced French aircraft designers, who had always been partial to monoplanes. This last biplane, the smallest and lightest in the 1914 competition, had been converted from a two-seater into a racing machine, with the second seat used for additional fuel containers. The recently-completed Gnôme-Monosoupape engine was so reliable that Pixton won the fifteen lap race on eight cylinders—one of the engine's nine cylinders was not functioning.

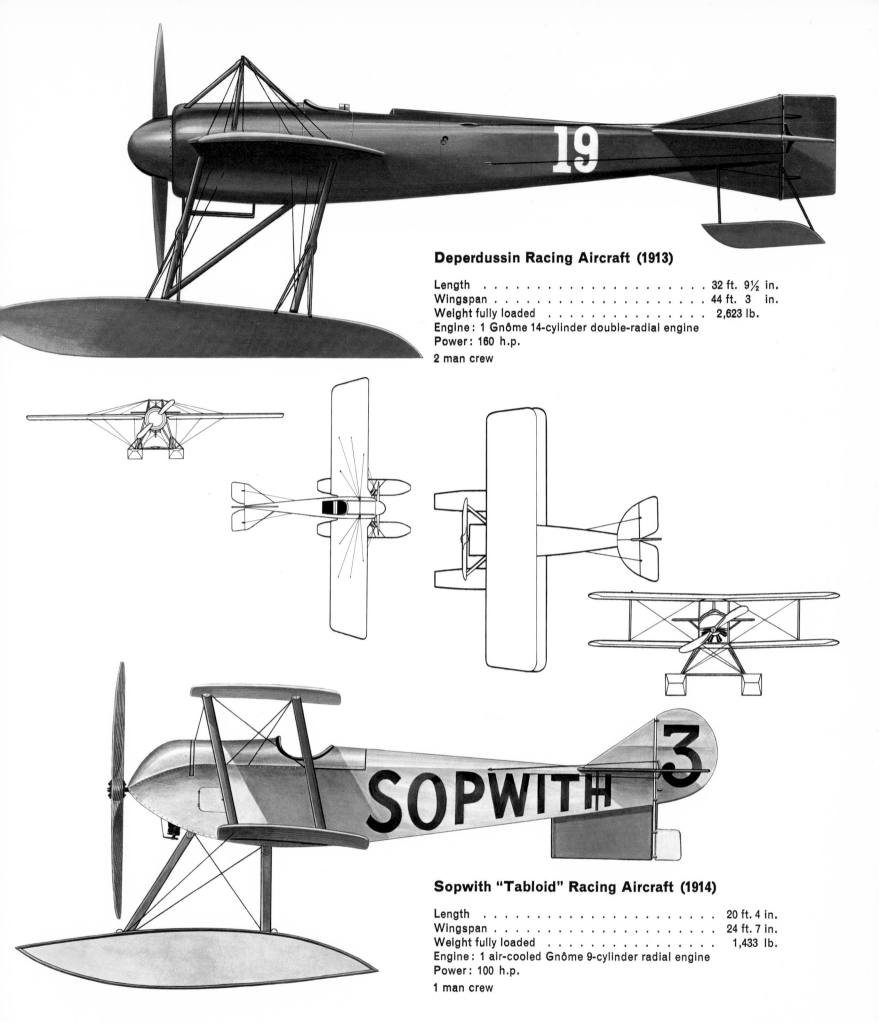

Deperdussin Racing Aircraft (1913)

Length . . . . 32 ft. 9½ in.
Wingspan . . . . 44 ft. 3 in.
Weight fully loaded . . . . 2,623 lb.
Engine: 1 Gnôme 14-cylinder double-radial engine
Power: 160 h.p.

2 man crew

Sopwith "Tabloid" Racing Aircraft (1914)

Length . . . . 20 ft. 4 in.
Wingspan . . . . 24 ft. 7 in.
Weight fully loaded . . . . 1,433 lb.
Engine: 1 air-cooled Gnôme 9-cylinder radial engine
Power: 100 h.p.

1 man crew

Curtiss CR-3 Navy Racing Aircraft (1923)

Length . . . . 25 ft. ⅜ in.
Wingspan . . . . 22 ft. 8 in.
Height . . . . 10 ft. 4 in.
Weight fully loaded . . . . 2,734 lb.
Engine: 1 water-cooled Curtiss V-12 in-line engine
Power: 450 h.p.

1 man crew

In 1921, the U.S. Navy ordered two racing planes for the Pulitzer Trophy race from the Curtiss Airplane & Motor Co. The Curtiss test pilot Bert Acosta, who later flew for Richard Byrd, made the first flight in August. He won the race with the CR-3. Both machines were modified for the Schneider Cup in 1923; Curtiss equipped them with pontoons and mounted the new V12 engine which developed 450 h.p. Lieutenant David Rittenhouse won the race for America in Cowes, England.

The large numbers painted on the planes are racing numbers and are not to identify specific models.

Macchi M-39 (1926)

Great Britain did not take part in the 1926 Schneider Cup race. Italy and the United States competed, and Major Mario di Bernardi carried off the trophy for Italy. His Macchi M-39 set a new record of 246.49 m.p.h.

Supermarine S-5 (1927)

Supermarines were the legitimate predecessors of the legendary Vickers "Spitfire" which gained such renown in World War II. In 1927, the Supermarine Aviation Works sent three Supermarines to the Adriatic to compete for the trophy donated by a French industrialist. The race became a duel between England and Italy. England's Flight Lieutenant Webster won the race with a record speed of 281.65 m.p.h.

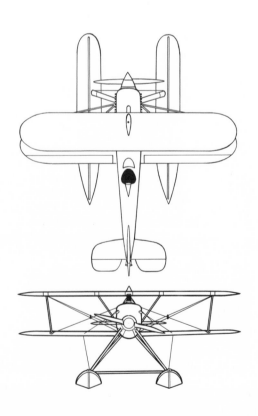

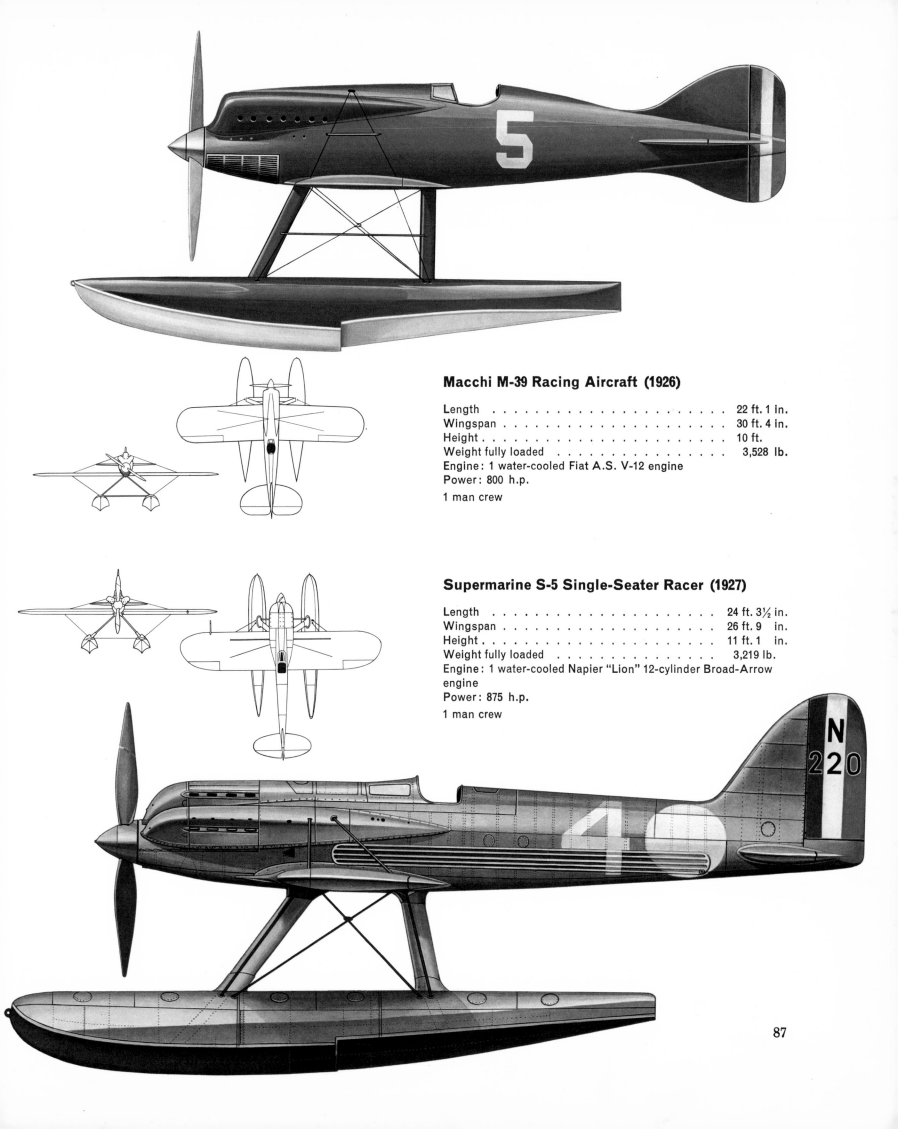

Macchi M-39 Racing Aircraft (1926)

Length . . . . 22 ft. 1 in.
Wingspan . . . . 30 ft. 4 in.
Height . . . . 10 ft.
Weight fully loaded . . . . 3,528 lb.
Engine: 1 water-cooled Fiat A.S. V-12 engine
Power: 800 h.p.

1 man crew

Supermarine S-5 Single-Seater Racer (1927)

Length . . . . 24 ft. 3½ in.
Wingspan . . . . 26 ft. 9 in.
Height . . . . 11 ft. 1 in.
Weight fully loaded . . . . 3,219 lb.
Engine: 1 water-cooled Napier "Lion" 12-cylinder Broad-Arrow
engine
Power: 875 h.p.

1 man crew

Supermarine S-5 N 220 plane at 281.65 m.p.h. His 12-cylinder Napier "Lion" VIIG engine had an output of more than 800 h.p., according to Kleffel in the "B. Z. am Mittag." Ernst Heinkel, host and witness of the race, was carried away by the "English Supermarine monoplane, which had been designed by Mitchell, an official in the British Ministry of Aviation. Its wings were still braced and not freely supporting, but otherwise the surface was so smooth and frictionless that I could literally 'see' its speed."

This happened — according to Heinkel — at a time when aerodynamics in aircraft design still played no decisive role. For aerodynamics was still largely an academic concept. Air flow, as far as it and its laws were known, was considered a virtually unexplored phenomenon; aircraft designers fell back on their prototypes. What could not be put down in black and white with slide rule and drawing board was replaced by power. The result: flying engines, around which sensitive frames were constructed, with the inevitable cockpit for the one who had to operate the whole thing. The problem has hardly changed up to the present day. Records, trying conditions, and lack of anything resembling comfort, go strictly together. Only, the wonder of it all has given way to a certain matter-of-factness.

"Alex Henshaw had prepared his 'Percival Mew Gull' especially for the race," a German reporter wrote of the winner of the "Race for the King's Cup" in England, "so that it deviated considerably from the standard design. He used an Original-Gypsy-Six 'R' of about 220 h.p. for an engine, adding a DH two-position variable pitch propeller. Additional extension of the crankshaft was necessary, likewise a longer propeller cap. The cockpit, located considerably back in the fuselage, scarcely extended above the sides, and frontal visibility was practically eliminated." Henshaw attained a speed of 236 m.p.h. in the "Race for the King's Cup" on July 2, 1938.

Eleven years after Ernst Heinkel had "literally seen" the speed of the Supermarine in Venice, the designers were still grappling with air resistance and ever faster, but still inadequate engines, while record-making pilots complained of bad frontal visibility. Had nothing changed since 1927? Nevertheless, the world's speed records for landplanes did not remain stationary; the American racing plane "Hughes," powered by a 1,000 h.p. Pratt & Whitney "Twin Wasp" engine, pushed the record up to 352 m.p.h. on September 14, 1935. Worthy of note was the machine's completely retractable landing gear, which marked a real step forward. As the development of the seaplane showed, it was a question of the long takeoff and landing strips, which only large surfaces of water could provide.

Methods of increasing lift, angle of climb, and speed, developments that were able to reduce landing speed and takeoff runs, were first discovered as the Schneider Prize

began taking a back seat to national races and individual records. The "magazine for all aviation," the "Deutsche Sport-Flieger," reported in October, 1938, with undisguised admiration that the Britons, R. J. Crouch and H. Bolas, had hit upon "very astonishing and satisfying results" in their "development of new ways of increasing lift." Crouch and Bolas had discovered that:

- "a notable increase in upthrust at low forward speeds occurred when the propeller slip-stream flowed over the greater part of the wings and when the propeller axis was inclined slightly downward toward the front."

The Englishmen built a test model, "whose two inner engines developed 420 h.p. each, but whose two outer engines developed only 145 h.p. each." Test flights revealed that an airplane so constructed:

- "reduced the takeoff run and time about 50 per cent, increased the angle of climb almost 100 per cent, hiked speed about 75 per cent, reduced the angle of vertical descent about 50 per cent, and lowered the landing speed and landing run by the same proportion."

It was 1934 when the Italians brought out their Macchi-Castoldi MC-72. Power above all was still the trump card. Mussolini, Air Marshal Balbo, and the hot-blooded national pride of the speed-obsessed nation made it impossible for them to reconcile themselves to the speed record's remaining in England.

Henceforth, the Italians were to concentrate their efforts on their air force "School of Speed" created in Desenzano on Lake Garda, where the process of testing, designing, rejecting, and improving continued. For a long time the engine designers faced a natural obstacle. Their engines, which were always souped up to the limit, often held up only just long enough to fly the standard 1.8 mile distance twice as required to break the world record, and for a long time they failed to last the distance even once. The Italians finally linked two engine units back-to-back on the MC-72, giving it the proud output of 2,800 h.p. Two counter-revolving propellers drove the Macchi through the air. On October 23, 1934, pilot Francesco Agello at last succeeded in bringing the absolute speed record back to Italy by attaining 440.5 m.p.h.

For five years, up until March 30, 1939, Agello retained the speed laurels. On March 30 the same year, Heinkel's 23 year-old test pilot, Hans Dieterle, hit 464 m.p.h. in a Heinkel He 100. Its DB 601 engine, developed by Daimler-Benz engineers, had 1,800 h.p. at 3,000 r.p.m.; a special oil and fuel containing an exceptionally high content of methyl alcohol were used. Ernst Heinkel recalled later that the life of the engine was "perhaps 60 minutes at the most." This was enough for Dieterle. And it was enough for the F.A.I.

In 1925 America's Lieutenant James Doolittle became famous overnight when he won his first great success in an army Curtiss CR-3, bringing the Schneider Cup to Baltimore, Maryland. As a lieutenant colonel in World War II, Doolittle led the first air attack on Tokyo on April 18, 1942; he also took part in preparations for the Allied invasion of North Africa.

Macchi-Castoldi MC-72 Record-Breaking Aircraft (1934)

Length . . . . 27 ft. 3½ in.
Wingspan . . . . 31 ft. 1 in.
Height . . . . 10 ft. 9½ in.
Weight fully loaded . . . . 6,417 lb.
Engines: 2 water-cooled Fiat A.S. 6 V 12-cylinder engines,
one behind the other, with reciprocal airscrew
Power: 2,800 h.p.

1 man crew

England's third victory in the Schneider Cup, which retired the trophy to her permanently, was a thorn in the side of the speed-conscious Italians. In the absence of further Schneider Cup racing, Italy set her sights on achieving the world speed record, and, on October 23, 1934, Francesco Agello attained it by flying at 440.5 m.p.h. in a specially designed Macchi-Castoldi type MC-72. The Air Force "School of Speed" on Lake Garda equipped the record-breaking machine with two back-to-back engines and two counter-rotating propellers. The record was to stand for five years.

The rules of the "Fédération Aéronautique Internationale" (F.A.I.) were very explicit: a 1.8 mile distance had to be flown twice in record-seeking attempts. Both ends of the stretch were marked by stationary semaphores. Another 1,640 ft. were allotted for approach and takeoff at both ends. The machine was not allowed to fly higher than 246 ft. over the distance, to prevent speeds from nose dives being greater than the engine's actual capacity. Officials under oath checked on the 246 ft. from the ground; aircraft controlled the 1,312 ft. altitude limit (the maximum height which the record-seeking airplane was allowed to attain during the entire flight between takeoff and landing).

The existing record was considered broken when:

- the new speed was at least five miles faster than the old record;
- and when the machine landed smoothly and undamaged after its flight.

Adolf Hitler sent Heinkel a telegram of congratulations, Hermann Göring spoke of an obligatory "glorious page in history." But 27 days later, Flight Captain Fritz Wendel broke this record in a Messerschmitt Me 209 V-1, flying 469 m.p.h. on April 26, 1939, a record for piston-engine aircraft that still stands today.

The He 100 developed 1,800 h.p. — likewise the Me 209 V-1. The two engines mounted back-to-back on Italy's Macchi-Castoldi MC-72 delivered 3,150 h.p., but this failed to prevent the intrepid Italians from being slower. The state of the technical progress in 1934 limited the speedy Francesco Agello's record because:

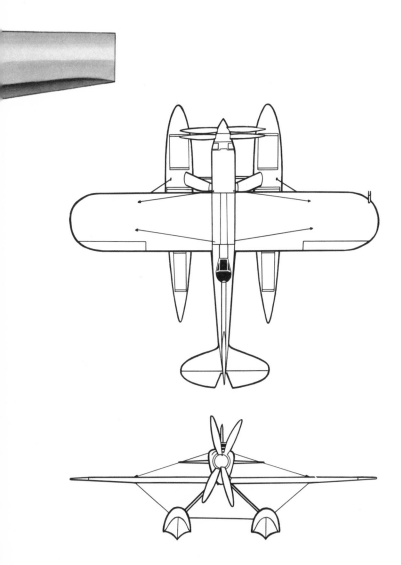

- his Macchi Castoldi MC-72 was a seaplane, whose huge pontoons could only be a hindrance in the air;
- the monoplane, braced from below and above, had too high an air resistance despite so-called streamlining;
- landing flaps and slats were not used; takeoff and landing runways were extended enormously.

However, the glory of the Messerschmitt machine, which broke the Italian record decisively for the second time, was marred. The records of the F.A.I. in Paris list not the Me 209 V-1, but the Messerschmitt Me 109 R. The Me 209 V-1 had been falsely registered for the record attempt in order to give the impression that the record had been made by the then standard German interceptor, the Me 109. This plane, however, had just barely succeeded in topping the 373 mile limit.

Thus the Macchi-Castoldi MC-72 not only went down as the last of the classic Schneider Prize machines (although it never actually competed for the cup itself), but it was also the last plane with piston engines to set a world record that had been entirely honest in its specifications.

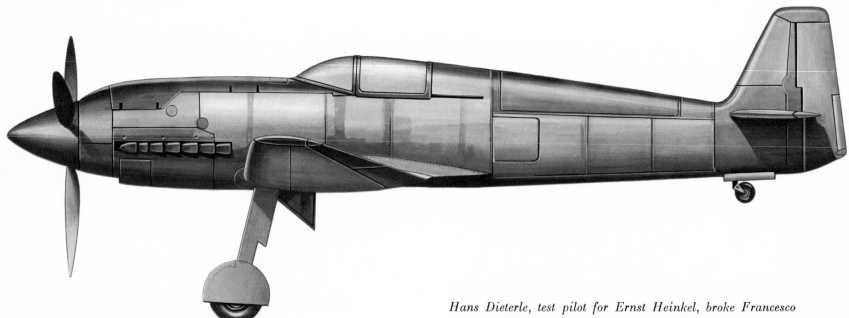

Heinkel He 100 V-8 Record Aircraft (1939)

Length . . . . 26 ft. 10 in.
Wingspan . . . . 24 ft. 11½ in.
Height . . . . 8 ft. 2½ in.
Weight fully loaded . . . . 5,600 lb.
Engine: 1 water-cooled Mercedes DB 601 A-1 in-line engine
Power: 1,800 h.p.

1 man crew

Hans Dieterle, test pilot for Ernst Heinkel, broke Francesco Agello's 1934 world record on March 30, 1939. He flew a Heinkel He 100 V-8 at a speed of 464 m.p.h. Hermann Göring immediately tried to exploit the German record for Nazi propaganda. The air marshal claimed that the He 100 was a standard model—as he did later with the Me 209. This was not correct. Heinkel, who, after Junkers, was Germany's most progressive aircraft industrialist in the thirties, was less interested in Göring's propaganda than in the record. Super-speedy planes had fascinated him all his life.

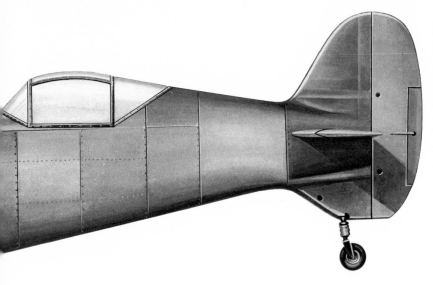

Messerschmitt Me 209 V-1 (Bf 109R) Low-Wing Record-Breaking Monoplane (1939)

Length . . . . 23 ft. 9 in.
Wingspan . . . . 25 ft. 7 in.
Height . . . . 9 ft. 4 in.
Weight fully loaded . . . . 4,673 lb.
Engine: 1 water-cooled Mercedes DB 601 ARJ 12-cylinder
suspended V engine with supercharger
Power: 1,800 h.p.

1 man crew

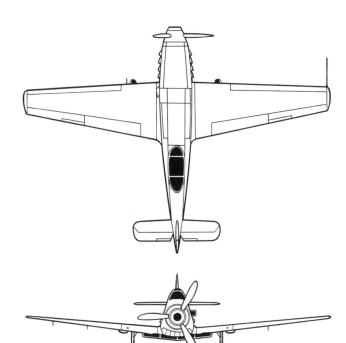

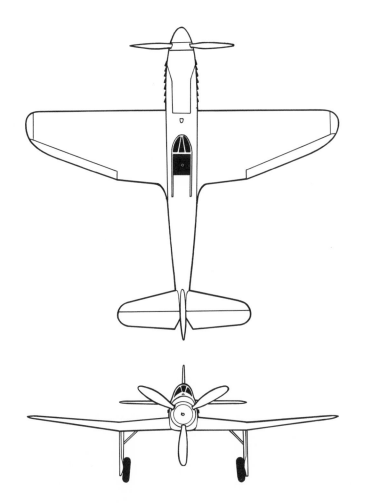

Dieterle's and Heinkel's He 100 record was short-lived; on April 26, 1939, Flight Captain Fritz Wendel broke the Heinkel record by 5 m.p.h. He was quite lucky, since world record attempts were only recognized if the new speed exceeded the old by at least 5 m.p.h. The Messerschmitt pilot flew 469 m.p.h. in a Me 209 V-1, which was designated officially as a Me 109 and entered in the F.A.I. record lists as such. It was a record for piston engine aircraft which still stands today.

93

"From here everything lies to the north!"

Richard E. Byrd flies over the South Pole

Richard Evelyn Byrd, born on October 25, 1888, in Winchester, Virginia, had two lifelong passions: polar exploration and flying. In 1926, with Floyd Bennett, he flew from Spitzbergen to the North Pole in "Josephine Ford," a Fokker F-VIIB-3M. In 1927 his Atlantic crossing in the "America," a Fokker tri-motor specially prepared for this attempt, ended in an emergency landing on the French coast. On November 28, 1929, Byrd, with three companions, became the first to fly over the South Pole. Shortly before the start of the expedition the explorer had decided against a Fokker in favor of a three-engined Ford 4-AT-B which he called "Floyd Bennett." The scientific knowledge gained by this flight opened up new horizons in polar meteorology, geography, and geology. The famous three-engined "Tin Goose" (as the model of the aircraft in which he flew was nicknamed by analogy to the "Tin Lizzy") made by Ford, was a close copy of the Dutch Fokker F-VIIB-3M. The American, William B. Stout, who is regarded as the "father" of this aircraft, once expressed the opinion that the "Tin Goose" itself did not represent a milestone in air travel; nevertheless, its forerunner, developed by Stout, had led to automobile constructor Henry Ford's interest in aviation and aircraft production.

"May the Sphinx of the North protect itself!" H. H. Houben, writer and expert on polar exploration, warned in 1927, the year when fliers of all nationalities were interested in discovering the two poles of our planet. Houben went on to describe enthusiastically, but not quite correctly, what had happened in the North: "In May 1926 [May 9] the Polar air rings with strange noises. The American flier, Commander Byrd, takes off from Kings Bay [Kongsfjord on Spitzbergen], reaches the Pole, circumnavigates it and, after fifteen hours' triumphant flight, returns to Kings Bay. There he is welcomed by Amundsen and his Italian companion, Nobile. Then on May 11 the new airship of Amundsen and Nobile, the "Norge," sets out and also reaches the Pole at 1 a.m. [May 12] in bright sunshine, descends as far as possible, but since it cannot land, flies on to Alaska and lands at Teller near Nome in fog, storm, and snow flurries. The propellers are almost completely iced over, the airship's skin is damaged, and no second flight will be possible. Nevertheless the first is a complete success.

"In its silent meditation the 'Sphinx of the North' felt fear and blinked its eyes, heavy with sleep, into the glimmering sunlight. What was that over there fluttering and spreading like a multicolored leaf over its white haze? Byrd's Stars and Stripes. Two days later the clatter of these alien birds approaches suspiciously near and once again colors flash in the sun: Amundsen's Norwegian and Nobile's Italian flag!"

Richard Evelyn Byrd was not satisfied to have been the first to have flown over the North Pole. Back in the United States he started making preparations to explore the South Pole, a feat he was to accomplish two years later. There was no long wait for the date which made history.

For the 38 men at the "Little America" Antarctic station, November 27, 1929, was a day like any other. The meteorologists recorded the usual temperature of minus 30° centigrade; the cook continued to tell his threadbare jokes; the medical officer, as usual, found everyone's health perfect and, as always, the huskies had begun barking for food at the crack of dawn.

On that morning four fur-clad figures and a handful of volunteers began work by sawing, hacking, and shoveling around a shapeless construction—half hut, half igloo. They had mixed feelings about that day, the icy prelude to a historic event. The igloo was visibly coming apart, and from it protruded the angular light metal fuselage of a 4-AT-B

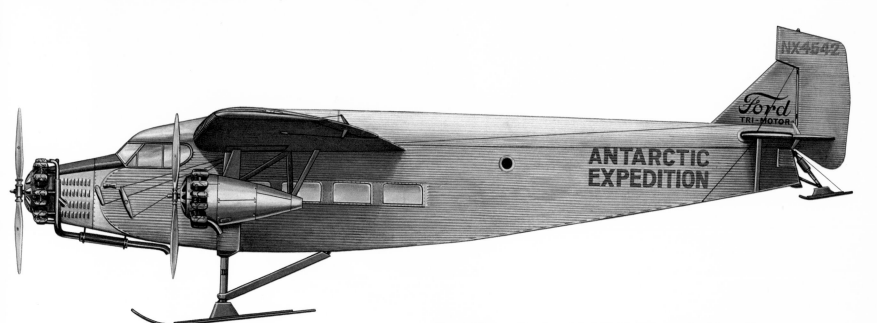

Ford Three-Engined 4-AT-15 Research Aircraft (1928-29)

Length . . . . 49 ft. 10 in.
Wingspan . . . . 74 ft.
Height . . . . 11 ft. 9 in.
Weight fully loaded . . . . 10,099 lb.
Engines : 3 air-cooled Wright J-6 9-cylinder radial engines
Power : 300 h.p. each

3 man crew — 11 passengers

Bernt Balchen, the pilot who had flown over the North Atlantic with Richard Byrd and Bert Acosta, also took part in Byrd's Arctic expedition. On November 28, 1929, he flew the "Tin Goose," Ford's tri-motor "Floyd Bennett," over the South Pole and back to the expedition camp. The fliers arrived over the Pole in pale afternoon sunshine. Byrd threw overboard an American flag weighted down with a stone from the grave of his North Pole pilot, Floyd Bennett. Harold June radioed the news back to the camp, and photographer McKinley attempted to take pictures of the earth's southernmost point. The Ford 4-AT-15 brought them back safely.

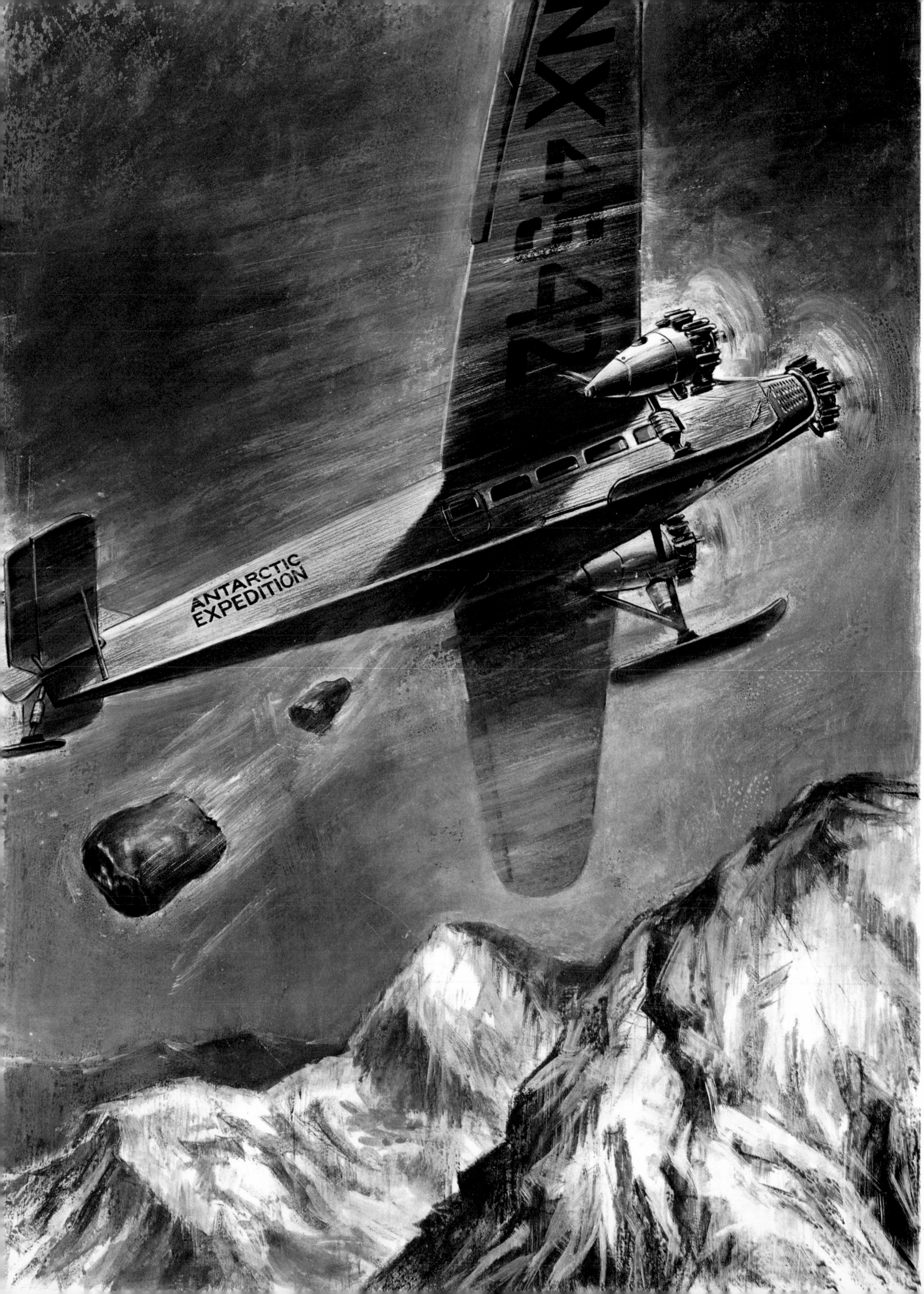
ANTARCTIC
EXPEDITION

on sprung runners. The men worked with a will, attaching the high wings to the monoplane and fitting the three engines. The cold paralyzed their fingers, but the ambition of making geographical history loosened stiff joints and made them oblivious to the icicles on their beards and eyebrows. At the start of the Antarctic night, beneath a sky glistening with colors ranging from steel blue to dark purple, they had finished their task. Byrd, navigator and leader of the expedition; Bernt Balchen, pilot; Harold June, radio operator; and Ashley McKinley, who was to operate the photographic equipment, withdrew with their aides into the safety of their station. On this particular night, there was little calm. The men kept asking anxiously questions such as: "Have we forgotten anything?" "Will the engines hold out?" and "Shall we ever get back at all?"

They did come back. The 4-AT-B, registration number NX-4542, which was to be the first aircraft to make the return journey over the mountains in the Queen Maud Range at the South Pole, had a reputation as a fully-developed and reliable model. From the test flight of the first 4-AT-B on June 11, 1926, this aircraft had won the Ford Motor Company a high reputation throughout the world. Henry Ford spared no expense on advertising to give his newest product a good image. Even more money was appropriated for preparation, delivery, and checking methods. William B. Stout, who in 1925 had sold Ford the first machine produced by his Stout Metal Airplane Company—the 2-AT with a Liberty engine—failed with his next aircraft, the 3-AT, which had a larger wingspan and three engines. Ford, enraged by this, replaced Stout and his team with Harold Hicks, who became the new head of aircraft production. Hicks, together with Tom Towles, produced the 4-AT as the definitive Ford three-engine aircraft.

When Byrd decided to attempt his flight over the South Pole, the plane had already made history. A Los Angeles automobile dealer, Jack Maddux, had purchased the first 4-AT-B in 1927. With it he founded Maddux Air Lines, and in October 1930 he entered into partnership with Transcontinental Air Transport. Maddux's contribution to this merger was his fleet of four aircraft. The new firm eventually grew into Transcontinental and Western Air Incorporated, the predecessor of the present T.W.A.

The Ford Aircraft Division was not only concerned with quality and safety. Aviation historian William T. Larkins reports a Ford-owned demonstration airfield complete with hangars, radio station for air traffic control, reception lounge, and airport hotel. In addition, a training school had been set up exclusively for aircraft pilots, where the rules of the course made the purchase of a "Tin Goose" dependent upon the qualifications of the prospective pilots: "Purchasers of planes are welcome to send their own men to our school for this special training, if they meet the requirements, but we must stipulate that our decision as to their fitness is final. So important do we regard this provision, that we reserve the right to decline to deliver a Ford airplane unless the pilot who is to fly it meets with the approval of our officials.

Bernt Balchen, Byrd's pilot on the South Pole flight, had already had considerable experience with the three-engined "Floyd Bennett" when the crew set off in November 1929. The measurements and specifications were standard for the lightweight version—which cost $65,000. The wingspan measured 74 ft. $1/3$ in., the length 49 ft. 10 in., and the height 11 ft. 9 in. Three Wright J-6 engines of 300 h.p. were the standard units. The 4-AT-B's normal flying weight of 10,099 lb. was admittedly somewhat exceeded by the "Floyd Bennett," which resulted in an appreciable reduction in speed of climb performance: standard, 7,182 ft. in ten minutes measured from sea level.

During the morning of November 28, skiers were called in who, in the event of an emergency landing, would aid the crew in returning to their home base or to outlying stations. Emergency rations were stored in the aircraft. The first trial runs of the engines appeared to confirm that all three power units had withstood the freezing conditions, and the crew made a first test by taking their seats and exchanging duties. McKinley found that, with the engines running, he was forced to lip-read any remarks shouted by June: he couldn't hear a word. "Either we shall have to make ourselves understood like the deaf and dumb," Byrd commented, "or we shall have to take a messenger dog along." The problem was solved by a double string which, running over two pegs in the air frame, enabled handwritten messages to be transported back and forth. Communications were kept as brief as possible. Since the engines caused heavy vibrations

Richard E. Byrd and his crew made the first flight to the South Pole in 1929, traveling in a three-engined Ford "Tin Goose." During their course over mountain barriers the "Tin Goose" developed engine trouble while trying to gain sufficient altitude, and forced them to cast off ballast in the form of fuel and emergency food rations.

in the comfortless machine, the writing was very shaky.

After making final preparations, Balchen turned the "Floyd Bennett" onto the bumpy runway. One last signal came from the ground staff—good wishes from all remaining behind. Takeoff was slow and laborious because of the excessive weight, but finally the aircraft was airborne and off into the Antarctic sky above the Ross Barrier.

By and large, the crew later explained, there was nothing very dangerous about the flight, "apart from the fact that we didn't know whether we would return, whether the engines might go dead on us, or whether the wings or the steering gear or the external controls would ice up."

This pioneering feat was not restricted to flying over the South Pole and obtaining abundant photometric and photographic material of the cold continent's whitest stretches. A Union Jack was thrown down (together with a stone from the grave of Byrd's North Pole pilot, Floyd Bennett) over the spot where Byrd shouted above the noise of the engine: "From here everything lies to the north!"

No less adventurous was a further step into new aviation territory, aerial mountaineering, which meant flying over mountain peaks. This was very important. Byrd's expedition confirmed the existence of a vast, high plateau with surrounding mountains of up to 13,156 ft. (Mount Fridtjof Nansen). When they were flying over the flat ice between "Little America" and the Queen Maud Mountains, the four men in the icy cockpit and the draughty fuselage debated whether they should sacrifice weight if the aircraft ran into difficulties while gaining height. What had been feared occurred, and Byrd, with Balchen's approval, jettisoned more than 500 gallons of fuel from the main tank in an attempt to lighten the aircraft. This did not help very much, and emergency rations were quickly thrown overboard. Even then the "Floyd Bennett" took a long time to gain height. "Unfortunately we had very little time," Balchen reported. "I don't think any of us gave a single thought to the fact that we should go hungry if we were forced to make an emergency landing. In those moments we did not see any so-called beckoning goals but threatening mountain crests—and turning round would have meant giving up."

A further problem was that shortwave ground navigation aids could not be used in the Queen Maud Mountains to detect passes at lower levels. Had Balchen, in fact, sought to find his way by use of the aids placed by the ground parties, the attempt, in reduced visibility, might have meant the end of the expedition. In unfavorable circumstances shortwaves can be reflected from rocks. The pilot—flying, as it were, by an echo-sounding system—takes his direction from them and may pilot his aircraft straight into a mountain.

Balchen had thoroughly familiarized himself with various observations of the Swiss mountain flier and airline pioneer, Walter Mittelholzer. He (following the Peruvian Chavez and the Argentinian Zuloaga) had systematically reported the circumstances surrounding this type of flying. Balchen was aware that weather and wind conditions in the mountains very often undergo unexpected reversals. At any height, gusts and turbulence from cliffs and on glaciers can have an unpredictable and highly dangerous effect on an aircraft's ability to keep on course or maintain height. Also, Balchen knew that for icy mountain flying use should be made only of solidly constructed aircraft equipped with powerful engines, and that the planes should be flown by pilots capable of meeting every possible danger.

The weather forecast from the far outlying meteorological station had predicted favorable conditions, and, in fact, throughout its entire flight the expedition remained free from excessively harmful weather.

10 a.m. on November 29, 1929, saw the return of the first men who had risked and lived through this adventure, a research flight for scientific purposes over the South Pole. The "Little America" base came into sight. Excitedly, the yapping dogs jumped up, and the men waved as if they themselves had taken part in the flight.

The United States government promoted Byrd to the rank of Vice Admiral. And following the successful exploit, the Ford Motor Company gave 4-AT-B NX-4542 a place of honor in the Henry Ford Museum at Dearborn.

The "Tin Goose" was, however, far from retirement. In 1932, when T.W.A. was replacing its Ford aircraft with Douglas DC-2's, and its peak period seemed to have passed, a spokesman for the Ford Aircraft Division rated the engine life of its tri-motored aircraft as "the 2,500 hours' flying time which only a three-engined plane can provide." Although sometimes condemned—John Collins, the Ford test pilot, had said, "I know the end has come for the old girl"—these aircraft flew in World War II, and even after it. Twelve "Tin Geese" are still in operation today, and three of them, two 4-AT-B's (N-7584 and N-7684) and a 5-AT-B N-1629-M, provide excellent service for the Island Airlines at Port Clinton, Ohio. They fly the shortest air route in the world, which lasts ten minutes from takeoff to landing. These planes carry an average of 35,000 passengers per year, and Island Airlines is the only line in the world carrying children to school every day in three-engined aircraft.

On the "Island Airlines" staff is Flight Captain Harold Hauck, who has logged more than 11,000 flying hours in "Tin Geese." But the N-1629-M beats him by far. Her log totals 22,900 hours, and she is still flying.

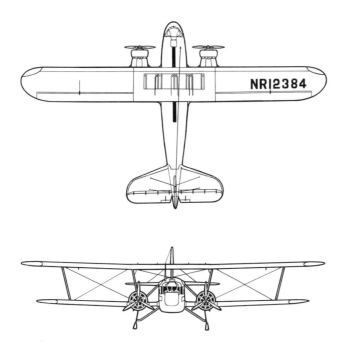

For his second Antarctic expedition, Admiral Byrd chose Curtiss-Wright's model T-32, which was considered to be one of the quietest passenger airliners of its day. It could take fifteen passengers. The explorer and his crew left Norfolk, Virginia, in October, 1933. Despite the acute business depression, Byrd not only succeeded in obtaining the materials he needed, but raised $150,000 in cash. When he and his group returned in March, 1935, they had explored no less than 450,000 square miles of Antarctic territory—mostly with the "Condor." Byrd selected this twin-engined biplane for its excellent flight properties, its roomy fuel tanks, and the conveniently large cargo space for his instruments. The Admiral had the plane modified with smaller propellers, reinforced interchangeable landing gear (pontoons, skids, wheels), additional navigation instruments and cowling engine designed for Antarctic conditions. Harold June, the radioman of the South Pole flight in 1929, was the pilot this time. The "Condor" lived up to its reputation for ruggedness; it spent the winter of 1933 to 1934 in a hangar of snow, and made its first flight over Byrd's camp, "Little America," in 1934.

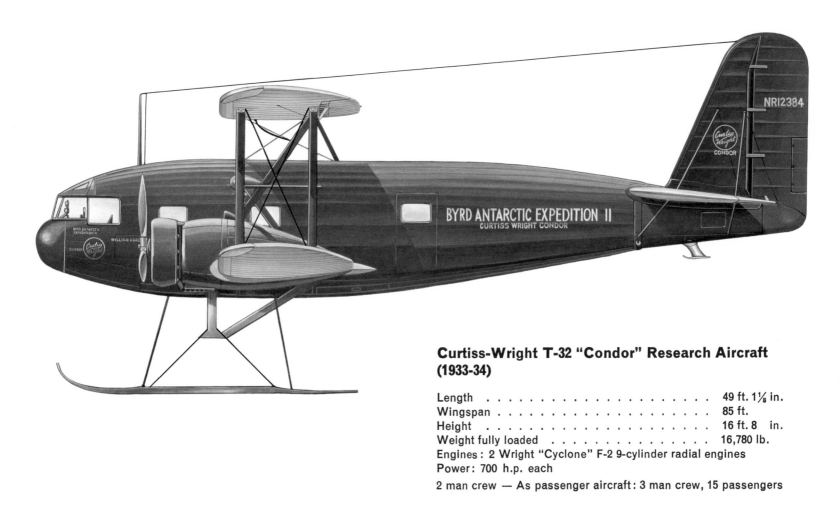

Curtiss-Wright T-32 "Condor" Research Aircraft (1933-34)

Length	49 ft. 1⅛ in.
Wingspan	85 ft.
Height	16 ft. 8 in.
Weight fully loaded	16,780 lb.

Engines: 2 Wright "Cyclone" F-2 9-cylinder radial engines
Power: 700 h.p. each

2 man crew — As passenger aircraft: 3 man crew, 15 passengers

DORNIER "WHALE", "DOLPHIN", DO-X

Whale above water

The world's air network
which was meant to take off from water

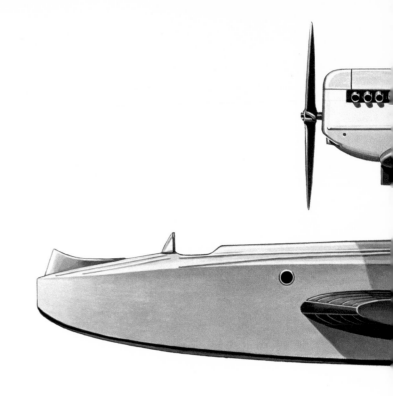

On May 25, 1966, a veteran American aircraft soared from Lake Washington in Seattle. It was the "B & W Seaplane," a 1916 Boeing and Westerhouse biplane with two imposing floats, flown by Boeing's ex-test pilot, Clayton Scott. The Boeing Company staged the event in honor of its founder, W. E. Boeing. The seaplane was a faithful reproduction, except that a modern 170 h.p. Lycoming replaced the original 125 h.p. Hall-Scott engine. Like young Boeing, many builders in the early years of flying thought that the future of aviation lay on the water. The early low-power engines of less than 100 h.p. were quickly developed into more powerful and faster types. Takeoff and landing runways could not keep pace with these high-speed developments, and, as a result, aircraft developers turned to water for the answer. In calm weather, the smooth runways provided by lakes stretched out almost without end. The United States made its contributions to progress with the flying boats of Glenn Martin and Igor Sikorsky, and Europe contributed to it largely with the designs of Heinkel and Dornier. The time when Claudius Dornier's "Whales" carried passengers on scheduled service down the coasts of South America have passed into history. The major role which seaplanes played then is over, but it is by no means forgotten.

Dornier Do J "Wal" ("Whale") Flying Boat (1930)

Length . . . . 57 ft. 3 in.
Wingspan . . . . 73 ft. 10 in.
Height . . . . 18 ft.
Weight fully loaded . . . . 176,400 lb.
Engines: 2 water-cooled BMW-VI engines in tandem (1 tractor screw, 1 pusher airscrew)
Power: 600 h.p. each
3 man crew

The young airman took out his penknife, looked suspiciously around the inside of the craft, and then attacked the red leather upholstery on the side walls of the cockpit. He threw the heavy armchair seat overboard, ripped out the carpeted floor, and, with hammer and pincers, removed all the non-essential iron fittings. Then he removed all the sand, dirt, and paint from the cabin.

Finally, Ernst Heinkel appeared to be satisfied. The pilot who had been signed up for his 100 h.p. Albatros monoplane, Hellmuth Hirth, could complain as much as he liked. It was he who had wanted the fancy cockpit, with the purpose of making a big impression at the Bodensee Hydroplane Competition in June 1913. The plane was certainly lighter now;

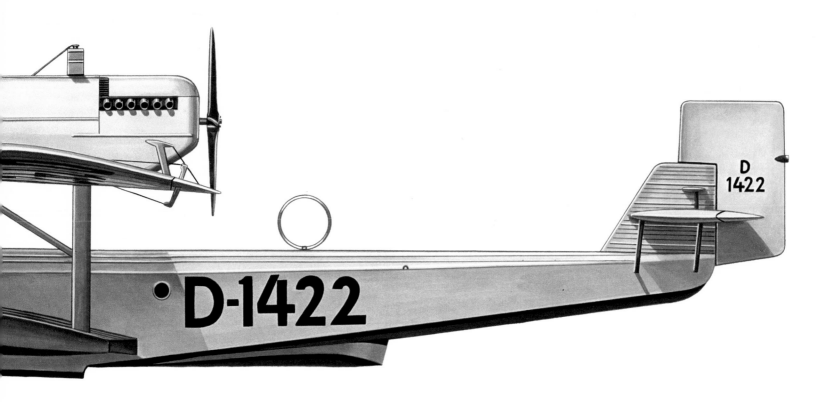

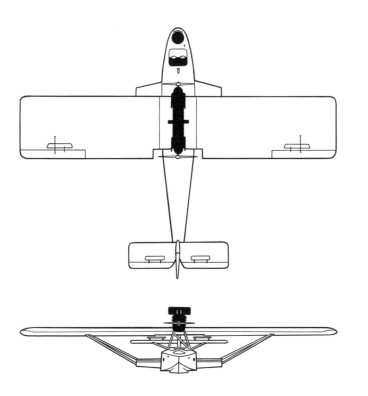

The twin-engined Dornier "Whale," a high-wing flying boat with an all-metal stressed skin construction, had a long series of noted predecessors. Ever since Dornier's Rs II of 1916, the designer had retained the tandem engine with push and pull propellers. Nevertheless, the Entente Commission, which controlled Germany's aviation, banned the "Whale," and Dornier went to Marina di Pisa in Italy where he began production of the J models in a newly-founded subsidiary. After the first flight, on November 6, 1922, contracts soon arrived from Spain and Italy, and the "Whale" went on to make aviation history. Amundsen made his dramatic polar flight to the 88th parallel in the northern hemisphere in a J type; de Beires and Franco crossed the South Atlantic in a "Whale" machine; and Wolfgang von Gronau, the chief instructor at Germany's official civilian flight leader school, pioneered a new route to New York in one. He took off from Warnemünde in a Dornier Do J with twin 450 h.p. BMW-VI engines on August 22, 1930, with a copilot, radioman, and a flight engineer on board. They flew over Reykjavik, Iceland, Ivigtut, Greenland, Labrador and Newfoundland, and landed the flying boat in New York near the Statue of Liberty. Thousands of New Yorkers welcomed the fliers. Gronau and his crew had covered 4,225 miles in four days, linking the United States and Germany in a route with relatively safe stopovers.

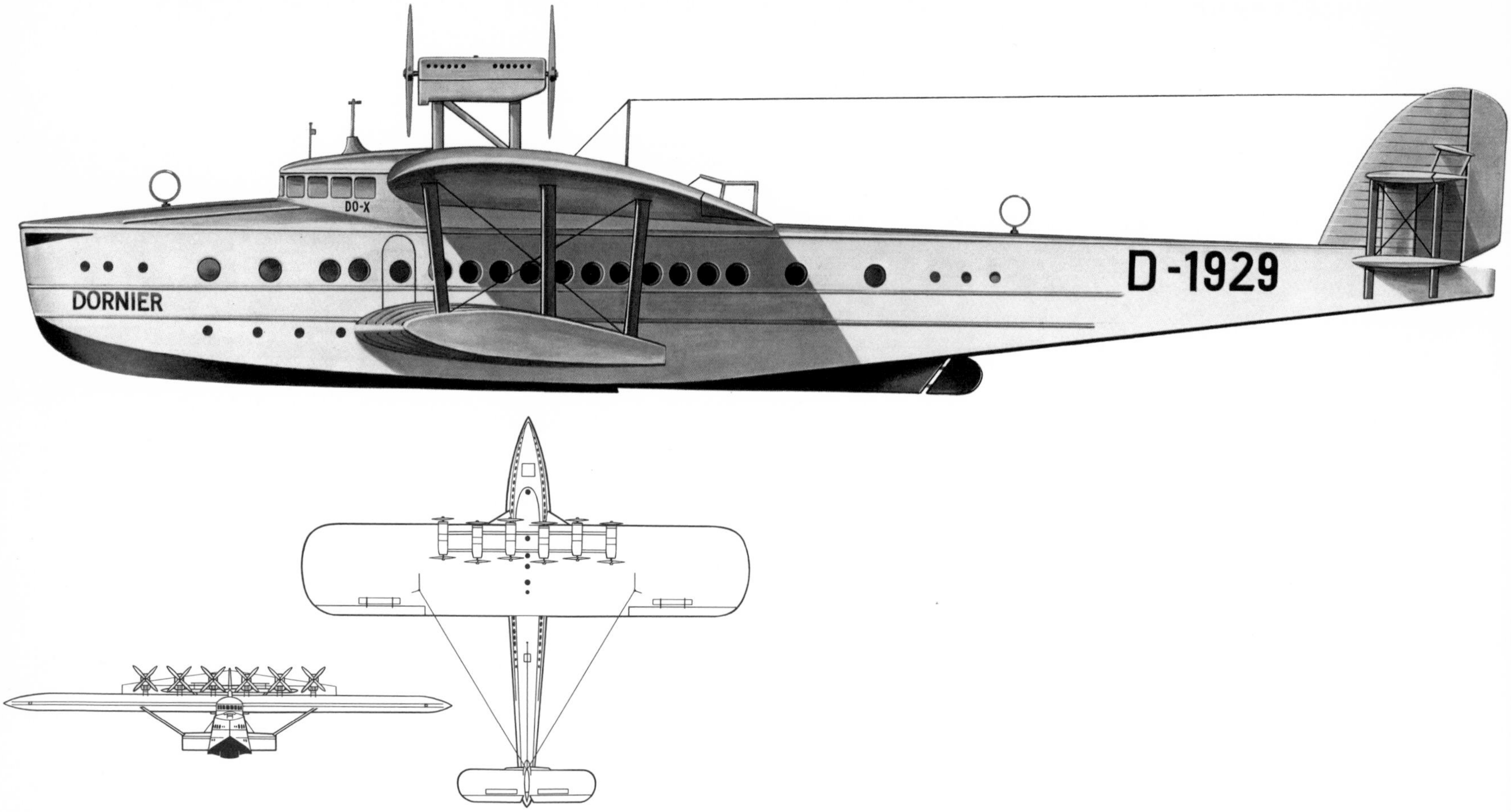
DO-X
DORNIER
D-1929

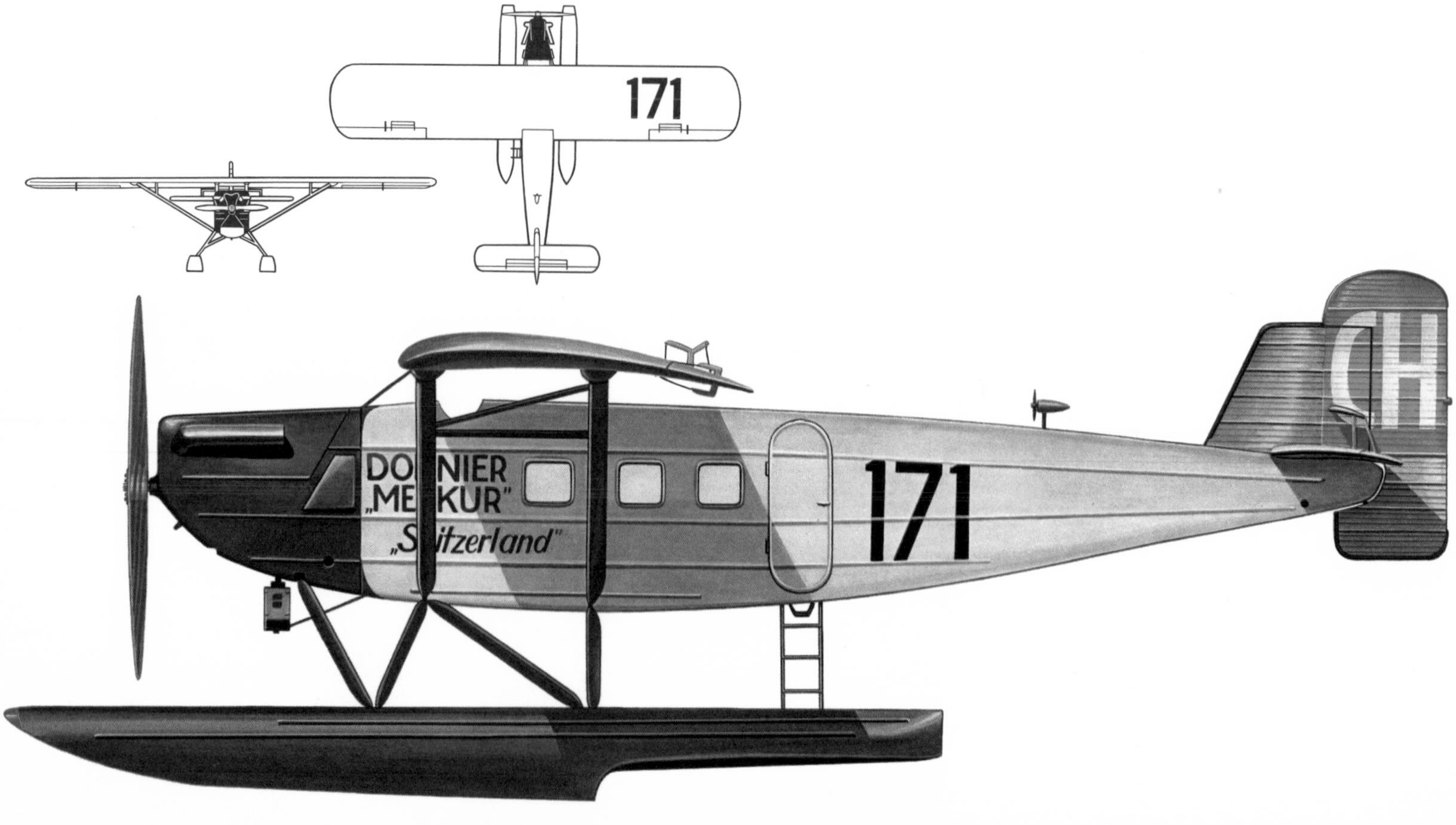
171
171
CH

Dornier Do X Airline Super Flying Boat (1929-31)

Length . . . . 131 ft. 5 in.
Wingspan . . . . 157 ft. 6 in.
Height . . . . 33 ft. 2 in.
Weight fully loaded . . . . 99,866 to 105,840 lb.
Engines : 12 Siemens "Jupiter" or Curtiss "Conqueror" or Fiat
engines in tandem on the wing
Power : 525 h.p. each (Siemens), 640 h.p. each (Curtiss) or 580 h.p.
each (Fiat)
14 man crew — 70 passengers

The huge flying boat, Dornier Do X, could accommodate up to 170 people. This machine made experimental flights to explore possibilities of connecting Europe and the New World more economically. The Do X also had the characteristic "Dornier stub wings" for greater stability on the water.

Dornier Do B "Merkur I" ("Mercury I") Passenger, Sea and Land Aircraft (1925-30)

Length : Land . . . . 41 ft.
          Sea . . . . 43 ft. 8 in.
Wingspan . . . . 64 ft. 4 in.
Height : Land . . . . 11 ft. 6 in.
          Sea . . . . 15 ft. 5 in.
Weight fully loaded : Land . . . . 8,158 lb.
                 Sea . . . . 7,938 lb.
Engine : 1 water-cooled BMW-VII in-line engine
Power : 460 h.p.

2 man crew — 6 passengers (for passenger service)

4 man crew (as Mittelholzer Research Aircraft)

Claudius Dornier's single-engined, multi-purpose Do B "Mercury" machine is linked to one of aviation's most versatile pioneers, Walter Mittelholzer, the Swiss pilot. Mittelholzer, co-founder and energetic promoter of Swiss aviation, was famed for, among other things, his long-range and research flights, which he nearly always conducted in Dornier machines. He made a spectacular exploratory flight through all Africa, after the pontoons of his "Mercury" had been exchanged for wheels during a stopover en route. The Swiss was also noted for his Alpine flights, and it was on one of these that his plane crashed and he was killed.

light enough, he hoped, to reverse the failure of the previous day when the aircraft, during a test flight, had failed to get into the air.

In his memoirs, written several decades later, Heinkel described the success that followed the stripping down of the Albatros cabin. On June 29, "Hirth won the first prize for rate of climb. He reached an altitude of 1,640 ft.—laughable today but tremendous at the time—in the seemingly unbelievable time of 11 minutes 6 seconds. He flew round the 124 mile course in 1 hour 46 minutes and 17 seconds. We were... far ahead of our competitors. The greatest success, as far as I personally was concerned, came when my aircraft was awarded the builder's prize."

In 1911, Lieutenant Colonel Hermann Hoernes had published a three-volume "Book of Flight." In one of the chapters, entitled "Mistaken Aerodynamic Concepts," Baron Roman Gostkowski, a college professor, expressed his views on the subject of weight. "What makes the flight of a mass less susceptible to external disturbances," he wrote, "is thus not its greater weight, but its greater energy, i.e. its greater mass *and* its greater speed." He minimized the effect of power producing motion; and, regarding time and speed, his views were that: "Both these concepts relate to things which are dissimilar and therefore cannot be brought into a numerical relationship with each other."

But Heinkel, two years later, had found it necessary to remove excessive weight from the fissures of his aircraft's body. And, at the same time, an official commission had made a new statement regarding values uniting *time*, *distance* and *speed* in a numerical relationship. Nevertheless, lightweight aircraft construction was still a long way off. Until then intuition and instinct had governed ideas and drawing boards; whether or not a plane would actually be able to fly was far removed from the theoretical calculations of the early designers. Only gradually did mathematics force its way into flight theory and aircraft construction.

In 1913, Algernon E. Berriman published a book entitled "Aviation," with an appendix containing reprints from the forward-looking British journal, "Flight." Accurate gliding angle diagrams were included in the book; and the author devoted a chapter to "Synthesis of Airplane Resistance." One "Flight" diagram illustrated the effect of centrifugal forces on an aircraft in a banked turn. In these early days, however, all such mathematical calculations and graphs remained theory; and much more was learned from experiments and the actual experience of pilots. At this time it was fundamentally unimportant which particular type of aircraft was to be developed. This was due to the fact that the successful construction of any plane that could become airborne and continue to be operative in the air represented an important step in the general development of aircraft design.

In Germany, hydroplanes were initially developed in the area around the Bodensee, which offered a fine stretch of water for takeoff and landing. The Bodensee attracted Count Zeppelin, whose ideas, incidentally, influenced lightweight aircraft construction long after his death and right up to the 1930's. Claudius Dornier also developed some of his best ideas there. In 1914, he had received instructions from Count Zeppelin to build giant aircraft for wartime use.

In 1911, Dornier had already begun the development of special light metal wing structures, and he was to discover practical answers to his theories on the problem of statics. However, a long way lay ahead before the Dornier Do L III "Dolphin" was born. This seaplane, accommodating eight passengers, finally came into being in 1921. Meanwhile Dornier developed several designs which were highly praised by experts. Before the first "Dolphin" was produced, Dornier's progress was marked by the following milestones:

- RS I Naval seaplane 3×180 h.p. Maybach engines, built 1914-1915;

- RS II Naval seaplane 4×240 h.p. Maybach engines, built 1916;

- RS III Naval seaplane 4×260 h.p. Maybach engines, built 1916-1917;

- RS IV Naval seaplane 4×260 h.p. Maybach engines, built 1917-1918;

- Cs I Naval two-seater combat plane, 195 h.p. Benz engine, built 1918;

- Gs I airline seaplane 2×260 h.p. Maybach engines, built 1918-1919;

- Do L III "Delphin" ("Dolphin") airline seaplane;

- The Do J "Wal" ("Whale") and the Do R "Superwal" ("Super Whale") built in 1923. The various versions of the "Dolphin" are the most outstanding ancestors of the legendary Do X.

Some 300 of the "Whale" flying boats, a stub hull high-wing monoplane with two engines mounted in tandem centrally on the wing, were built at Bodensee. Over 20 different water- and air-cooled engines were used in building the craft. Up to the end of 1932, according to a Dornier press release of that date, "Whales" had "covered more than six million miles for airline companies both in and outside Europe" on regular scheduled flights. A later release suggested that it must be unique in the history of flying for the same aircraft design to have remained unchanged for fifteen years without having become technically out-dated.

Success came easily to Claudius Dornier; and often it was not merely success, but triumph. Sometimes it happened that the individual achievement of a pilot flying in one of his machines made the pilot's name even better known than that of the publicity-shy designer. An example was the Swiss pilot, Walter Mittelholzer, whose name was a household word at the time for his flying expeditions over the Alps and world travels—in a Dornier machine. Mittelholzer even overshadowed his compatriot, Oskar Bider, who made the first flight across the Pyrenees, and the first from Berne to Madrid and from Berne to Milan.

Mittelholzer (who in partnership with Alfred Comte set up, in 1919, the "Ad Astra Aero" flying company, the forerunner of Swissair) took off in the winter of 1926 in a Dornier Do B "Mercury" for the Cape of Good Hope. This flight has its place not only in the history of flying, but also in that of scientific research. Mittelholzer chose the Dornier six-passenger airline plane, with its 460 h.p. BMW engine, because the various "Mercury" models had already proved their value on scheduled Swissair flights. His crew consisted of a flight mechanic, the Swiss geologist Dr. Arnold Heim, and the geographer, René Gouzy. The plan was to investigate geographical, geological and zoological aspects of the African continent. From Zurich, the air route of the "Mercury" included Pisa, Naples, Athens through to Abukir in Egypt. From there, stops were made at Luxor, Aswan, Khartoum, Malakal and Mongalla in the Sudan. Further stages at Butjaba and Lake Albert brought the crew to Jinja on Lake Victoria, where the schedule was interrupted because a member of the crew had developed malaria.

Eventually the four men flew on to Kisumu in Kenya, and to Mwanza and Bukoba in Tanganyika. Bukoba was chosen as their long-term base, and they made local exploratory trips into the region surrounding Lake Tanganyika. Then Mittelholzer flew the two scientists, Heim and Gouzy, to Rhodesia where they planned to collect material for their research; and with his flight mechanic he made various air trips up and down through regions in East and South Africa which led him as far as Capetown.

On his return to Zurich, Mittelholzer made the headlines, and Dornier came in for a share of publicity, his great reputation as a pioneering aircraft manufacturer being even further strengthened both at home and abroad.

The "Mercury" was originally a landplane, but for the Swiss research flight it was fitted with floats. In less than a hundred flying hours it had covered some 12,500 miles without incident. America's seaplane designers were duly impressed with the performance of the "Mercury," which had contributed one more milestone to the history of flight. Meanwhile, in November 1926, the German Ambassador to the United States had agreed to be flown in a Dornier machine, the "Atlantico," along the coast of South America from Buenos Aires to Rio de Janeiro. This Dornier "Whale" was owned by the Brazilian airline, Condor Syndicate. The flight was successful, and as a result the Brazilian Ministry

During the mid-thirties, the Dornier Do J "Whale" was used to speed up airmail services. The flying boats, carrying mail and freight, made stopovers on stationary ships and passenger liners equipped with catapult takeoff facilities. Eventually these planes were superseded by Short and Boeing Clippers with greater range.

of Transport granted the airline (with its single "Whale") an airmail permit. Before the end of the year a further concession was granted to extend the service to Rio Grande do Sul on the Uruguay border, and ultimately to Natal.

This success encouraged Dornier to start work on fresh projects, and, prompted by Lufthansa's interest, he began experimenting with bigger craft. The result of this development was his flying liner, Do X. Franz Ludwig Neher, the air historian, wrote:

"A whole year was spent by the Dornier design department on detailed drawings for the liner and its individual components; a whole year was taken up by tests and construction work at the Schweizer Werft. A further year was spent by the airliner in countless hours' flying over the Bodensee to test its reliability before it was released to carry out a task far more difficult than any up till then assigned to an aircraft." This task was to cross the ocean with passengers and demonstrate the profitability and comfort of an Atlantic air crossing, "an ideal combination of safety and speed." In his book, "The Miracle of Flight" (published in 1938), Neher also pointed out that "the liner's flights from 1930 to 1932 had nothing in common with any record flight." Records were not, in fact, Dornier's aim. Nevertheless, records show that the service flights of the Do X were spectacularly successful. A few technical details on the machine are as follows:

- 12 Curtiss "Conqueror" engines each of 600-700 h.p.;
- Wingspan: 157 ft. 6 in.;
- Length: 131 ft. 5 in.;
- Weight fully loaded: 105,840 lb.
- 70 passengers and crew (on a flight over the Bodensee a Do X carried 170 passengers.)

On November 5, 1929, Friedrich Christiansen, a World War I Pour-le-Mérite Naval flying ace and later Luftwaffe General, took over command of the plane, which had made its maiden flight on July 13 of that year. Then in the summer of 1930, the huge flying boat, piloted by Horst Merz and Cramer von Clausbruch, took off on a projected 20,505 mile trip from Bodensee via Lisbon and the Cape Verde Islands to the Americas, and from there back to the Muggelsee

near Berlin. Early in the trip, at Lisbon, a short circuit caused a fire on board which damaged part of the wings, and, as a result, any thought of continuing the flight for the summer had to be abandoned; spare parts had to be procured and assembled. Further delays were caused by the winter weather and spring storms over the Atlantic, but finally, on June 20, 1931, after a perfect flight, the aircraft landed in Rio Bay. A huge crowd of people was on hand to welcome and applaud its arrival. About nine weeks later, the Do X landed in New York Harbor. The reason for the time it took was a publicity experiment; the liner covered the distance in short stages, "anchoring" at every town of any size en route. The flight was a demonstration intended to break new ground.

On June 21, 1932, after having made flights all over the United States and along its coasts, the aircraft took off from Newfoundland on its last stage, the flight back over the Atlantic to Berlin.

Wherever the 12-engined giant landed, sightseers flocked in crowds to the dockside, some sailing out in pleasure boats for a closer look at the giant. Yet, eventually, the Do X passed into oblivion, which was in accordance with the wishes of its research-minded creator. Dornier explained: "Our main object was to supply practical proof, proof that the upper limits set on increasing the size of aircraft are far greater than theorists suppose."

However, following Dornier's Do X, the "Luftwaffe's largest hydroplane," the BV 222 Blohm and Voss "Viking" turned out to be somewhat smaller, instead of larger as some had expected. This double-decker transport plane was designed by Richard Vogt, and was equipped with six BMW Bramo 323 or six Junkers Jumo 207 engines. Its length was 121 ft. 4 ¾ in. compared with the 131 ft. 5 in. measurement of the Do X, and its wingspan was 150 ft. 11 in. as opposed to the predecessor's 157 ft. 6 in.

As a casualty and troop transport plane, the BV 222 "Viking" needed to be only as economic as a war budget required it to be. Whether or not, in its day, the Do X was an economic proposition remains unknown. No balance sheet was ever published of a trip covering 20,505 miles.

Of the Do X not a shred remains today. The plane ended up at Berlin's Aircraft Museum. During World War II the Museum was heavily bombed during a night raid, and both the building and the Do X were completely destroyed.

Boeing 314 "Yankee Clipper"
Passenger Flying Boat (1939)

Length . . . . 106 ft.
Wingspan . . . . 152 ft.
Height . . . . 27 ft. 7 in.
Weight fully loaded . . . . 82,400 lb.
Engines : 4 air-cooled Wright GR-2600 "Cyclone" double-radial
engines
Power : 1,500 h.p. each

10 man crew — 74 passengers

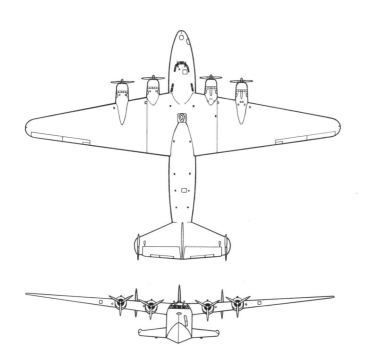

The Boeing 314 was the largest flying boat that Pan American Airways ever put into service. These Clippers flew both Atlantic and Pacific runs up to the end of the Second World War, and were then replaced by landplanes. The first "Yankee Clipper," christened by Eleanor Roosevelt, wife of the U.S. president, was introduced to the public at San Francisco's Golden Gate International Exposition in 1939. From there, the machine flew over San Diego and New Orleans to Baltimore. An "Atlantic Clipper" and a "Dixie Clipper" were introduced soon afterwards, but the "Yankee Clipper" was the first of these shapely flying boats to fly a regular service over the Atlantic. When World War II broke out, the P.A.A. "Clippers" provided a welcome means of escape from the Old World. The ten man crew made two round-trip Atlantic flights weekly in the four-engined planes. One flight stopped at Newfoundland; the other took a southerly route by way of the Azores.

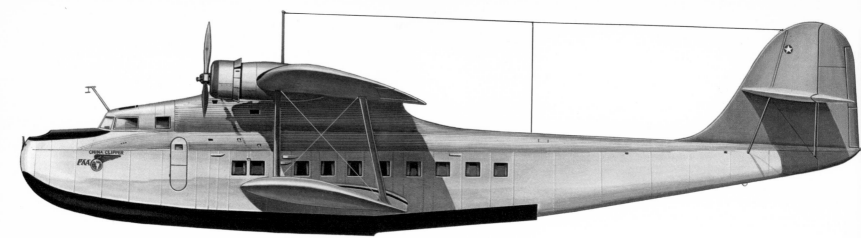

Martin 130 "China Clipper" Airline Flying Boat (1934-36)

Length . . . . 89 ft. 7 in.
Wingspan . . . . 130 ft. 3 in.
Height . . . . 23 ft. 11 in.
Weight fully loaded . . . . 52,015 lb.
Engines : 4 air-cooled Pratt & Whitney "Twin Wasp" S1A4G double-radial engines
Power : 830 h.p. each

6 man crew — 46 passengers (18 berths)

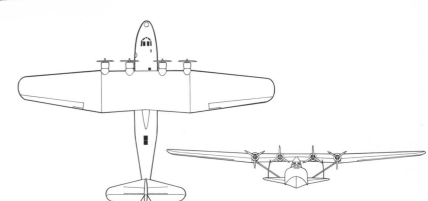

Blohm & Voss Ha 139B Catapult-Launched Long-Distance Postal Aircraft (1937-38)

Length . . . . 64 ft. 6 in.
Wingspan . . . . 96 ft. 9 in.
Height . . . . 15 ft. 9 in.
Weight fully loaded . . . . 38,587 lb.
Engines : 4 Junkers Jumo 205C Diesel engines
Power : 600 h.p. each

4–5 man crew

108

Aviation accelerates

Far-sighted Fokker and the passenger network

After his first exhibition flight over Haarlem in August 1911, his father gave him a gold watch. It was a characteristic gesture. Anthony Fokker was to face many difficulties during his pioneering life, and his father was always ready to encourage him, and to help him—except once. On February 22, 1912, young Fokker, the most outspoken flier in Berlin's Air Pilots' Association, declared his independence by setting up the "Fokker Aviatik GmbH." (later to become "Fokker Flugzeugwerke GmbH."). The company's initial capital was 20,000 Reichsmark. Fokker gave hair-raising demonstration flights, but they won him few customers. Time and again his father came to his rescue with cash. But finally Fokker senior, fearing that if this drain on his resources continued he would not have enough money left for his retirement, wrote to Anthony: "You can stand me on my head if you like, but don't expect another penny from me!" Somehow young Fokker managed, and soon he managed so well that shortly after the outbreak of World War I he was able to pay his father back not only the borrowed capital, but also interest that had never been requested.

On April 6, 1890, Anthony Herman Gerard Fokker was born into a wealthy family of Dutch planters in Blitar-Kediri, Java. Four years later the family moved to Haarlem, Holland, and by 1910 young Fokker had built his first aircraft: "Spin No. 1." A year later, when he was 21, Fokker obtained his flying license on "Spin No. 2." This aircraft, as opposed to the earlier one, had lateral controls. Soon he became proud owner of an aircraft factory near Schwerin and in 1919 he set up a new one at Veers in Holland, to which he managed to smuggle out of Germany 400 aircraft engines, 200 finished aircraft types D-VII, D-VIII, and C-1, 100 parachutes, and enough material to fill some 350 railway trucks. A few years later Fokker went to the United States and worked there for a time as a designer, and upon his return to Holland was in a position to license out seventeen aircraft designs to his competitors. On December 23, 1939, Fokker died in New York, and the aviation industry lost one of its most daring, gifted and business-minded pioneers.

After setting up his first factory, the going was tough for young Fokker; he starved from one order to the next. In August 1912, he took a chance and traveled to St. Petersburg where he attempted to sell six of his aircraft to the Tsar's army. He succeeded in disposing of one M-3 aircraft in Russia; not to the army, however, but to an enthusiastic young lady named Liuba "Pushka" Galanshikova. The girl followed him from St. Petersburg to Johannisthal, and he fell in love with her. However, Liuba's first thoughts were for Fokker; aviation was much further down on the list of her interests. Fokker, of course, was obsessed by flying, and the technical jargon he used without end increasingly irked the Russian girl until the romance finally foundered.

At the factory, the 22 year-old planemaker found himself badly in the red, and when the German Ministry of War continued to show no concrete evidence of placing an order, he gave flying lessons in partnership with his school friend, Fritz Cremer, in order to earn some money. The latter's teaching record was 83 pupils in one day! Up until July 1913, Fokker flew, taught, and built aircraft, losing money all the time. Then his first real break came when the German Army at last came through with an order. They bought ten aircraft at a price of 45,700 Reichsmark each.

The order gave a great boost to the morale of the Fokkers, both father and son, and to Fritz Cremer and Bernard de Waal who had joined the Fokker team. Yet the early M types (M-1 to M-4) brought the flying Dutchman little luck, and it was not until the M-5L was developed that a turning point in Fokker's fortunes was reached. Anthony, who later admitted that initially his aerobatic flights terrified him, completely overcame this fear in the summer of 1914 when he made his first loop-the-loop in an M-5L. The plane's performance also impressed the skeptics in the Ministry of War. Their Excellencies not only acknowledged the maneuverability of the

Junkers F 13 Passenger Aircraft (1919)

Length . . . . 33 ft. 3 in.
Wingspan . . . . 58 ft. 3 in.
Height . . . . 14 ft. 9 in.
Weight fully loaded . . . . 5,071 lb.
Engine: 1 Junkers L-2 engine
Power: 230 h.p.

2 man crew — 4 passengers

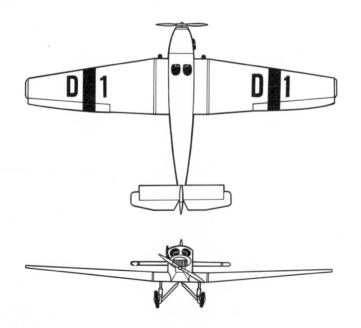

The Junkers F 13 was the world's first all-metal airliner. Even in the first year of manufacture, the internally-braced F 13 monoplanes with a body of light metal ribbing covered by corrugated tin plating, made flights to Austria, Poland, and the United States. In 1920, the new Junkers machines opened up routes to Columbia and Hungary, and in 1921 they were flying to Albania, Argentina, Italy, Japan, Persia, and the Soviet Union. This airplane combined economy, safety, and comfort to the utmost degree, and its design, shape, and materials became guidelines for aircraft development. In 1919 a crew of six established the world's altitude record at 22,146 ft. and two years later, an F 13 broke the world endurance record with a flight lasting 26 hours and 19 minutes. The Junkers creation encouraged Fokker and Stout to develop models on similar lines. The wing mounting stumps were provided with bolt fastenings. Junkers was the first to assemble aircraft by this method.

Schwerin aircraft, but thought highly of its climb perform-ance and its advanced technical equipment. Orders began to pour in to Fokker.

Then World War I broke out, and by December 1914, the German fighter pilot ace, Oswald Boelke, among many others, was singing the praises of the M-5K/MG —which had been given the military designation E-1. In a letter home Boelke wrote: "My best Christmas present is the new Fokker, about which I am as delighted as a child!"

Fokker was now 24 years old. The war was to bring him increasing renown, and, through orders for mass production fighter and combat aircraft, the kind of operating capital he needed. He put most of the money into his products, and the stock comment among pilots in Germany's Official Acceptance Committee was: "The aircraft industry's worst-looking factory produced the best-looking aircraft."

Fokker's fame rapidly grew up around:

- the M-14 (E-III), an improvement on the Service Mark E-1 (some 130 to 150 of these units were built from August 1916 onwards) which helped to put the factory on a sound economic basis;

- the V-4 (Dr-I), the only German triplane to be sent in large numbers (320) to the Western Front—where it made its mark in the Richthofen Squadrons from August 1917, until the end of October (when surprisingly two of them fell to pieces in the air);

- the V-24 (D-VIIF) single-seater fighter biplane, with its 185 h.p. BMW-III engine, of which some 4,000 units were built from May 1918, until the end of the war.

After the war, when the Allies ordered German war mate-rial to be handed over as part of the reparations agreement, the D-VII was the only aircraft to be mentioned by name. In fact, the U.S. Commission at Coblenz specified that 114 of the 200 aircraft to be surrendered must be of this type. The fighter planes, which still had a lot of service left in them, were transferred to the United States.

Fokker was a Dutchman, but during the war he had accepted German nationality under official pressure. Now that the hostilities had ended, the astute Dutchman quietly arranged for several freight trains, each 60 cars long, to transport a complete factory across the border to Holland. A restaurant car chef smuggled part of Fokker's fortune out of Germany, while his private yacht sailed across the North Sea to the Netherlands with another sizable portion. The flying Dutchman packed the rest of his fortune into a D-VIIF (fitted with additional fuel tanks) and took off for Holland under the eyes of the police guarding his factory.

"Fokker smuggles 100 million marks abroad," cried the German press, and the British Foreign Office warned the Netherlands Government at the Hague that "Anthony Fokker has cheated the Allies." The hundred million marks was an exaggeration, however, and the British Foreign Office, after first attempting to apply pressure, decided to withdraw.

Fokker had acted wisely in turning his back on Germany. Article 201 of the Peace Treaty of Versailles prohibited Germany from manufacturing aircraft or air engines, and it severely limited flying altitude. And in 1921 the "London Ultimatum" paralyzed Germany's aviation or, at least, was intended to do so.

Meanwhile, the young designer set about giving wings to civil aviation in Holland. However, in most countries during the early post-war days, passenger planes were frowned upon by the civil authorities. A former U.S. military pilot, Dick Depew, clearly expressed the plight of fliers when he was asked: "What is the most dangerous thing in aviation?" De-pew answered: "The danger of starving to death!"

To earn some money, many of the pilots went in for aerobatics, and the audacious demonstration flights they performed began to arouse a new interest in flying.

In February 1919, one French and one British company flew regular flights between London and Paris. In the United States, Aero Limited, founded in August 1919, earned a somewhat meager livelihood carrying holiday makers from New York to Atlantic City. At about this time, Finland founded its "Aero O. Y." Company, Austria its "Österrei-chische Luftverkehrs A.G.," and Switzerland its "Ad Astra Aero" Company. Each of these organizations was a pioneer in the field of commercial air passenger service.

The practical Swiss, with their "Ad Astra Aero" operation, were ahead of all competitors in demonstrating sound economic instinct. They started out with a small airfield at Schwamendingen, and in three years they had built up scheduled services to include takeoffs from Dübendorf, near Zurich, and from Berne, Basle, and Lausanne. Plane harbors had been built in Zurichhorn, Geneva, Ouchy, Lugano, Locarno, Rorschach, and Lucerne as well as on Lake Maggiore. A major influence on the explosive growth of both "Ad Astro Aero" and Swissair was the Swiss research flight pioneer, Walter Mittelholzer. He acquired for the company Junkers F 13 aircraft and also planes from Fokker and Dor-nier. One of Mittelholzer's countless air adventures occurred on January 8, 1930, when, carrying Baron Rothschild as a passenger, he became the first to pilot a flight over Mount Kilimanjaro. The successful trip contributed a great deal to promote passenger air travel.

Before 1920, Fokker already had a keen eye on K.L.M. ("Koninklijke Luchtvaart Maatschappij") or Royal Airline Company. On October 7, 1919, Dr. Albert Plesman had signed a paper setting up the "Maatschappij" (the full name in Dutch: "Naamlooze Vennootschap Koninklijke Luchtvaart

Maatschappij voor Nederland en Kolonien") and the following year on May 17, the company was to start regular passenger operations between Amsterdam and Croydon.

On that same day in May, Fokker took a group of Dutch journalists on board his F-II, and gave a demonstration flight not only for them, but for various representatives of Government Departments especially assembled for the occasion. As Fokker had hoped, his plane received an enthusiastic reception. Plesman was sufficiently impressed to order two F-II's from the Veere plant, and on September 30, for the first time, K.L.M. started flights to England with its own Dutch aircraft.

The history of the F-II is an eventful one. The aircraft derived from the V-45 (V means "Versuchsmuster" or experimental design), and had made its maiden flight in October 1919, piloted by Adolf Parge. At the end of that year, the F-II had remained behind in Schwerin, and Fokker was legally unable to remove it from Germany. However, his friend Reinhold Platz was still in Schwerin, holding the fort for him. Fokker was determined to get the plane to Holland at no matter what cost, and he persuaded Platz to work with him on a scheme that would outwit the Germans.

Fokker sent Bernard de Waal to Holland, where, wearing a false beard and dark glasses, he checked in at the Niederländischer Hof in Schwerin. De Waal contacted Platz. "The Spartacus League's Workers' Councils and the police are my main headaches," Platz complained. "We've got to pull the wool over their eyes. Two men from the Workers' Council are on my side, but there are police all around the runway!"

Platz managed to smuggle de Waal into the factory as a foreign visitor, and a few days later this foreign visitor flew straight out of the hangar in front of the startled police guards who began to run after the plane, shouting and gesticulating. Meanwhile, de Waal had decided that the F-II by itself was insufficient booty. There was a shortage of sewing machines in Holland, so he took one along with him.

De Waal's flight turned out to be a series of hops from one emergency landing to another. After half an hour in the air, while still over Germany, de Waal had to make his first landing. He did so in an open field, and managed to fix the faulty carburetor and take off again unnoticed. An hour later, the carburetor was acting up again, and he was forced to come down, this time, however, in front of two policemen.

"I made it perfectly clear to them," de Waal said later, "that I had lost my way and was a Dutch pilot. One of them went away to get orders. I told the other that as soon as I'd finished the repair I wanted to test the engine and see whether it was running smoothly. The policeman helpfully swung the propeller and suddenly the engine started. Then I simply set the plane in motion and when after a turn I flew over the meadow I saw the policeman below jumping wildly about and waving madly—probably not from amusement!"

De Waal's adventure ended in another emergency landing, but fortunately he had alighted on Dutch soil, and the F-II was soon back in the delighted Fokker's hands.

Even later the aircraft (with its K.L.M. registration H-NABD) seemed to have a way of attracting problems, but not all of them quite so amusing. On the airline's maiden flight with the F-II to Croydon on September 30, 1920, cooling difficulties delayed the takeoff; then the flight mechanic found that he had forgotten his tools and that the log book was temporarily mislaid. Yet, essentially, the jump to England over the "Blériot Line" and Dover was a complete success, and in Cricklewood, even Fred Handley-Page had words of praise for his competitors. The pilot on this flight to Croydon happened to be a one-eyed Englishman named W.G.R. Hinchcliffe.

Albert Plesman was a tough businessman, and on December 30 of that same year he created a big problem for Fokker when he "invited" him to buy back, at the original cost, the two aircraft K.L.M. had purchased and flown hard ever since. The argument was that K.L.M. would prefer later to purchase the up-to-date F-III. This, Plesman explained, was also in Fokker's interests, because K.L.M. would then be flying the best that his factory had produced. Fokker declined.

This *contretemps* was not the only one between Fokker and Plesman. The latter saw his task not merely to build up an air fleet for the honor of Holland, but to act as a shrewd businessman. Frequently this resulted in clear avarice. Plesman would calmly return aircraft that had been delivered to K.L.M. in exact accordance with the specifications and within the time-limit, requesting alterations—at the expense of the manufacturer.

Fokker's foreign clients proved less difficult to handle. One of these was the "DERU-Luft" (German-Russian Air Traffic Company) which Germany slyly used as a way to get around the Versailles Treaty regulations. The company bought twelve Fokker F-III's for its air network between Central Europe and Moscow. For a long time the experts of this company were puzzled by the aircraft's amazingly long takeoff runs—until one day they discovered the solution to the problem. The takeoff weight of the planes was always being exceeded because the pilots were smuggling watches, cheese, meat, perfume, and silk into Russia!

The U.S. pilots, too, got to know Fokker well. In May 1923, two of them, Kelly and McReady, flying a Fokker F-IV, made a non-stop coast to coast flight from San Diego to New York. This 36 hour flight set a world record for endurance.

Gradually flying shook off its earlier reputation as a mere novelty, useless for civilian purposes. Nevertheless, for a long while aircraft designs worked out solely for carrying passengers remained few and far between. Inventive airmen and zealous businessmen went on converting outdated combat aircraft into air transports as best they could. Their

Farman F-60 "Goliath" Passenger Aircraft (1919)

Length . . . . 47 ft.
Wingspan . . . . 86 ft. 10 in.
Weight fully loaded . . . . 10,519 lb.
Engines: 2 air-cooled Salmson CM.9 radial engines
Power: 260 h.p. each
2 man crew — 12 passengers

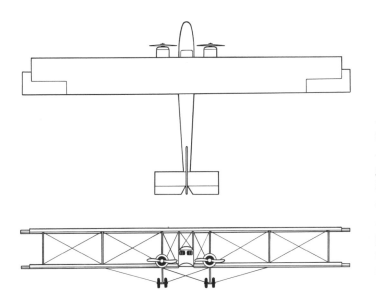

A Farman biplane made the initial flight on the Paris-London run, taking off from Le Bourget, near Paris, on February 8, 1919. Air France developed from this service. Farman's F-60 giant airplane, originally planned as a bomber but converted by the designer into a passenger machine, took fourteen people, comfortably seated in cane chairs, on the first flight to the English capital. The "Goliath" remained in service for many years, with various types of engine. A Farman F-60—together with numerous other entries—was once a candidate for the Orteig Prize, offered for the first non-stop Atlantic flight.

ARMY AIR S
NON S
COAST TO

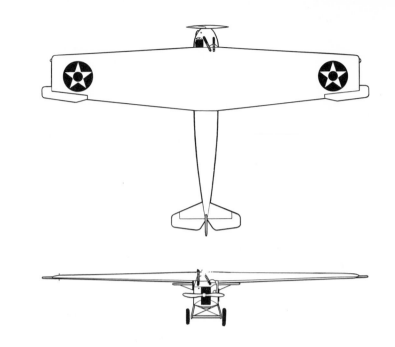

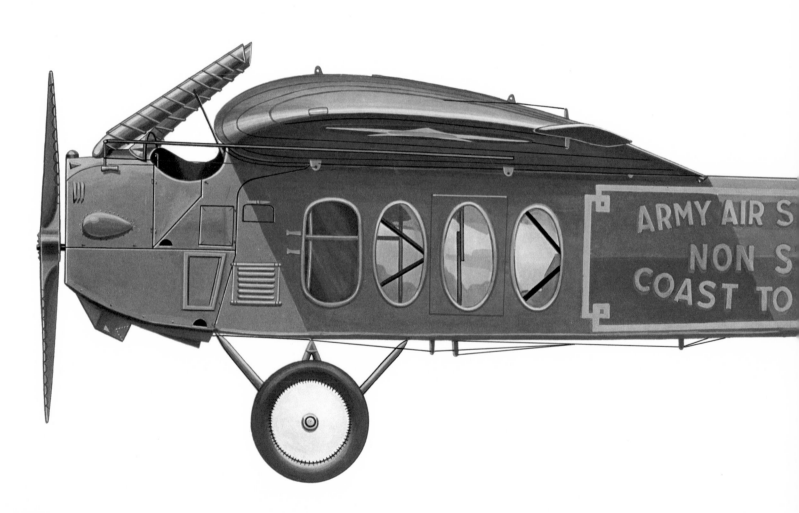

Anthony Fokker's T-2 was the first cargo machine planned and built in the Netherlands by his Dutch friend, Reinhold Platz. Fokker hoped that the airline companies would order it: the machine could transport ten passengers. But the huge plane proved to be a miscalculation and Fokker sold both finished models to the U.S. Army Air Service for use as cargo planes. The T-2 would probably have been forgotten if it had not unexpectedly set a world record. On May 2, 1923, Lieutenant Oakley Kelly and First Lieutenant John McReady took off from New York on a non-stop flight to San Diego. Their flight book, now on display in the Smithsonian Institution, Washington, records that they landed in California on May 3, 1923, after 26 hours, 50 minutes and $38^3/_5$ seconds. Kelly and McReady believed in precision!

Fokker T-2 Passenger and Freight Aircraft (1922-23)

Length . . . . 49 ft. 2 in.
Wingspan . . . . 74 ft. 10½ in.
Height . . . . 11 ft. 10 in.
Weight fully loaded . . . . 10,672 lb.
Engine: 1 water-cooled Liberty V-12 engine
Power: 420 h.p.

2 man crew

cargoes were usually passengers wearing helmets and glasses, or else a collection of mail bags and parcels. However, as early as August 25, 1919, Aircraft Transport and Travel Limited, which made daily flights on the London-Paris route with open former De Havilland DH 9 bombers (from which the armaments had been removed) carried passengers at a £21 fare. In Germany, Rumpler's Ru-C1 provided a less draughty service. The pilot, Adolf Doldi, had knocked together a kind of cabin roof which at least protected the passengers from the worst of the wind.

Fokker had seen his great chance to go one better than anyone else in providing passenger comfort. In 1921 he exhibited the F-III, an enclosed high-wing monoplane with a 230 h.p. Siddeley "Puma" engine (later: 350 h.p. BMW and, in 1922, 360 h.p. Rolls-Royce "Eagle" engine) which was designed to carry five passengers. The F-III resulted in praise for Fokker, and also for the reliability of K.L.M.'s service. Technical journals went overboard: "All pilots are unanimous in their enthusiasm about the F-III's behavior and in saying that its passenger cabin is at present the most luxurious on offer," stated "The Airplane" in April 1921.

The journal also praised the airline's punctuality: "During the appallingly bad weather in the last few weeks a strikingly favorable impression was made by K.L.M.'s regularity. A combination of good pilots and reliable Fokker aircraft appears to make it possible to fly in virtually any weather. In addition, all the signs point to the fact that K.L.M. genuinely works to a profit: there is no lack of passengers or freight."

Lack of money and talented people to work for him had become a thing of the past for Anthony Fokker. Remaining as one of his guardian angels was Reinhold Platz, his design chief and constant companion from 1912 to 1931. The two men made an ideal team. Fokker flew, and Platz planned; Fokker discovered weaknesses, and Platz removed them. It was Platz's job to translate Fokker's sensitivity into slide-rule terms, and the result of their cooperative efforts was extremely successful.

The Veere factory also began to bring out hidden talents. John Tjaarda, an ex-pilot and instructor in the Royal Dutch Flying Corps, worked for Fokker as an engineer from 1921 to 1923. The same Tjaarda later achieved fame in the United States, designing for Briggs—just as Fokker himself did later for Edsel Ford. Tjaarda designed streamlined "Sterkenburg" motor vehicles, and it would appear that these may have influenced Professor Porsche's much later Volkswagen and Dr. Ledwinka's Tatra.

Fokker loved showmanship, both for his own amusement and for profitable publicity purposes. Whether it was an event like the F-VII with its 360 h.p. Rolls-Royce "Eagle" engine, the first aircraft to be sent from Amsterdam to Batavia, or whether it was a trial flight of the untested F-V (which never actually went into full production) when his

passengers were ordered forward into the narrow cockpit to compensate for an overweight tail, Fokker always used every event to the best advantage for the image of his company.

Then the tireless Dutchman decided he wanted to see America again and get to know it better. He had been there in October 1920, supposedly on a private visit, but actually he ended up founding the Netherlands Aircraft Manufacturing Company of Amsterdam, a sales organization with a registered office in New York.

At the suggestion of the U.S. Army Air Corps, Fokker had one of his best-known aircraft built in the United States. It was the F-VIIA-3M, which was to give rise to a long line of successful three-engined aircraft. In the twenties, and even well into the thirties, these three-engined planes played an equivalent role to the later Douglas DC-3's. Edsel Ford took over the F-VIIA-3M and made it available to Richard Byrd for his flight over the North Pole in May 1926.

Meanwhile, Fokker's American subsidiary had put its "Universal" high-wing monoplane on the market. This had a 220 h.p. Wright "Whirlwind" engine, four passenger seats and an additional seat in the cockpit; and it offered an undercarriage with exchangeable wheels, snow runners or floats. The design was by Robert Noorduyn, Fokker's manager in the United States, who made a great hit with it.

In 1927, the "Universal" was followed by the "Super Universal," a more powerful plane, with a 410 h.p. Pratt & Whitney "Wasp" engine, a strengthened undercarriage, and accommodation for six passengers. Airline companies in many countries were attracted by this aircraft. The type flew, among others, for:

- the American companies: Western Air Express, Universal Airlines, Southern Air Transport, Standard Airlines, National Park Airways, Mid-Continent Air Express, Pan American Airways, Dominion Airways, and West-coast Air Transport;

- the Western Canada Airways, Ltd., which started scheduled services for Canadian mining and the country's Northern Territories;

- the Nakajima Aircraft Company in Japan, which itself built 43 "Super Universals" under license;

- the Japan Air Transport Company, Ltd., which took over the aircraft built by Nakajima;

- the Manchurian Airline, which used "Super Universals" to build up its air network in the Far East.

At that time Fokker aircraft accounted for more than 40 per cent of the North American passenger and freight air fleet. Fokker had broken new ground both in civil and military areas. For Richard Byrd he equipped the three-engined

Engine trouble forced Anthony Fokker's friend, Bernard de
Waal, to make several emergency landings during his historic
escapade to remove an F-II from Schwerin in Germany to
Holland shortly after World War I.

F-VIIA to complete an Atlantic flight. His B-IVa (designated in the United States as F-11a), an amphibious plane dating from 1929, was used as a private aircraft by two millionaires, Harold Vanderbilt and Gar Wood. Western Air Express operated Fokker's biggest aircraft (and the largest built in the United States up to that time), the four-engined F-32, which could carry 32 passengers.

Despite his other successes, the most famous of all Fokker's civil aviation aircraft prior to World War II were the many three-engined types. Among these was the F-VIIB-3M, which flew into history on May 5, 1935, when Sir Charles Kingsford-Smith and his copilot Captain Taylor (later Sir Gordon) made the first airmail flight from Australia to New Zealand. Just like Brown, who during his 1919 transatlantic flight with Alcock had crawled out onto the "Vimy's" wings to prevent the pilot from crashing because of an iced-up carburetor, Taylor several times risked crawling from the port of the "Southern Cross" to the starboard engine and back. The right engine was out of action, and the left was losing oil. Kingsford-Smith was flying the "Southern Cross" at some 32 ft. above a relatively calm sea. Taylor, suspended from the right engine gondola, let out oil from it, caught it in a thermos flask, crawled with the flask through the cockpit to the left-hand engine and poured in the oil. Just like Alcock and Brown, the two men reached their destination safely, and some of their fame was to rub off on Anthony Fokker.

In May 1929, General Motors acquired a 40 per cent holding in the U.S. production of Fokker's machines. For the next five years, Fokker, who held only 20 per cent of the shares, became technical director at an annual salary of $50,000. Then in May 1930, his name disappeared from the firm's title, which became General Aviation Corporation.

Fokker was to suffer other disappointments. The following year, on March 31, a T.W.A. three-engined Fokker crashed in Kansas. One of the seven passengers killed was Knute Rockne, the football hero. For days disaster headlines filled the press, and Fokker came in for his share of the blame. Then, on May 4, 1931, all Fokker three-engined aircraft built in 1929 were grounded by official order. The reason given was that they did not meet safety requirements; it was reported that there were serious defects in the wings. The decision affected not only Fokker, but some 35 aircraft owned by Pan American Airways, Western Air Express and American Airways.

This blow to the Fokker image wounded the Dutchman's vanity and publicity sense, and headlines announced his resignation as technical director of General Motors. He did not, however, give up his 20 per cent share in the company, which assured him a seat on the board. "Time" magazine reported that "the explosive Tony did not always conduct his business with good taste and tact." And Fokker's biographer and friend, Henri Hegener, wrote later, a little

harshly perhaps, that "he was continually avid for a profit from air travel and determined to do very well out of it."

Dispirited, Fokker lost his urge to continue contributing to the development of passenger aircraft construction. He was still in his prime, but he began to look back at the pioneering days that had led up to the general recognition of world air travel in the middle 1920's. The greatest advance at the time was in Europe, on which Fokker had turned his back. International organizations came into being, while smaller companies collapsed for economic reasons. Nations which only a few years previously had fought each other coordinated their interests in the newly-born transport and traffic market. In 1924, the following countries operated regular passenger and freight services through their own companies: Belgium, Denmark, Danzig, Germany, Estonia, Finland, France, Great Britain, Columbia, Latvia, the Netherlands, Austria, Poland, Russia, Sweden, Switzerland, Czechoslovakia, Hungary, and the U.S.A.

In England the air scene was dominated by Imperial Airways Ltd.; France initially used a mainly internal air network through the "Compagnie de Lignes A. Latécoère," the "Compagnie de Messag. Aéronautique," the "Compagnie Franco-Roumaine (Int.) de N.A.," and the "Compagnie L'Aéronavale, Société Générale de Transport Aérien." Leaders in Germany at this time were the "Deutsche Aero Lloyd A.G." and the "Junkers Luftverkehrs A.G.," which in January 1926, with their countless subsidiary companies, joined together as the "Deutsche Lufthansa."

Washington first limited its official recognition of civil air services with the Trans Continental Air Mail Service. Only in 1927 did the United States inaugurate a regular air freight service, although already two years later more than 40 regular airlines were operating in the U.S.A. Besides the American companies, small and medium-sized flight enterprises existed in all the air-minded countries. In some cases amazingly large profits were reported.

At this time, when not only Fokker but Boeing, Dornier, De Havilland, Heinkel, Junkers, and Morane-Saulnier were planning for passenger traffic on air lanes, the first really encouraging steps were being taken toward international cooperation, or what a contemporary expression described as "inter-state operational partnerships"!

It was realized that a tight air network, flown by all the cooperating lines, could only be achieved by dovetailing the respective interests. In the second half of the 1920's, when Fokker, Dornier, and Junkers aircraft formed part of almost every European company's fleet, this cooperation took the following form:

- London-Berlin-Moscow:
  Imperial Airways Limited; "Deutscher Aero Lloyd"; "Danziger Aero Lloyd"; "Deroluft."

Fokker F-II (V-45) Passenger Aircraft (1919-20)

Length	38 ft. 2½ in.
Wingspan	56 ft. 7 in.
Height	12 ft. 5 in.
Weight fully loaded	4,145 lb.

Engine: 1 water-cooled BMW in-line engine
Power: 185 h.p.

2 man crew — 6 passengers

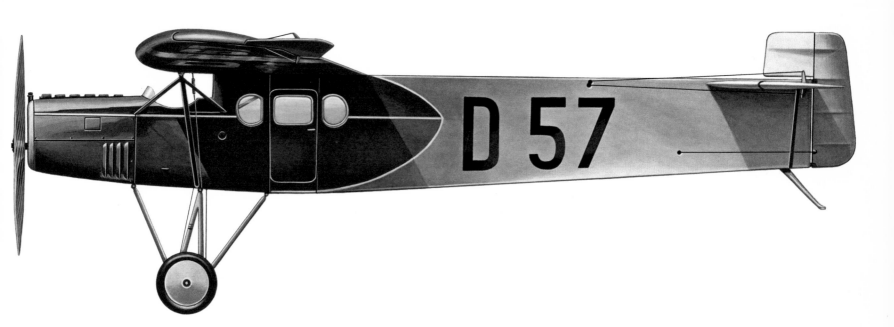

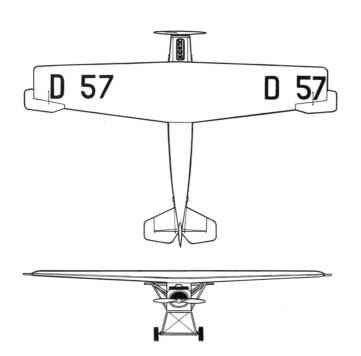

Immediately following the armistice, Fokker and his designer Reinhold Platz began a project in Schwerin to build a passenger and cargo aircraft. Some 20 units of the newly designed F-II were quickly sold. One machine remained in Schwerin. Fokker needed it in Holland so that he could offer it as a cargo plane there. Bernard de Waal took off in the direction of Holland under the flabbergasted eyes of a policeman. After a crash landing following engine trouble, the machine was repaired and sold to the budding Dutch airline, K.L.M., which then bought another one. Although the plane was not a commercial success, it was long-lived. One F-II was still in the service of the Aviation Research Company in the Netherlands at the outbreak of World War II.

Fokker "Universal" High-Wing Passenger Aircraft (1925)

Length . . . . 33 ft. 7¹/₅ in.
Wingspan . . . . 47 ft. 11 in.
Height . . . . 8 ft. 7 in.
Weight fully loaded . . . . 4,300 lb.
Engine: 1 air-cooled Wright "Whirlwind" 9-cylinder radial engine
Power: 220 h.p.

1 man crew — 4–6 passengers

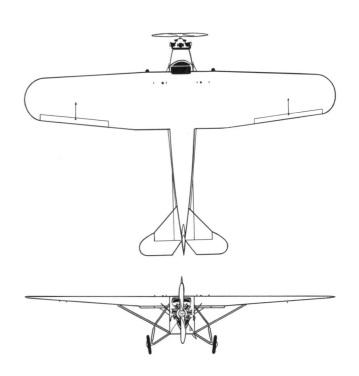

In 1925, R.B.C. Noorduyn, Fokker's agent in the United States, designed the four- to six-seater "Universal" for the U.S. market. It was a cabin passenger machine with open cockpit, wood-covered wings, and fuselage and tail shaped out of a canvas-covered steel tube frame. The "Universal" could be equipped with pontoons, wheels, or skids, which made it especially attractive for Canada's snowy landing fields. Following the success of the "Universal" with America's domestic airlines, in 1927 Fokker drew up plans for a "Super Universal." This was a continuation of the "Universal"—a braced high-wing monoplane with a more powerful Pratt & Whitney "Wasp" engine (410 h.p.) and longer, wider, and higher measurements.

120

- (London)-Rotterdam-Hamburg-Copenhagen: "Koninklijke Luchtvaart Maatschappij"; "Deutscher Aero Lloyd"; "Danske Luftfart Selskab."

- Trans-Europe Union with the following companies: "Ad Astra Aero A.G.," Zurich; "Rumpler Luftverkehrs A.G.," Munich; "Österreichische Luftverkehrs A.G.," Vienna; "Aero-Express R.T.," Budapest; "Bayerischer Luftloyd GmbH.," Munich; "Südwestdeutsche Luftverkehrs A.G.," Frankfurt-am-Main; "Sächsische Luftverkehrs A.G.," Dresden; "Junkers Luftverkehrs A.G.," Berlin.

- North Europe Union with the following companies: "Danziger Luftpost GmbH.," Danzig-Langfuhr; "Lettländische Luftverkehrs A.G.," Riga; "Aeronaut A.G.," Reval; "O.Y. Helsingfors," Helsinki; "Junkers Luftverkehrs A.G.," Berlin; "Junkers Luftverkehr Russland."

These operational partnerships formed the essential basis for ensuring regular air traffic from country to country.

"The present picture of European air travel will certainly represent the foundations of all traffic for many years ahead," said Karl Grulich, at that time a director and the Technical Head of the "Deutsche Lufthansa A.G." Grulich added: "If air policy is to lay down the direction in which the desired developments are to take place, it must follow the three leading European countries, Britain, France and Germany, representing three different systems. In France we find air traffic built up solely from French resources and using exclusively national air travel organisations; in Britain a system in part purely British (lines to Cologne and Paris) and in part traffic under settlement arrangements with Germany and the Netherlands as a result of successfully concluded agreements; Germany's service relies mainly on operational partnerships of an international nature."

Even at that early date, the attitude of each country toward air travel, and the relationship between the country or state and the aircraft industry, was extremely important. In this area, too, differing systems could be distinguished in the three countries. France had many private air companies aided financially by the government; for economic reasons the same arrangement persists with many prestige airlines today. Only two of the French airline firms were based on the French aircraft industry. In Britain, the state, the aircraft industry and aircraft operators worked in close cooperation. Aircraft services were provided by a trust

company, Imperial Airways Limited, which maintained a monopoly. Obviously, state influence on these air services was unavoidable; on the other hand, there was no direct connection between the trust and the industry.

In Germany, the scene was dominated by the "Deutsche Lufthansa A.G.," which had emerged from the Junkers and "Aero Lloyd" companies. This merger was so arranged that it was closely tied up with aircraft construction. Nevertheless, at that time the "Deutsche Lufthansa" was a private company in which relatively small sums of public money were invested. Private capital predominated, and no government representative sat on the advisory boards.

While Fokker cast his lot with the United States, the Dutch company of "Tony the Great" let out countless licenses. Today's firmly-established civil aviation would have been unthinkable without this Daedalus of modern times. Fokker divided his time between New York aboard his yacht "Helga" on the Hudson River, and Haarlem, with his mother.

Anthony Herman Gerard Fokker was a pioneer with diverse interests. He designed, manufactured, flew, carried out tests with gliders, shot impressive films of air exhibitions and flying displays, took part in motorboat races and had a 118 ft. yacht built to his plans. Even today, any Fokker F-27 "Friendship" turboprop aircraft taking on or landing passengers at an airport anywhere in the world, or any S-14 "Mach Trainer" jet used by students in the Netherlands Royal Air Force, is a reminder of the pioneer whose name it bears. The Flying Dutchman whom the British journal "Air Service" described as "a genial personality, democratic phenomenon and boundless enthusiast," was as proud as a peacock and always ready to prove what a perfect flier he was.

When Kingsford-Smith crossed the Atlantic in June 1930, a reception was held for him on an airfield near New York. Fokker was present, and one of the guests, thinking him to be out of earshot, remarked that he considered Fokker's days as a great flier were over. Fokker overheard him and strode off, jumped into a nearby Curtiss P-1, and took off. The exhibition Fokker gave then could hardly have been forgotten by those who witnessed it. He flew 10 ft. above the spectators' heads; he made two landings and immediately took off again; he looped the loop, and, on landing, taxied right up to the flabbergasted crowd.

A breathless airfield official came up to Fokker and accused him of breaking a whole set of regulations which would set him back $500 in fines. Fokker paid up. He was asked to surrender his pilot's license, but Fokker no longer had one.

Fokker F-32 Passenger Aircraft (1929)

Length . . . . 69 ft. 10 in.
Wingspan . . . . 99 ft.
Height . . . . 16 ft. 6 in.
Weight fully loaded . . . . 22,468 lb.
Engines : 4 air-cooled Pratt & Whitney "Hornet" radial engines
Power : 575 h.p. each

3-4 man crew — 32 passengers

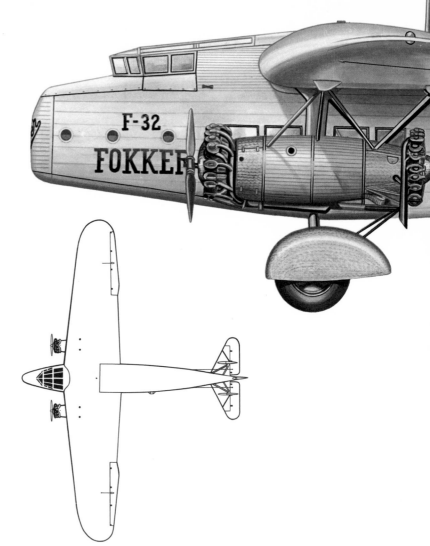

The four-engined F-32 was the biggest plane built by Fokker in the United States. The large monoplane carried 32 passengers. Ten machines of its type were built, with four 575 h.p. Pratt & Whitney "Hornet" engines mounted in twin tandem gondolas under the wings. The plane also had two push and two pull propellers, and was provided with four compartments, each furnished with eight seats.

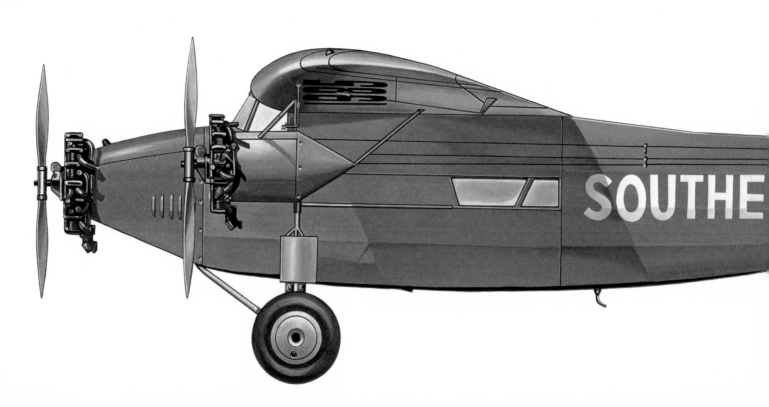

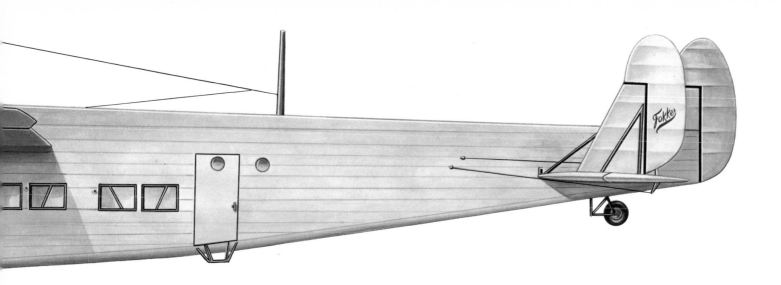

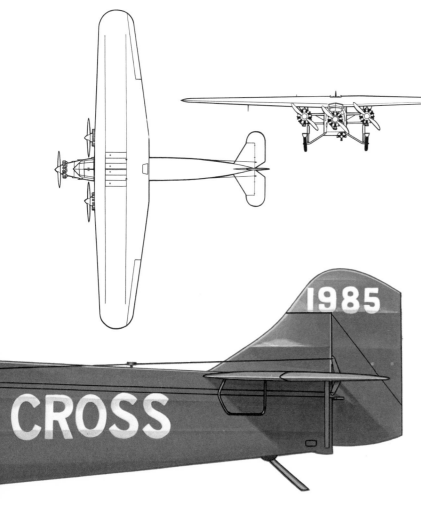

Fokker F-VIIB-3M "Southern Cross" Atlantic and Pacific Aircraft (1928-35)

Length . . . . 47 ft. 7 in.
Wingspan . . . . 71 ft. 2 in.
Height . . . . 12 ft. 10 in.
Weight fully loaded . . . . 15,302 lb.
Engines: 3 air-cooled Wright "Whirlwind" J-5C 9-cylinder radial engines
Power: 575 h.p. each
4 man crew

The F-VIIB-3M is one of Fokker's most renowned models, and particularly famous is the three-engined cargo version known as the "Southern Cross." Australian commander and pilot, Charles Kingsford-Smith, made the first Pacific crossing in three long stages with this plane. He and his crew, copilot Charles T.P. Ulm and two Americans: radio operator James W. Warner and navigator Harry W. Lyons, flew 7,938 miles from America's west coast over Honolulu and Suva between May 31 and June 9, 1928. Seven years later, the same "Southern Cross" flew the first mail from Australia to New Zealand. The plane can be seen today in the Commonwealth Museum in Canberra.

Partiality to greatness

A flying laboratory over the Pacific

In 1889 Sir Hiram Maxim built a rotor aircraft—with no practical results. But on May 25 of that same year, Igor Ivanovitch Sikorsky—whose name was to make history in aviation—was born in the Ukrainian town of Kiev. Today Sikorsky is a successful manufacturer of helicopters. In 1913, when he was 24 years old, he designed the first giant aircraft, "Russkiy Vitiaz." Six years later the young aircraft maker emigrated first to France, then to the U.S.A., where, in 1923, he set up his own Sikorsky Aviation Corporation. Anyone building aircraft at that time found the going tough—but Sikorsky literally always remained on top. In June 1930, Charles Lindbergh, using a Sikorsky S-38, was the first to fly the Miami-Jamaica-Barranquilla route over the Caribbean, opening up this service for United States postal and passenger traffic. Sikorsky pioneered airline services over the Pacific; his S-42 "Clipper" operated as a pathfinder for the route between San Francisco and Honolulu. Flight records and successes confirmed the soundness of Sikorsky's designs, but he did not neglect work on the development of rotary wings. His S-55 series rapidly became famous and, under the designation HRS-1, these transport helicopters proved their worth in Korea and also gave good service as civilian passenger or rescue aircraft. Today the word Sikorsky means helicopters, but the pioneer's greatest pride was his S-42 B.

Today, names such as Ernst Heinkel, William E. Boeing, Anthony Fokker, or Donald Douglas are, like Sikorsky, well known to virtually every schoolchild. They were aviation pioneers whose aircraft are more famous than the men themselves. Like his great competitors, Igor Sikorsky, when only 20 years old, had already turned his thoughts to aircraft heavier than air. His first fully-developed design immediately marked an aviation milestone. This was the first four-engined aircraft in the world, the "Russkiy Vitiaz" which, with its four 100 h.p. Argus engines, made its maiden flight on May 13, 1913. Karlheinz Kens, an aviation history research worker, described it thus:

"In the spring of 1914 the 'Ilya Murumetz,' increased in size, went into line production at the Russian Baltic Wagon Factory. Production was nearly stopped because the first sortie after the outbreak of war ended in a fiasco. But Major General M. W. Shidlovski, Superintendent of the Wagon Factory, begged that a second chance be given to the giant aircraft. He then founded the 'Eskadra Vosduschnich Korablei' (E.V.K.), or Flying Ships Squadron, which was to become the star unit of the Imperial Russian Air Force. The 'Ilya Murumetz' aircraft had bomb sights of a quality unequalled at the time, enabling between 60 per cent and 95 per cent of the chosen targets to be hit accurately. These aircraft were first used operationally in February 1915, for sorties on towns and railways in East Prussia and on the German seaplane station on the Angernsee. The E.V.K.'s greatest achievement was the destruction of the German Supreme Headquarters in Lithuania, and as a result the unit specialized in attacks upon enemy headquarters. The aircraft proved to have tremendous strength, and only one of them was ever shot down by the Germans. These successes aroused considerable interest among Russia's allies, who wanted to build them. In 1915 the French, and in 1916 the British, sought manufacturing licenses for them and on December 17, 1916, these plans were approved by Tsar Nicholas II."

Right up to the outbreak of the Revolution in October 1917, the "Ilya Murumetz" aircraft carried out bombing raids with increasing success. Then all were destroyed by their crews, which numbered from four to seven men each.

In 1919, Igor Sikorsky left Europe for the United States, where, far-sightedly, he applied his creative talents to the peaceful uses of aircraft. Sikorsky's first milestone added nothing to his reputation, however: in 1926, René Fonck, France's successful World War I fighter pilot, had a severe

Sikorsky "Ilya Murumetz V Bomber" (1917)

Length . . . . 56 ft.
Wingspan . . . . 101 ft. 3 in.
Height . . . . 15 ft. 6 in.
Weight fully loaded . . . . 10,473 lb.
Engines : 4 Sunbeam or Renault engines
Power : 150 h.p. or 220 h.p. each

7 man crew

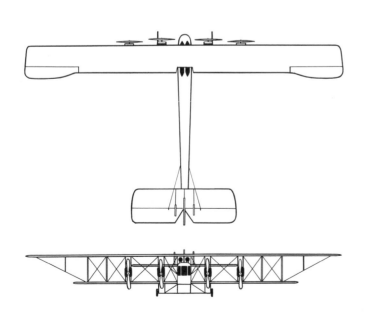

Sixteen passengers and a dog were on board when the first "Ilya Murumetz" machine set a new high-altitude record of 6,857 ft. on February 12, 1914. The world's second four-engined giant aircraft, created by the 25 year-old Russian designer Igor Sikorsky, was the direct successor to the "Russkiy Vitiaz"— also a four-engined Sikorsky design. Cabin and cockpit of the "Ilya Murumetz" were closed; the nose of the biplane, almost tucked in under the front edge of the wings, gave the appearance of being tail heavy. This was deceptive. After initial difficulties (a number of machines were wrecked because of faulty maintenance), technical officer Shidlovsky obtained a reprieve for the big bomber, and under his direction an entire fleet of the "Ilya Murumetz" was created along with maintenance shops, a flight school, a testing department, meteorological stations, and aerial gunnery training. The Sikorsky machines were to have a demoralizing effect on the enemy because of their apparent indestructibility. Only one of them was ever reported to have been shot down; on September 12, 1916, a solitary "Ilya Murumetz" fell victim to seven fighter planes—but not before shooting down three of them and heavily damaging another.

accident with a three-engined Sikorsky. Fonck was a competitor for the hotly contested $25,000 Orteig Prize, offered in 1919 by the New York hotel owner, Raymond Orteig, for the first person to fly non-stop from Paris or the French coast to New York, or vice versa. Two of Fonck's crew members were killed in a crash on takeoff from Roosevelt Field. A year later the Orteig Prize went to young Charles Lindbergh who flew a single-engined biplane made by an unknown San Diego firm, Ryan Airlines Inc. Sikorsky then dropped the idea of long-distance flights in favor of passenger air routes around South America. Air travel had long ceased to be a cause of great wonder, and Sikorsky followed the trend of the day: he built flying boats, which were immediately introduced into Pan American Airways services, among others. Along with the Dutchman, Anthony Fokker, and the German, Claudius Dornier, Sikorsky supplied the aircraft for the Latin American routes. He then turned to the Pacific Ocean.

Sikorsky and the American air companies were neither the first nor the only ones to campaign for and actually open up air routes to the Far East. Air France, whose 102 flight captains of 82 aircraft flew some 6.2 million miles on freight and passenger services in 1934, had done exploratory work, not only with flights over the South Atlantic but also for its "India Service."

A Couzinet "Arc en Ciel" ("Rainbow") was to span the two continents. In January 1933, it made its maiden flight with a crew of five, captained by Jean Mermoz, an Air France pilot and a pioneer of the South Atlantic route. In 1930 Mermoz had taken less than 22 hours to fly this route from Saint-Louis in Senegal to Natal, Brazil. The Couzinet 70 "Arc en Ciel" was a streamlined high-speed passenger aircraft with three water-cooled 650 h.p. Hispano-Suiza 12 Nb 12-cylinder engines. It was designed to explore the possibility of a regular mail service to South America. Though both the outward and the return flights were successful, the "Arc en Ciel" was ultimately used as the standard aircraft on the Air France India passenger service. Meanwhile, Sikorsky quietly concerned himself with the vast distances he hoped to bridge across the Pacific.

In 1935, Sikorsky's S-42, a "flying laboratory," made its maiden flight from San Francisco to Honolulu. The best Pan American Airways pilots, who had gained years of experience in scheduled flights over the Caribbean, flew for Sikorsky and his company. Meanwhile Pan American had ordered three flying boats: the "China Clipper", "Philippine Clipper," and "Hawaii Clipper"—all type 130—from the Glenn H. Martin Company in Baltimore. In the future, these aircraft were to be Sikorsky competitors on the major airline routes.

From then on, Pan American flew regularly from San Francisco to the Philippines. This was not a non-stop route: points in Honolulu, the Midway Islands, Wake Island and Guam divided the itinerary into relatively short stages. Its

total length was 8,050 miles; the shortest stage, from Midway Island to Wake Island was 1,260 miles, and the longest, from San Francisco to Honolulu, was 2,410 miles. These flight distances were staggering for the years before World War II. From Manila, Pan American's terminal, only Sikorsky aircraft flew to Hong Kong and other points in China. The machines were the improved S-42 B, known as the S-43, a twin-engined amphibious aircraft that carried a crew of three and fifteen passengers, or a crew of two with 25 passengers. The S-43 was used on long-distance postal services along with the old S-42 in its original form.

The trip from California to the Middle Kingdom took five days. The pioneering achievement of developing this route brought about several other all-time firsts:

- the first reconnaissance flights with Sikorsky S-42's;
- practical recommendations for the building of four-engined comfortable passenger aircraft which would be profitable in operation;
- the construction of island airfields and flying boat harbors;
- the setting up of accurate meteorological stations in Manila, Guam, Honolulu, and San Francisco using, among other devices, manned weather balloons providing their own typhoon warning system.

Sikorsky's urge to build big came out again in his S-42 "Clipper." This had only the name "flying boat" in common with the legendary Curtiss NC-4, a U.S. Navy machine designed to prove the great range and capacity of sea planes. On May 8, 1919, a Curtiss NC-4 flew from Newfoundland via the Azores to Portugal and then on to England with two intermediate stops. By contrast, Sikorsky took advantage of all the progress and experience of the preceding fifteen years and put it to profitable use when he announced details of the construction of his flying boats:

"Our latest development is made of light metal right up to the wing and the horizontal tail plane. The vertical fins are similarly made of light metal with a fabric covering.

"In building the wings alone, 57,000 rivets were used and 90,000 for building the floats. In all roughly 400,000 rivets were processed in this aircraft [S-42], which incorporates 5,262 sq. ft. of sheet metal. Each of the floats alone would make a four-seater motorboat. More than 1,500 sq. ft. of plywood with walnut veneer were used for the passenger quarters alone."

At a press conference given by the Sikorsky Aviation Corporation, a journalist, as a joke, asked a question which to his amazement was conclusively answered:

"Perhaps you can also tell us," said the reporter to the Sikorsky spokesman, "how many components the S-42 has in all?"

The giant "Russkiy Vitiaz" had four engines and was the first
operable big airplane in aviation history. It made its appearance
in 1913. Praise for the youthful Russian designer, Igor Sikorsky,
was also big: it came from the Tsar himself.

"Certainly," the public relations officer replied. "In round figures one and a half million, excluding engine and propeller. If you like, you can count them all from the 1,855 single-spaced sheets of typewritten specifications.

"A few more points: the anchor weighs 220 lb. Some 620 gallons of paint, enamel and varnish were used in building the S-42. Three hundred and fifty photographs were taken during the various stages of construction. The oil tank holds 60 gallons, the fuel tank 1,000 gallons. The landing speed is 68 m.p.h. On test flights from New York to San Francisco and back a cruising speed of 160 m.p.h. and frequently the maximum speed of 180 m.p.h. was recorded."

The S-42 B's produced in 1935 and 1936 showed improvements. The four Pratt & Whitney "Hornet" engines, each of 670 h.p., were replaced by S1EG "Hornets," each of 750 h.p. (nominal performance at 7,000 ft.). Inside the ailerons were trailing edge flaps which could be adjusted to specific positions for takeoff, cruising, and landing, with setting determined by flying speed. The fuselage (with nine bulkheads) was a keeled, two-deck structure. The front section had an emergency compartment with full sea rescue equipment, behind which were quarters for two pilots, a radio operator-navigator, and a steward. The partitioned passenger accommodation was 9 ft. 6 in. wide and could take 32 passengers. The cockpit rear wall was fitted with an instrument panel connected to all the equipment for controlling and monitoring the engines. All eight fuel tanks were mounted in the wings and held a total of 1,200 gallons.

Couzinet 70 "Arc en Ciel" ("Rainbow") Passenger Aircraft (1933)

Length . . . . 53 ft.
Wingspan . . . . 98 ft. 5¼ in.
Weight fully loaded . . . . 37,022 lb.
Engines: 3 Hispano-Suiza 12 Nb water-cooled V 12-cylinder engines
Power: 650 h.p. each
4 man crew

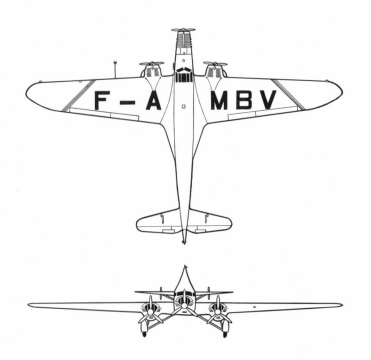

During the twenties, Marcel Maurice Drouhin decided to take part in the east-west transatlantic flight competition. He joined forces with 23 year-old designer René Couzinet, who created a three-engined machine specifically for that purpose. He called his machine "Arc en Ciel" ("Rainbow"). The first Couzinet 70 had a touch of the romantic about it. Its youthful designer, penniless, ambitious, and enthusiastic, raised two million francs through a nation-wide fund-raising campaign to cover construction costs. Together with Drouhin, he made innumerable test flights until, one fatal afternoon in August 1928, the "Arc en Ciel" crashed at Orly airport, and Drouhin was killed.

Short "C" "Caledonia" Empire Passenger Flying Boat (1936)

Length	88 ft.
Wingspan	114 ft.
Height	31 ft.
Weight fully loaded	40,439 lb.

Engines : 4 Bristol "Pegasus" Xc 9-cylinder radial engines

Power : 910 h.p. each

4 man crew — 24 passengers : 12 berths

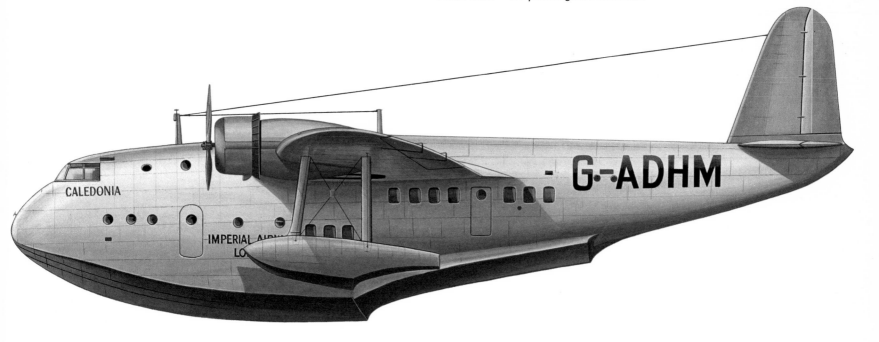

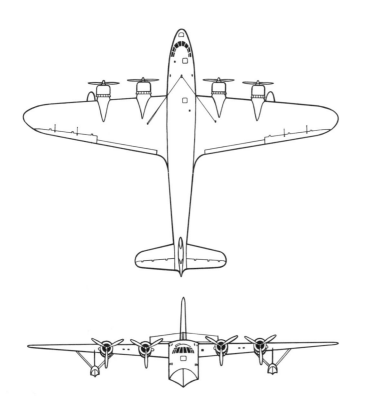

At the beginning of the thirties, the situation in the large-plane market was tighter than ever. Douglas DC-2 machines and Boeing's 247 had made such a good showing in the long-distance London-Melbourne race that Britain's aircraft industry began to fear that it might be squeezed out. Greater efforts had to be made to attract passengers, and it was decided that competitive Clippers of the Sikorsky and Martin class were to be built. The Short brothers received the order, and they designed the noted "C" class flying boats, of which 44 were produced up to 1940. The planes were used in passenger and postal service. A Short "C" flying boat, the "Maia," made aviation history in 1938 as the pickaback carrier of a four-engined Mercury seaplane. During flight over the ocean, the Mercury took off from the back of the "Maia" carrying mail for America. The "Caledonia" also achieved fame by setting a trans-ocean speed record of 15 hours 3 minutes in a flight from Shannon to Botwood on July 5, 1937. The flight was under the command of Captain Wilcockson. A Sikorsky Clipper attempted to break this record, but failed, and the Short "C's" remained the speediest of the time.

129

Sikorsky S-42 B Passenger Flying Boat (1934-39)

Length	67 ft. 11 in.
Wingspan	118 ft. 5 in.
Height	17 ft. 4 in.
Weight fully loaded	42,115 lb.

Engines : 4 air-cooled Pratt & Whitney "Hornet" S1EG 9-cylinder radial engines

Power : 750 h.p. each

5 man crew — 32 passengers

Igor Sikorsky had one great advantage: his aircraft's generous 4.31 ton payload proved a decisive factor in giving his company a profitable position in the ever-hardening competition for contracts.

His unshakable faith in aircraft as transport for the masses and his long experience enabled Sikorsky to see far ahead. In 1938 he announced that future airliners would provide a new type of travel. "A person living in New York or Berlin would be able during his week's holiday to visit the primeval forests of Central Africa or South America, to fly over the North Pole or even to fly right round the world."

At the same time, Sikorsky said that the "highest possible speed for an aircraft" was "about 500 m.p.h." He was closer to the mark when he prophesied "stratosphere flights for passengers and mail." He expressly encouraged airlines to start "many departures at brief intervals, for instance one a day between the major towns of Europe and America."

Today's Sikorsky Aircraft Division no longer builds "China Clippers." Long since the American from Kiev returned to his 1909 love—the helicopter. Like its competitors, the Sikorsky Aviation Corporation attempts to prove performance by setting records, such as in October 1954, when it startled the world with its type S-59 helicopter which made an altitude record of 24,704 ft.

Water, cloud, and distance have never lost their attraction for this grand old man of aviation history. On June 1, 1967, nearly 40 years after Lindbergh's epoch-making flight, four Sikorsky S-61 (HH-3E) helicopters flew from New York across the Atlantic to Paris for the Le Bourget Air Show. They flew non-stop, just like Lindbergh.

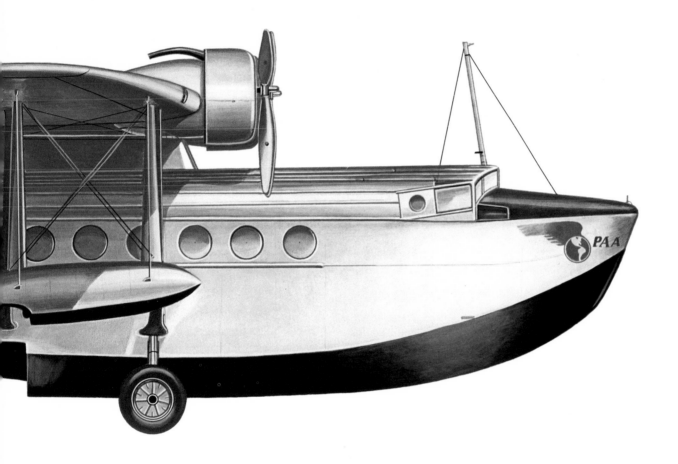

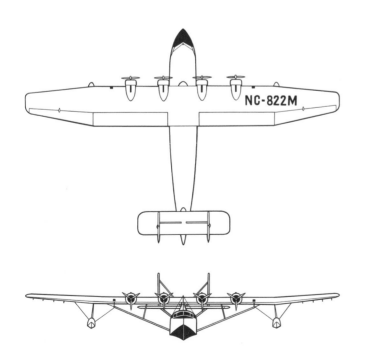

NC-822M

When Igor Sikorsky presented his first S-42, everyone was convinced that no larger aircraft could be built. This opinion had to be revised when Glenn Martin brought out his Clipper. But the clever Russo-American still remained ahead of the game with his flying boats. The first test flights of the Sikorsky S-42 prototypes broke eight world records, and the planes were soon commissioned for regular service between New York and Buenos Aires. Señora Getúlio Vargas, wife of the Brazilian president, christened the first of these machines the "Brazilian Clipper." The second flying boat of this type, the "Clipper Pioneer," flew as a research plane in the Caribbean, exploring the conditions for a Pacific run. At the same time, the crew tested a new shortwave radio, which Pan American Airways had developed for Pacific air travel. The company opened its first Pacific flights in 1936 with Martin 130 Clippers over Hawaii, Midway, Wake Island, Guam, and the Philippines. They flew passengers and mail to Manila, the end of the line. In 1937, Sikorsky expanded the Pacific routes, and flew his S-42 B boats as far as Hong Kong. The flights between the United States and Asia had now grown to a total of 8,050 miles.

POLIKARPOV I-16

The hawk and the mule

The Soviet Union's first prototype hunter in World War II

In the spring of 1932, the Soviet "Central Institute for Aero- and Hydrodynamics" was ordered to design a superior and advanced fighter that was both easy to build and to fly. Pavel Sukoi came up with the I-14, and this was the predecessor of the "Rata." It remained a museum piece. Then designer Nikolai Polikarpov continued the project and the first prototype of the I-16 flew on December 31, 1933, attaining a maximum speed of 222.5 m.p.h., and its takeoff and landing speeds were relatively high. A final version, the type 4, with a 600 h.p. M-25 engine of Soviet design, appeared in June 1934. The "Rata" flew and fought in the Spanish Civil War (where she got her name) and in China and Mongolia. She went into action in Finland in 1939 to 1940, and was used against the German Luftwaffe during World War II up until the Battle of Stalingrad. The I-16 was withdrawn from front-line service at the end of 1943. According to Soviet pilots, "Yaks and Ilyushins were a cinch if you could fly the I-16."

Every Soviet pilot had to take the "Red Army Oath": "To learn the art of war conscientiously, to defend the welfare of the army and people by every means, and to dedicate myself till the last breath to my people, my homeland, and the workers' and peasants' government."

The vow was hard to live up to in the case of the pilots of Polikarpov's I-16. In combat they had not only to cope with the enemy, but sometimes with the cussedness of their machines. Eventually the one-seater fighter was replaced by more advanced models, but by then the I-16 had already become famous. The planes were given high-sounding names from the animal kingdom:

- "Yastrebok" ("The Hawk")—the name of the I-16 when it was fledged in the Soviet Union in 1934;

- "Ishak" ("The Mule")—an early nickname of the squat 22 ft. long aircraft, with a 33 ft. wingspan and a height of 9 ft., that could be so awkward, but fulfilled all its obligations faithfully;

- "Abu" ("The Gadfly")—the Japanese name for the I-16's when they flew against it in China;

- "Mosca" ("The Fly")—the name the pilots gave it during the Spanish Civil War in 1936-39;

- "Rata" ("The Rat")—the name given by the German pilots of the "Condor Legion," and used again by the Germans throughout World War II.

As the first one-seater monoplane with a closed (or semi-open) cockpit and fully retractable landing gear (equipped with skids for takeoff from field airports in winter), the Polikarpov I-16 attained an honorable place in the history of Soviet aviation. But its technical drawbacks were undeniable. When the Russian pilots were confronted with the I-16 for the first time in 1934, they could not resist the temptation of calling it "Ishak," the mule, instead of "Yastrebok," the hawk, because of its obstinate ways.

The pilots, who were used to the short takeoff and landing runs of their biplanes, found it difficult to adjust to the "Rata." It needed 984 ft. to take off and 755 ft. to land. The poorly kept Russian airstrips were too short for it. As a result, the pilot had to wind up the landing gear into the fuselage while trying to keep the somewhat unstable craft on course. When landing, trainee pilots often forgot to crank down the landing gear before the descent. Moreover, the machine had a disconcerting tendency to stall because of directional instability. The pilots soon developed a strong aversion to the unconventional monoplane and preferred the old one-seater I-6 and I-13 biplanes.

The Red Army Air Force Supreme Command arrived at a somewhat unconventional decision: instead of calling on designers to help overcome its defects, they fell back on three famous pilots. Shkalov, Suprun, and Stefanovski were three fliers who enjoyed great prestige in the world of aviation, and they were given the difficult task of convincing their reluctant colleagues of the virtues of the I-16. They were accordingly sent off on a tour of all training centers where "Ratas" were stationed.

Shkalov, Suprun, and Stefanovski worked individually. They sat down with the young pilots and flew with the experienced ones. They showed the fledglings what could be done with the "Rata" and under their guidance, "Ishak" again became "Yastrebok."

Objections to the aircraft were removed once and for all during an air exhibition near Moscow in September 1935. Shkalov, Suprun, and Stefanovski took off in triple formation, their wing tips linked by colored bands. Maintaining formation, they went through a series of aerial acrobatics. When they landed, the bands were still intact, wing tip to wing tip—to the amazement and pride of the young pilots who had witnessed the show.

After passing her baptism of fire in the Spanish Civil War, the "Rata" gained the full confidence of her pilots, and in 1938 was incorporated into the "Voyenno-Vosdushniy Sili Rabotsho-Krestyanskaja Krasnaya Armiya" (Air Force of the Red Workers' and Peasants' Army) as the training of pilots continued. The Soviet Union offered comprehensive schooling at:

- the Air Combat Academy, Moscow, with a faculty of engineers and officers,

- the Military Aviation Academy, Moscow,

- the Advanced School of Air Navigation, Leningrad,

- the Advanced Tactical Fliers School, Lipezk,

- the Advanced Chemical Academy, Moscow,

- theoretical military schools,

- military aircraft commander schools,

- seaplane commander schools,

- aircraft observer schools,

- aerial gunnery and bombardment training academies,

- Air Force naval technical schools,

- Air Force special branch schools,

- 64 brigade schools for young "aerial specialists,"

- 1,500 aircraft commander schools of the "Osoavyakhim,"

- 2,000 seaplane commander schools of the "Osoavyakhim," and

- nine schools for women commanders of aircraft.

The organization of the air corps into 60 air brigades of 184 squadrons and five naval brigades with sixteen squadrons, (including 63 flights for special purposes), with each squadron made up of three flights and nine aircraft, reflected sound military thinking. In the event of war, the Air Force Command under the Army High Command would have three independent air forces of which one with four to five corps had already been established.

The Soviet Union had one-seater and two-seater fighters, reconnaissance and cargo aircraft, light and heavy bombers, one-seater fighter seaplanes, bomber flying boats, and torpedo bombers, as well as training and courier aircraft. Polikarpov's I-16's formed the mainstay of the interceptor command. The "Rata" had to fight hard.

German fighter pilots were never to forget the rotund single winger—not because of its combat effectiveness or superiority, but because of the skill demonstrated by the Russian pilots in coping simultaneously with the enemy and their own machines. As far as possible, the Red combat fliers tried to overcome the technical disadvantages, but at first they were unable to offset the limitations of the machines ready for combat. In point of fact, only 1,160 German combat aircraft faced the Soviet's 1,800 combat planes (of which 1,000 were obsolete) when the Germans launched their offensive against the Soviet Union on June 22, 1941. The fighting strength of the Soviet Air Force was based on 2,000 fighters (of which only 300 were modern types) as opposed to 720 German fighter planes. Hundreds of I-16's were destroyed on the ground immediately after the German attack on the U.S.S.R. And during the first major assault the Soviets lost the "iron ore basin of Krivoli Rog, a number of steel works in the Ukraine; they were forced to evacuate aluminum works on the Dnieper and in Tichwin, an engine factory and two aircraft factories in Leningrad. These factories [could not] resume production in new locations for seven or eight months" (according to Stalin in a personal letter to the then British Prime Minister, Winston Churchill). In Stalin's opinion, new aircraft production was not in view for the time being.

The "Rata" was no knight in shining armor able to rescue the situation. Although a respected opponent during the Spanish Civil War (when the German and Italian fighters were of the same vintage), 1937 was a long time ago, and the I-16's were inferior to the faster German machines of 1941. Consequently, the hawk again became the mule, and was given the most unpleasant tasks as combat fighter flying support sorties for infantry.

During this time of dire straits for the "Rata," the newly developed Ilyushin Il-2 "Sturmovik" was the Soviet Union's most effective fighter plane. The machine was designed by Sergei Ilyushin, and is still considered one of the best all-purpose combat aircraft of World War II. The "Black

Polikarpov I-16/24 B Fighter (1939-45)

Length . . . . 20 ft. 1¼ in.
Wingspan . . . . 32 ft. 3³/₅ in.
Height . . . . 8 ft. 5 in.
Weight fully loaded . . . . 4,189 lb.
Engine: 1 air-cooled 9-cylinder Shvetsov M62 radial engine with
two-stage compressor
Power: 1,100 h.p.

1 man crew

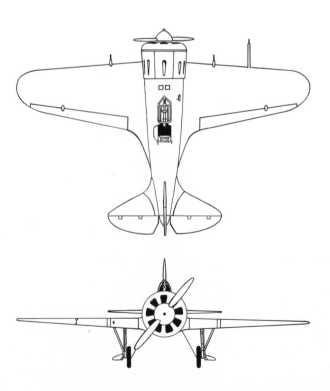

*Even though they had become obsolete, Nikolai Polikarpov's
I-16 types still formed the backbone of the Soviet Air Force
in 1941. These planes had a disconcerting peculiarity; the
pilot had to make no less than 44 crank turns before the landing
gear was completely lowered or retracted. However, over the
years, the Soviet fliers had grown more than accustomed to the
idiosyncrasies of the I-16, and had scored notable successes
with the plane in the Spanish Civil War. When Hitler attacked
the Soviet Union, the cranking procedure of the I-16 had become
routine, and the Red fighter pilots did a heroic job against the
more technically advanced enemy aircraft.*

ANT-25 "Stalin Route" (1936-37)

Length . . . . 44 ft.
Wingspan . . . . 112 ft.
Height . . . . 18 ft.
Weight fully loaded . . . . 24,850 lb.
Engine: 1 water-cooled AM-34-R V 12-cylinder engine
Power: 900–1,000 h.p.

3 man crew

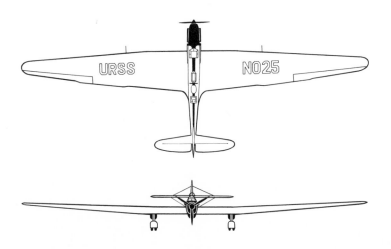

In 1936, Soviet designer A.N. Tupolev's ANT-25 attracted attention when one of these machines was flown nearly 6,000 miles on a non-stop run from Moscow to Kamchatka. At about the same time, Sigismund Levanevsky, the "Lindbergh of the Soviet Union," and his copilot Viktor Levchenko, flew from Los Angeles to Moscow over Alaska and Siberia. Then on June 18, 1937, the ANT-25 "Stalinskiy Marshrut" ("Stalin Route") demonstrated even more clearly the excellent long-range properties of Tupolev's creation when the hero of the Soviet Union, Valeriy Shkalov, with his copilots Baidukov and Belyakov, flew some 5,288 miles from Moscow to Vancouver via the North Pole without a stopover. This was pioneer flying in the real sense of the word. Using oxygen equipment, the trio flew their single-engine machine continuously at altitudes of between 14,108 and 20,670 ft. The icing of the rudders and a temporary shortage of oxygen almost caused the daring exploit to fail. Shkalov had hoped to land in Oakland, California, but had to come down in Canada because of bad weather.

Death," as the German soldiers called the low-level attack plane, had come into being in 1939. That year a Soviet test pilot made the first flight of the one-seater prototype of the Il-2, only to discover that the machine was underpowered. The water-cooled V 12-cylinder AM-35 engine with 1,370 h.p. was too weak for the more than four ton machine. With a more powerful AM-38 engine developing 1,700 h.p., however, the combat aircraft was to give excellent performance.

For a time, the "Sturmovik"—the Soviet designation for combat planes—bore the experimental insignia CKB 57. It attained a speed of 292 m.p.h. at an altitude of 6,500 ft. Nevertheless, only 249 of these models could be built before the Germans attacked the Soviet Union: production had only begun in March 1941. Even so, the few Il-2 models that went into combat proved to be a great success. The drawback, that the planes were vulnerable from the rear, resulted in the development of the two-seater Il-2. In the new model, the designers put a second seat behind the cockpit and installed a 12.7 mm. machine gun to defend the rear. Engine compression was increased. The improved machine, with the type designation Il-2m3, went into action in August 1942.

Meanwhile, the "Ratas" still had to bear the brunt of the fighting. The removal of the aircraft factories to the Urals had—as Stalin complained—cost precious time. Even increased production and rationing were unable to make up for this. By 1943, however, production figures had increased significantly. The armament of the "Sturmovik" was also reinforced. Not only did the plane now fire 37 mm. aircraft cannons (installed in addition to the MG armament), it also introduced a novel way of dealing with pursuers. Self-igniting infantry projectiles were released in tiny parachutes, which meant that if a pursuing machine flew into such a swarm, it unleashed a chain of deadly explosions.

The Il-2m3 also became the terror of enemy tanks during one of the greatest tank battles of World War II—the Battle of Kursk from June to July, 1943. Ilyushin's "Sturmovik" became for the Germans what the Junkers Ju 87 "Stuka" had been for the Soviet tanks. According to the Russians, the Wehrmacht's 9th Tank Division alone lost 70 tanks during a massive 20-minute attack by the "Sturmoviki" on July 7. The 17th Tank Division, consisting of about 300 tracked vehicles, had only about 60 tanks left intact

after a four hour attack by the Il-2m3's. These were victories with which Polikarpov's faithful old I-16's could not possibly have competed.

The failure of the summer "Citadel" offensive was largely due to the successes of the Soviet Air Force. At Kursk on July 19, its "Sturmoviki" had command of the air. The Junkers Ju 87 and Ju 88, the Messerschmitt Me 109 and the Focke-Wulf Fw 190 were no longer coming up against the "Rata," but against the Ilyushin Il-2m3 with its increased fire power and improved armor. Loaded with both bombs and rockets, it was a tough machine to shoot down. Again and again, the "Sturmoviki" returned to their bases, tails, wings, and bodies riddled with holes, but with the cockpit and fuel tanks unscathed.

The Ilyushin Il-2m3 soon became known as "Ilyusha" among her pilots, who fondly adopted a girl's name. But from the frog's eye view of the infantrymen, she was called the "Flying Tank" or alternatively the "Flying Infantryman" or "Hunchback."

The Ilyushin Il-2m3 rolled out of the factories in ever-increasing numbers. Russia, after losing more than 8,000 aircraft by the end of 1941, succeeded in improving production by virtue of the fact that the new factories in Irkutsk, Semenovka, Kasan, and Novosibirsk were out of range of enemy bombers. And from March until July 1942, while the Germans made uninterrupted raids on the Arctic port of Murmansk, the Red Army Air Force was able to recuperate even further.

The Soviet Union had depended on her own resources in the air. The British Allies had promised to send her 400 fighters, but as time began to run out, Stalin, on September 3, complained to Winston Churchill that "these aircraft, which obviously will not be ready so soon or together... will be unable to make a serious change in the situation on the eastern front."

Meanwhile, the decimated Soviet Air Force scored impressive victories in defensive actions with their belittled Polikarpov machines, which were to remain on the front for another two years. The "Rata" fliers made up in the lack of maneuverability and speed of their machines by tricks, skill and sheer courage, spurred on by their anger at the German attacks. The "Rata" became an increasing threat to bombers and reconnaissance planes flying without escort. The First Fighter Regiment of the Soviet Air Force equipped

"Rata rams Ju 88" became a familiar phrase to German pilots in World War II. They had to fend off ramming attacks from Russian pilots in Polikarpov I-16 planes, following the opening of the German offensive against the Soviet Union.

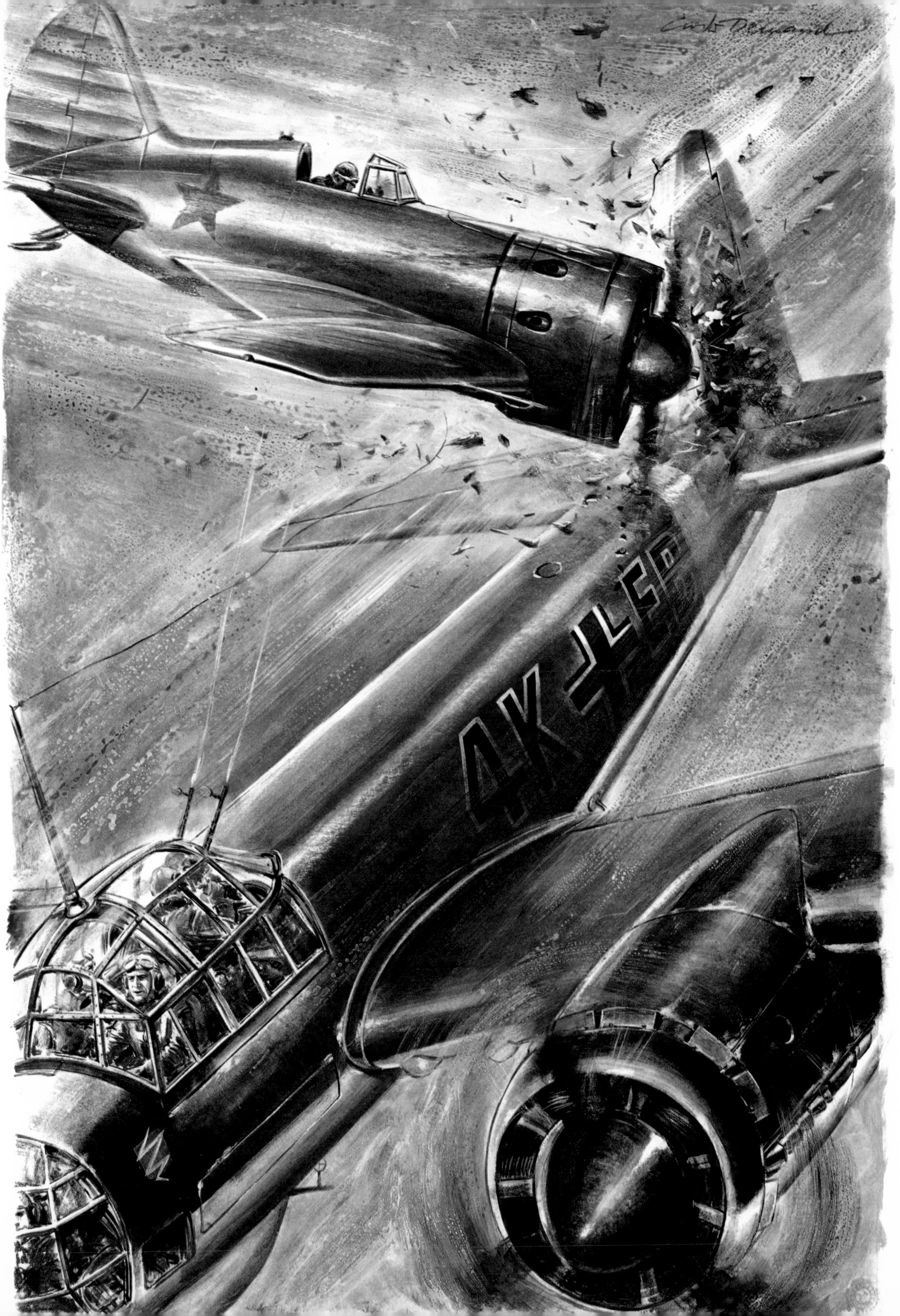
4K

Junkers Ju 88 A-4 Bomber (1940-45)

Length . . . . 47 ft. 1½ in.
Wingspan . . . . 65 ft. 10½ in.
Height . . . . 15 ft. 9 in.
Weight fully loaded . . . . 26,680 lb.
Engines : 2 water-cooled Junkers Jumo 211J-1 12-cylinder
injection engines
Power : 1,100 h.p. each

4 man crew

The twin-engine, horizontal and dive bomber Ju 88 was, with the Ju 87 "Stuka," the best-known product of the Junkers works. It was not of purely German design. After a long period in the United States as an aircraft designer, W. H. Evers returned to Germany with an American citizen, Alfred Gassner, to work at the Junkers factory. He and his U.S. colleague designed the tactical fighter-bomber for the Luftwaffe. The internally braced low-wing monoplane proved to be an excellent tactical bomber. But as a strategic bomber, a task for which it had never been conceived, the Ju 88 failed. Between 1939 and 1945, when 15,000 Ju 88's were manufactured, more than 3,000 modifications on this popular type were made. The mass production version of the A-4 series of horizontal and dive bombers had a longer wingspan, increased armament, greater bomb load capacity, reinforced landing gear, and more powerful engines than the type A series. The aircraft proved to be a practical multi-purpose model; it was manufactured as a bomber, fighter-interceptor, and reconnaissance plane.

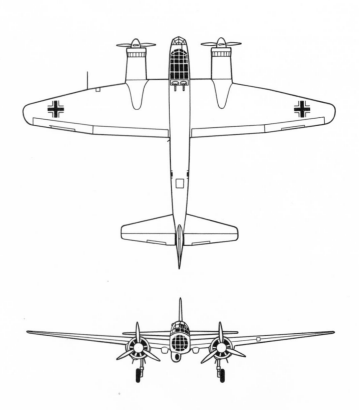

Ilyushin Il-2 Fighter-Bomber (1939-45)

Length . . . . 38 ft. 3 in.
Wingspan . . . . 47 ft. 11 in.
Height . . . . 10 ft. 9 in.
Weight fully loaded . . . . 12,237 lb.
Engine: 1 water-cooled AM-38F in-line engine
Power: 1,700 h.p.

1 man crew

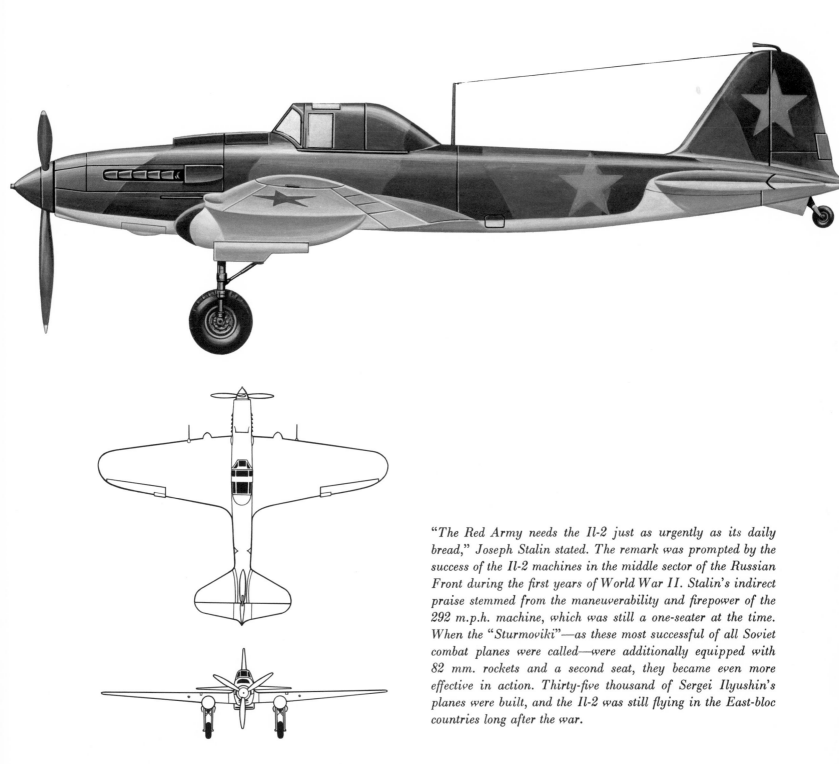

"The Red Army needs the Il-2 just as urgently as its daily bread," Joseph Stalin stated. The remark was prompted by the success of the Il-2 machines in the middle sector of the Russian Front during the first years of World War II. Stalin's indirect praise stemmed from the maneuverability and firepower of the 292 m.p.h. machine, which was still a one-seater at the time. When the "Sturmoviki"—as these most successful of all Soviet combat planes were called—were additionally equipped with 82 mm. rockets and a second seat, they became even more effective in action. Thirty-five thousand of Sergei Ilyushin's planes were built, and the Il-2 was still flying in the East-bloc countries long after the war.

139

with "Ratas" was made a Regiment of the Guards, partly for its victories scored over the German Heinkel He 111's and Junkers Ju 88's.

As "Yastrebiki", "Ishaki," and "Ratas," the Polikarpov fighters—too often the object of unjust scorn from German soldiers—gained new laurels on all sectors of the front. "Rata" aces among the Red Air Force combat fliers came to represent what Captain Alexander Kasakov had represented in the Tsarist Air Force in the First World War. They employed a hazardous technique also developed during World War I—ramming.

Lieutenant Viktor Talalikin was the first pilot to revive the technique. An unescorted Heinkel He 111 was reported to be heading for Moscow on the evening of August 7, 1941. After taking off on alert, Talalikin engaged the German and made three unsuccessful attacks. The He 111 remained steady on course until suddenly the "Rata" pilot decided to ram it. The He 111 crashed between buildings in a Moscow suburb. Talalikin was made a "Hero of the Soviet Union with Gold Star."

Like Talalikin, most of the Soviet Air Force aces had, at the beginning of their combat careers, flown the I-16. Although the plane ended up being used only for low-level

sorties and as as an interceptor for the defense of cities and industrial plants behind the lines, the "Rata" fliers received praise and medals even for routine milk runs. One of these pilots, Captain Alexei Meresyev, lost both legs when he was shot down in a I-16. The officer was made a "Hero of the Soviet Union," not because of the loss of his legs, however, but because of his later successes in La-5 combat planes, which he continued to fly undaunted with artificial limbs until the end of the war.

Another fighter pilot, Sachar Sorokin, likewise a "Hero of the Soviet Union with Gold Star," achieved notable victories in the far north, shooting down five German machines in patrol flights over the Barents Sea. His comrade, Captain Khlobistov, who was among the defenders of Murmansk, continued ramming even after he had ceased flying "Ratas," and in a single sortie knocked down three German planes with a Curtiss P-40.

These spectacular victories caused the Soviet pilots to give names to their squadrons which reflected what has commonly become known as the "Russian Soul." Among the squadrons were those named "For the Glorious Soviet Union", "For the Motherland", "Victory will be Ours", "For Leningrad", "For Stalin," and "We shall never give up Leningrad."

Nikolai Polikarpov's fame grew up around the I-16 which had typically Russian characteristics: it was robust, aerodynamically not very sound, and placed unreasonable demands on the skill of Soviet pilots. Thousands of these aircraft were destroyed during the surprise attack by Germany on the Soviet Union; nevertheless, the remainder of these planes fought on undaunted.

The Russian Polikarpov I-15 had served in the Soviet Air Force since 1933. The double decker was especially designed to give the pilot better all-round visibility, a feature which had hitherto been all too neglected by aircraft constructors. The air speed of this aircraft, which was still operational in World War II, reached 177 m.p.h. Nevertheless, the I-15 was to be overshadowed by the I-16.

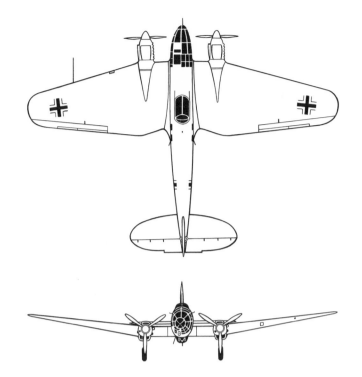

Heinkel He 111 H 6 Bomber (1939-45)

Length	53 ft. 9 in.
Wingspan	74 ft. 1½ in.
Height	13 ft. 2 in.
Weight fully loaded	30,870 lb.

Engines: 2 water-cooled Junkers Jumo 211F-2 12-cylinder in-line engines

Power: 1,340 h.p. each

5 man crew

By the time World War II broke out, two-thirds of all German combat units had been supplied with the He 111—the Heinkel works' medium horizontal bomber. When production ceased in 1944, Heinkel had turned out 5,656 He 111 types. These machines developed from a fast Lufthansa airliner, and externally resembled the well-known He 70. They soon attracted the interest of the German Air Ministry, which chose the type for its future standard horizontal bomber. On May 4, 1937, the first He 111 left the production lines of the Heinkel plant at Oranienburg. Despite two interruptions in production, it remained a "work horse" up till the end of the war. Even though increased bomb loads and armament slowed it down, the He 111 retained its popularity among German combat fliers. At the end of its career, no longer fast enough for a bomber, the He 111 was converted into a carrier for parachute troops and replaced the Ju 52/3m which had grown too slow for this purpose.

They did not give up in Kiev, either. Lieutenant Ilya Borisov became a hero there in an action that the Russian people still remember. In September 1941, when the battle was raging around Kiev, Borisov's flight, equipped with I-16's, was behind the front. The pilots flew their missions without interruption, scarcely taking time out to refuel and reload ammunition. On September 10, a few days before the German Army penetrated the city after bitter fighting, Borisov took off once more with two comrades with orders to intercept a formation of nine Junkers Ju 88's.

The three "Ratas" headed toward the Ju 88's, spotted them, and then split up. Everybody was now on his own. Borisov had a Junkers in his sights and attacked twice, flying out of the afternoon sun. He fired all barrels; both 7.62 mm. Shkas machine guns in the body and the two 20 mm. Shvak automatic cannons in the wings. The Ju 88 showed no effects of the barrage. Its gunner, seated behind the pilot, shot back—also without any luck. Borisov took his "Rata" up and in an Immelmann turn, rolled off to the right and took on the Ju 88 again. He saw the enemy's face a few feet away as he shot over the fuselage of the Junkers machine while attempting to ram its tail. Borisov just missed.

The Soviet lieutenant now showed that he had more than just a fighting spirit. With the stick pulled hard back he went into a normal roll without transition (an innovation attributed to his countryman Nesterov) while the Ju 88 flew on, still sticking to its formation.

Borisov then flew into his fourth attack, and for the second time without firing. He rammed the tail of the German plane with his propeller, causing it to fall into a spin. It crashed and exploded. Borisov had also gone into a spin, but he righted his "Rata" at about 980 ft. above the ground and managed to land safely in a meadow behind his own lines—with a dead prop and shaky crankshaft. Borisov flew no more sorties that day. Neither of his comrades returned; his flight had become a unit without aircraft. This situation was not uncommon, especially in view of the devastating losses suffered during the first days of the war.

About 20,000 of Polikarpov's I-16's were built, in many variations:

- Type CKB 12, equipped with two 7.62 mm. machine guns, had a speed of 224 m.p.h.
- Type I-16-1, equipped with two 7.62 mm. machine guns, could climb to 16,404 ft. in 9.24 minutes.
- The I-16-4 attained a speed of 286 m.p.h. at an altitude of 9,842 ft.
- The I-16-6 (also used in the Spanish Civil War) flying with a Wright F. 54 Cyclone "master" engine.
- The I-16-10, with more armament: two 7.62 mm. machine guns fired from the body between the landing gear, and two others fired out of the wings.
- Type CKB 18, a test model, equipped with four 7.62 mm. machine guns mounted with their barrels pointing straight down. Two bomb racks could carry a 110 lb. bomb each. The cockpit and fuel tanks were plated with armor.
- The Polikarpov I-16/180, of which only a few test models existed, attained a speed of 342 m.p.h. in 1938.
- The I-16 UTI, a two-seater trainer, used by pilots learning to fly the "Rata."

Nikolai Polikarpov's aviation milestone, the unbraced monoplane I-16 with its many names, was made with a wooden fuselage and wings and metal tail. With the type I-16/24B the designers finally turned out a genuine hawk which lived up to its predatory name. The 4,189 lb. machine (loaded) had an air-cooled 9-cylinder Shvetsov M63 radial engine, which developed 1,000 h.p. at 2,300 r.p.m. on takeoff, and 820 h.p. at 14,764 ft. Cruising speed of this I-16/24B, which was built and used up until the end of the war, was 184 m.p.h. The armament, consisting of two 7.62 mm. Shkas machine guns in the body and two 20 mm. Shvak automatic cannons in the wings, was effectively and progressively supplemented by two 82 mm. RS82 rockets under the wings, of which up to six in number could be taken.

Thus what was once the "Rata," or rat, became the hardworking mule "Ishak" and the fighting hawk "Yastrebok." That valiant animal never got a medal. But it helped some of those that did.

MESSERSCHMITT ME 323 "GIANT"

Elephants with a tender skin

The largest World War II transporter

At first they were only gliders. Then they were changed into the largest powered transport aircraft of World War II. These were the six-engined Messerschmitt Me 323 "Giants." In March 1941, five months after the creation of a Special Aircraft Construction Unit at Leipheim under an engineer named Fröhlich, the first 59,525 lb. monster, towed by a Ju 90 with American engines, took off. The Ju 90 was not powerful enough, and it was thought that a successful tow might be provided by three Me 110 C's in "Troika Formation," but this proved too dangerous. Eventually, when two He 111's were built into an He 111 Z, a perfect answer appeared to have been found. Until July 1941, 200 "Giants" sailed as gliders on the Western Front, ready to take part in the projected invasion of England—which was never to materialize. From then on, the Me 321 freight glider, with its 22 ton payload, proved itself on various sectors of the Eastern Front. The gliders were finally fitted with engines for unassisted takeoffs. Four French Gnôme-Rhône 14N-48 engines each with 1,000 to 1,180 h.p. at takeoff were built into the gliders. The combined power of these engines was still insufficient, so two more were added. By 1944, 201 Me 323 aircraft had left the Leipheim and Obertraubling assembly plants.

Airman Fred Rabe was proud, very proud. "We fly with a crew of five, seven, nine, or eleven men," he told his fiancée one day, "and we can carry 130 fully equipped soldiers, or a complete 8.8 cm. anti-aircraft train, or 52 barrels of fuel, or 8,700 loaves, or..." The girl interrupted him: "All those loaves? That would be enough to feed our part of town for two days," she said incredulously.

For a moment the young airman appeared embarrassed; but soon his enthusiasm returned. "And when we make a specially sharp turn," he went on excitedly, "the flight mechanic in one wing can see his mate in the other one grinning his head off!" The reason for this particular phenomenon was a tendency of the aircraft, with its wingspan of 180 ft. 4 ¾ in., to oscillate. The young girl, who had seen the "Giant" in flight over Breslau, did not share her fiancé's delight at flying such an oversize monster. But she managed to contain herself. After the war, if Fred landed himself a job at a filling-station, he would be easier to handle, she thought hopefully.

For the German infantry the Messerschmitt "Giant" proved a big headache. If the infantry had to fly, they flew, but they preferred riding in the "Auntie" Ju 52. "Auntie" was quieter; furthermore she seemed more solidly built, and not as if a good poke with a finger would pierce the stiff linen

covering. The Junkers factory had much longer experience in the construction of large-size transport planes than the Messerschmitt plant. This was probably known to the soldiers, and so they naturally had much greater confidence in the Junkers aircraft.

The Ju W-34, a transport and passenger aircraft developed from the Junkers Ju W-33, remained an "old friend" as a trainer in the Luftwaffe right up until the end of World War II. Again, the Junkers Ju G-38, a large four-engined transport plane with a wingspan of 144 ft. 4 ¼ in., a length of 76 ft. 1 ⅝ in., and a height of 23 ft. 7 ½ in., was extremely popular with Lufthansa passengers long before it undertook transport duties for the Luftwaffe.

In its numerous versions, the Junkers Ju 52 surpassed all other German transport planes. The three-engined aircraft, which shared almost equal fame with America's legendary Douglas DC-3, was familiar even to the general public, who had no particular interest in aviation. This plane, developed from the single-engined Ju 52/1m, made its first international appearance at Zurich in 1932 as the winner of the "Airline Aircraft" group flight over the Alps. The machine was piloted by Willi Polte, and its success ensured the designer Zindel a niche in aviation history. Some 30 companies in 25 countries were to operate "Auntie Ju." The aircraft had proved itself as

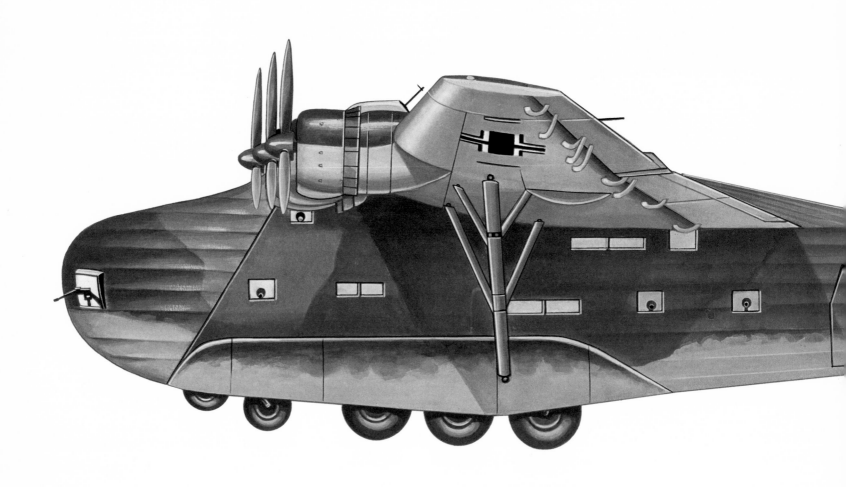

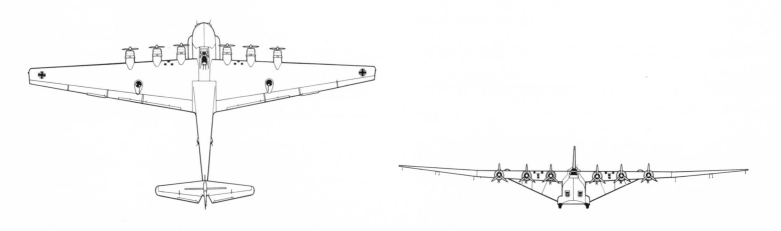

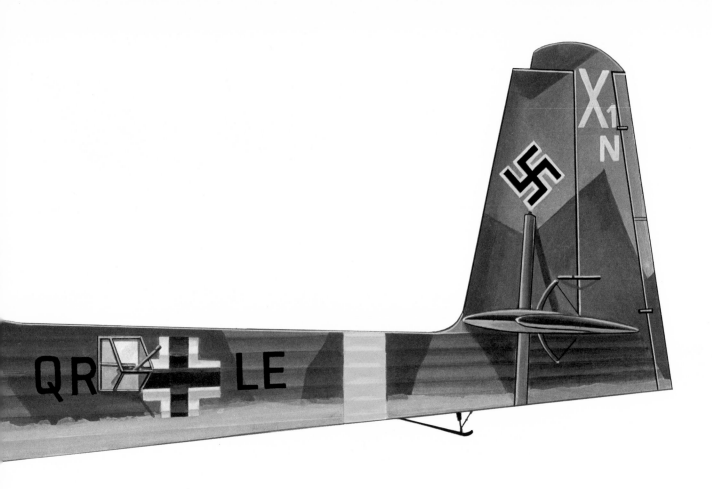

Conceived as a silent glider, and famed as a six-engine monster, Messerschmitt's "Giant" Me 323 distinguished itself as a cargo plane during World War II, and with its immense size it lived up to its name. Its armament consisted of nine machine guns (seven MG 131's, two MG 151/20's), to which six more could be added in the sides of the fuselage. The bow could be separated into two compartments accommodating 120 fully equipped infantrymen. De-planing ramps were included in its equipment. As soon as a "Giant," swinging on its rear wheels, was brought into horizontal position, the cargo shifted to the exact center of gravity and could be secured. In 1942, the re-established Zeppelin aircraft makers had the engineers of Leipheim continue the development of the "Giant" after serial production had begun at Messerschmitt. As earlier, the Zeppelin enthusiasts wanted to make the giant even bigger, and under the designation ZSO 523, they began work on the design of a larger aircraft, based on the essential features of its Me 323 predecessor. The Allied drive into France—where the project was being carried out in cooperation with the French SNCA.SO company —stopped further work on the super "Giant." Often derided as an "adhesive tape bomber," the Me 323 nevertheless remained a satisfactory combat cargo plane and one of the largest and most bizarre air spectacles in World War II.

Messerschmitt Me 323 E-2 "Gigant" ("Giant") Transport Aircraft (1942-44)

Length . . . . 93 ft. 5¾ in.
Wingspan . . . . 180 ft. 4¾ in.
Height . . . . 31 ft. 5¾ in.
Weight fully loaded . . . . 99,225 lb.
Engines: 6 Gnôme-Rhône 14N-48 and/or 49 radial engines
Power: 1,180 h.p. each
11 man crew

On April 22, 1943, Allied fighters over the Mediterranean engaged
the German Messerschmitt "Giants" in their last battle; they shot
down fourteen out of sixteen of these massive cargo planes in the
short stretch between Africa and Sicily.

146

a transport plane, and, after World War II, it continued to be built in France at Villacoublay.

The Junkers Ju 52 and the Messerschmitt Me 323 obviously could not alone handle the transportation of entire armies. Furthermore, neither aircraft could be used except within certain runway restrictions—unlikely to be found on unfortified tactical airfields. A story is told of one Me 323 which, in order to escape from approaching Soviet troops, was forced to take off from prefabricated barrack parts laid down on the ground.

Badly needed was a serviceable plane somewhere between the Ju "maid-of-all-work" and the excessively oversized "Giant." As a stop-gap, a cantilevered two-engined high-wing monoplane was developed by Arada from 1941-42. This was the Ar 232, with its retractable three-wheel under-carriage. The main wheels were drawn up hydraulically inwards into the wings and the nose wheel disappeared backwards. This device, plus the 22 rigid low pressure balloon wheels, was designed to make takeoff and landing possible on any kind of unprepared terrain. Large and bulky loads could be stowed in the squared fuselage. However, the "Centipede," as it was nicknamed, was built only in small numbers and could not compete either with the Ju 52 or with the "Giant."

At this time, only 40 years after the first powered flight, any passenger or transport plane with more than three engines aroused the skepticism of the average passenger who had to be, or desired to be, flown. Meanwhile, the twin-engined Douglas DC-3 developed from the DC-1 achieved popularity for its reliability, and so did the Ju 52. The two aircraft had another thing in common: a long life-span.

The Messerschmitt "Giants" were viewed with much suspicion by the German soldiers, even before hair-raising stories began to be circulated about the young pilots who took off with a full weight of 99,225 lb. and whose lives,

along with those of their fellow passengers, often depended upon the copilots' skill at trimming. While the copilot was trimming the control surfaces, the pilot, with help from the servomechanisms, struggled with the extremely high control forces. These forces first became apparent in the Me 321 glider version, and were never effectively reduced.

Some of the stories bandied around about the "Giant's" pilots sounded like sheer fantasy. One of these, which was quite typical, told of an entire crew that took off with their pilots on a "special flight" to loop the loop over Mount Etna in their six-engined aircraft. The furious commander of the transport squadron allegedly radioed the Me 323 in person and called it back to base. The crew only just escaped court martial, and were lucky enough to get off with a lenient eight-day close arrest.

During the Africa campaign, infantry and wounded, who along with many other loads were often carried in "Giants," shuddered at such stories. "Fly in a thing like that?" one infantryman remarked. "You must be mad!" The story of a crash at takeoff from Kecskemet which Fred Rabe related merely stressed what crews of the M 323 were always saying: "It's not everyone that can handle a 'Giant.'"

"The copilot failed to turn up," Rabe explained to his audience, "and because the flight was urgent, the flight captain was assigned an He 111 man. So we took off, with a fully-loaded weight of about 99,225 lb.; the entire freight space was taken up with vats of fuel for the Me 109's in Budapest. The flight captain couldn't get the plane off the ground, not by an inch. 'Trim her, trim her, she's nose heavy, you idiot!' he shouted. So the man from the He 111 kept on trimming as if she were tail heavy, and by the time the penny had dropped, the 2,625 ft. runway and a bit more was behind us. Ahead lay a wood. To make it worse, the Me 323's lateral controls were combined with trimming flaps driven by an electric servomotor in each wing.

Next to the all-metal Junkers F 13 and Fokker F-VIIB-3M machines, the most favored combination for the construction of passenger or freight aircraft was corrugated sheet-iron and three engines. This remained popular for many years, and Richard Byrd's Ford tri-motor in which he made his famed South Pole flight was no exception. The Junkers Ju 52/3m also came under this category, and proved to be most successful.

"The plane crashed and the jets of flame were enormous," Rabe went on. "Only one of the seven members of the crew came out alive, with legs broken."

"That's a tall story!" an infantryman in the audience objected. "No one could come out alive from a sea of flame like that!"

"Right," Rabe agreed, "but the flight mechanic in the right-hand wing somehow smelled a rat and after about 1,900 ft. he jumped out of the aircraft as it taxied. I suppose I ought to tell you the flight mechanic's station in the wing has a cover: he jumped out through that."

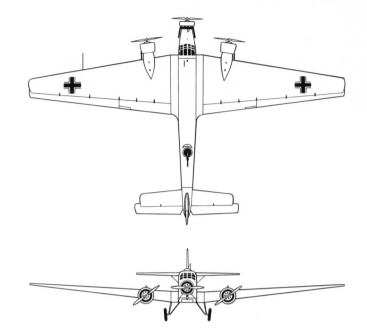

Fact and fiction were not widely separated. Nothing seemed impossible, and some of the most unlikely sounding feats of the crews of the Me 323 were indeed true.

The fabric, steel tube, and plywood "adhesive tape bombers" flew at a service ceiling of 14,760 ft. and with a range of 807 miles at a cruising speed of 155 m.p.h. After the war, rough statistics showed relatively high loss of human life. However, one safety virtue credited to the "Giant" was that it could not be set alight, even by the heaviest fire, provided that the fuel tanks were not hit.

For months the TG 5 Me 323 E aircraft had flown between Trapani and Palermo in Sicily and the Africa Corps airfields in Tunis and Bizerta, carrying reinforcements to Africa and wounded from there to Italy. Meanwhile orders had been issued to discontinue dangerous individual flights and, instead, to fly in close formation. Since the "Giants" carried five to nine machine guns (13 mm. MG 131) and were thus better armed than the Ju 52's, a large formation seemed advisable.

April 22, 1943 was a black day for the TG 5's. Four days previously the Luftwaffe had lost 24 Ju 52's over the Mediterranean, and 35 other "Aunties" were so severely damaged that they broke up after emergency landings. Then the last sixteen aircraft of No. 5 Transport Squadron took off from Trapani for Tunis, with crews totalling 140 men. The "Giants" were carrying fuel for Rommel's Africa Corps.

The North African coast came into view. The planes were due to fly over Cape Bon, and it was there that British fighters attacked the formation. The more maneuverable "Spitfires" and "Marauders" massacred the Germans, and only two "Giants" escaped. The fourteen remaining aircraft either crashed in coastal waters or were destroyed after emergency landings. Two days later, the fifteenth "Giant" was destroyed on the Tunis airport during an air raid. Only nineteen out of 140 pilots, radio operators, air gunners and flight mechanics were rescued; the others were killed or drowned. In one fateful month a great idea which had been turned into reality was irrevocably destroyed.

A single Me 323 returned to its base at Trapani, filled with wounded from Rommel's Africa Corps. Among the crew was Fred Rabe, then 22 years old.

It was said that the noise of the Ju 52 in flight resembled "six motorcycles wide open in first gear going downhill." Junkers' "Auntie Ju" stemmed directly from the 1915 all-metal Ju 1. After the Douglas DC-3, Ju 52/3m airplanes became one of the most familiar sights at airports throughout the world. Meanwhile, the "Auntie Ju" had been used for military purposes. Junkers delivered models to Bolivia in 1932, and they served as transport machines in the Bolivia-Paraguay conflict. The "Auntie Ju" flew with Diesel and fuel engines, and took off and landed on skids, pontoons, or wheels. Whatever she was assigned to do—in peace or war—she did well: observer, bomber, reconnaissance, cargo, trainer, and tug for cargo gliders. The Short brothers built ten booty Ju 52/3m's for British European Airways in Belfast after World War II, and, at the same time, the French Société Amiot manufactured her as the A.A.C. 1 "Toucan."

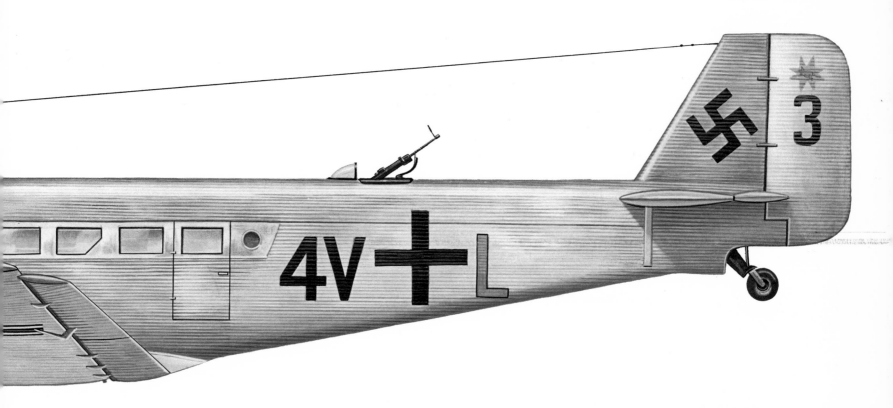

Junkers Ju 52/3m Passenger and Freight Aircraft (1932-47)

Length . . . . 62 ft.
Wingspan . . . . 95 ft. 10 in.
Height . . . . 18 ft. 2 in.
Weight fully loaded . . . . 20,944 lb.
Engines : 3 air-cooled BMW 132T 9-cylinder radial or other engines
Power: 660 h.p.

2 man crew — On airline service: 15 passengers

Douglas DC-3 (C-47) Passenger and Freight Aircraft (1935-68)

Length . . . . 64 ft. 5¾ in.
Wingspan . . . . 95 ft. 6¼ in.
Height . . . . 16 ft. ⅓ in.
Weight fully loaded . . . . 24,365 lb.
Engines: 2 air-cooled Wright "Cyclone" G-102A (R-182a)
9-cylinder radial engines
or 2 Pratt & Whitney R-1830-92 radial engines
Power: 1,200 h.p. each
2 man crew — 21 passengers

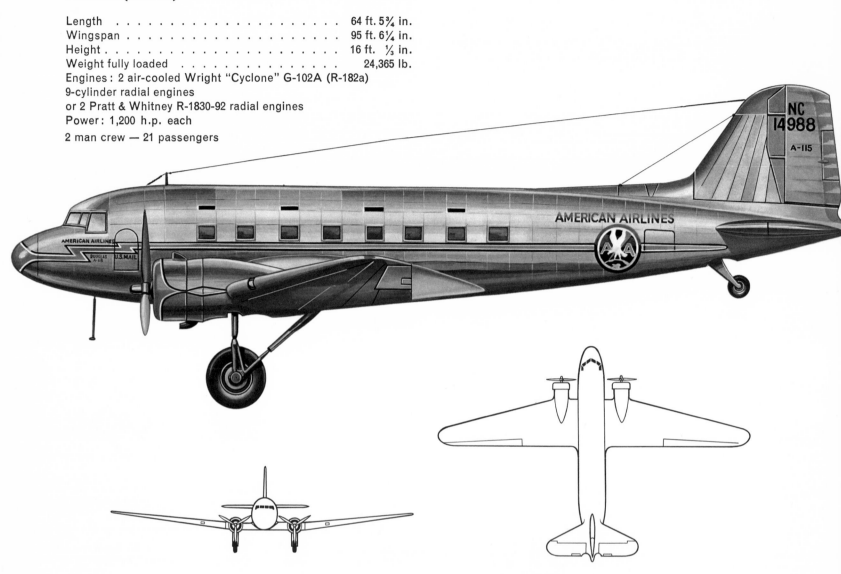

This shapely plane resulted from a telephone call from C.R. Smith, President of American Airlines, to his friend Donald Douglas. Business with the Ford, Fokker, and Curtiss machines was going badly; his company had lost more than a million dollars to competitors within a year after the faster and quieter Boeing 247 appeared. A new and better plane than the good DC-2 was needed. Smith promised to purchase 20 aircraft of the new type as soon as they were finished, and he took an option on 20 more at a price of $110,000 per machine. Douglas named Fred Stineman as director of the project, and the remainder of 1935 was spent in studying, planning and testing. On December 17, 1935, 32 years after the Wright brothers had made their first flight, the Douglas DC-3 prototype made its maiden flight from Clover Field, near Santa Monica in California.

On June 7, 1936, American Airlines inaugurated the first DC-3 run—a non-stop service between Chicago and New York. This saw the beginning of a long string of successes over the continents, in all the world's airline companies, at every corner of the earth suitable for landing and takeoff strips. Large and small airline companies throughout the world ordered the twin-engine, all-metal monoplane, which could take 21 passengers. They were made under license abroad, and, in the end, total production amounted to more than 13,000 DC-3's. As a cargo and passenger machine, DC-3's continued to fly after World War II, and a few of them are still used today by private owners. During the war, the trim Douglas transported soldiers, ammunition and supplies on all fronts. She is not just a part of aviation history, she made history herself.

Hell's angels

The aircraft which helped win World War II

New bombers were constantly being designed and developed: planes that could transport death by the ton. Famous in World War I were such bombers as the Handley-Page 0/400 and the Gotha GV; and in World War II among others to make their appearance were the Avro Lancaster Mk I, the Consolidated B-24 "Liberator," the Focke-Wulf Fw 200 and the Junkers Ju 88. But particularly feared by the enemy—and loved by its crew—was Boeing's B-17 "Flying Fortress." A total of 12,731 machines of the B-17 type was built, 6,981 by Boeing, 3,000 by Douglas, and 2,750 by Lockheed. They dropped 640,000 tons of explosives on European targets during 291,508 missions. As the war neared its end, B-17 production figures practically attained automotive standards—in 1944 an average of sixteen machines came off Boeing's production lines in Seattle every 24 hours in the all-out war effort.

The excellent flight properties and stability of Boeing's B-17 "Flying Fortress" were established at the very outset, when the plane was still in the drawing board stage. The U.S. War Department issued the original requirements for the type in August 1934. The specifications called for a multi-engined machine "with a 20,000 to 26,000 ft. service ceiling, a flight duration of between six and ten hours and a top speed of between 200 and 250 m.p.h. at an altitude of 10,827 ft."

Boeing's design team, led by 24 year-old Edward C. Wells, saw a chance in the Department's specifications for their four-engined type 299. Wells' B-299 was the ancestor of the B-17 "Flying Fortress," and was later to be followed by the B-29 "Superfortress," the B-52 "Stratofortress," and the Boeing 707 airliner.

The B-299, bearing the test number X 13372 on its fuselage, took off on its maiden flight on July 28, 1935. Test pilot Les Tower pushed forward the gas lever for the four 600 h.p. Pratt & Whitney "Hornet" engines, and, according to one report, "It wasn't long before it became apparent to Tower and the observers waiting impatiently below that this machine was one of the good ones." But later this first B-299 "Flying Fortress" crashed and burned, killing Tower and his copilot Major Ployer P. Hill. The cause was attributed to pilot error.

Despite this mishap, the B-299 (B-17) machine was considered to be of advanced design and, as test flights continued totalling 9,923 flight hours and covering more than a million miles without further losses or notable mishaps, the U.S. War

Department ordered its first 119 machines: 39 type B-17's, 38 type B-17C's, and 42 type B-17D's. The Army Air Corps (which had tested the tactical possibilities with twelve "Flying Fortresses" in the Second Bomber Squadron at Langley Field) was pleased.

The B-17's had already made headlines in 1938 when six Y-17's (the original designation) made a 5,000 mile "Goodwill Flight" from Miami to Buenos Aires and back under the command of Lieutenant Colonel Robert C. Olds. One of the navigators on this flight was Curtis E. LeMay, eventually to become U.S.A.F. Chief of Staff and initiator of the Strategic Air Command (S.A.C.).

In 1938 the heavy bomber under its initial designation Boeing YB-17, was described as having four air-cooled 9-cylinder radial Pratt & Whitney "Hornet" engines of 700 h.p. each, or "Cyclone G" engines of 1,000 h.p. each, mounted in engine nacelles (two each on the right and left sides of the fuselage at the wing leading edges level), and triple-bladed "Hamilton" variable pitch, constant speed propellers. But no information was published at the time on the bomb load capacity, and data on weights and performance came from the manufacturers in an inexact form, since precise information was secret.

At the beginning of 1941, the United States supplied Britain's Royal Air Force with some 20 type B-17C's, and the plane went into action over Europe. Historian Steve Birdsall, writing of this, the first practical trial of the "Flying Fortress," said that "they were too lightly armed

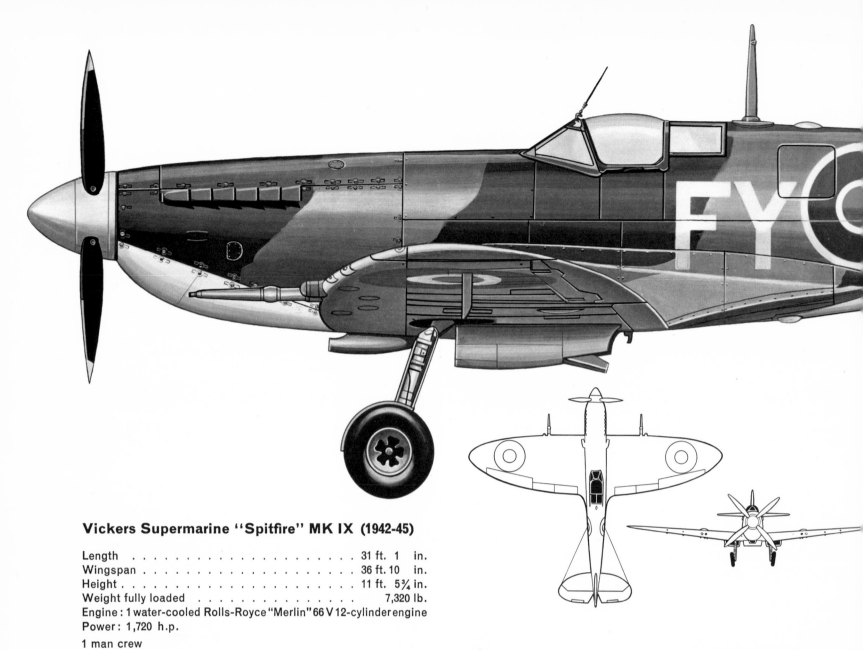

Vickers Supermarine "Spitfire" MK IX (1942-45)

Length . . . . 31 ft. 1   in.
Wingspan . . . . 36 ft. 10   in.
Height . . . . 11 ft. 5¾ in.
Weight fully loaded . . . .   7,320 lb.
Engine : 1 water-cooled Rolls-Royce "Merlin" 66 V 12-cylinder engine
Power : 1,720 h.p.

1 man crew

*Britain's most famous fighter plane in World War II, the
Vickers "Spitfire," followed in the glorious tradition of the
"Supermarine" aircraft, which, years earlier, had brought the
Schneider Cup to Great Britain. The "Spitfire," a further
development of the machines designed for that race, was manufactured in a number of variations, each of which enjoyed great
success. The type IX was designed to challenge Germany's
Fw 190, just as the older type V "Spitfires" had been designed
to challenge the standard German fighter Me 109. The new
"Spitfire" MK IX differed externally only by the longer engine
structure. The more powerful "Merlin" engine increased the
machine's speed to 401 m.p.h., enabling the "Spitfire" pilots
to inflict heavy losses on German fighter units. The "Spitfire"
MK IX remained in combat until the end of the war. In addition
to their bravery, many British fighter pilots owe their high
decorations to this superb fighter.*

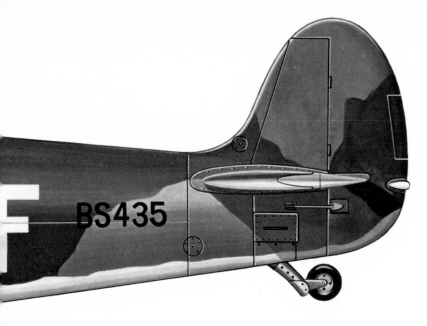

A team of designers from the Bavarian Aircraft Works—later Messerschmitt—led by engineer W. Rethel, went into action in 1934, the year when Germany's standard fighter in World War II was first conceived. The group surrounding Professor Messerschmitt and Rethel planned the Me 109 (Bf 109), which eventually became the German Air Force's most produced combat plane. By 1945, 30,573 machines had been built. The racy monoplane gained combat experience from 1936 to 1939 during the Spanish Civil War. The first type to go into mass production was the Me 109 E, and by the end of 1939 the Air Ministry had supplied all squadrons destined for the front with the new fighter. The Me 109 served till the end of the war, and was linked with many of Germany's air heroes.

Messerschmitt Me 109 E Fighter (1938-45)

Length	29 ft. 4 in.
Wingspan	32 ft. 4 in.
Height	8 ft. 2 in.
Weight fully loaded	5,865 lb.

Engine: 1 water-cooled Daimler-Benz DB-601A V 12-cylinder in-line engine (suspended)
Power: 1,100 h.p.

1 man crew

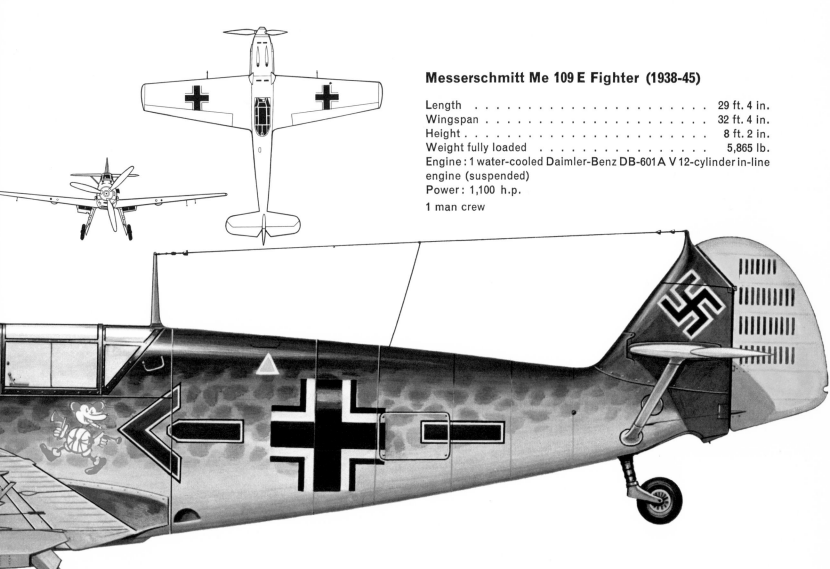

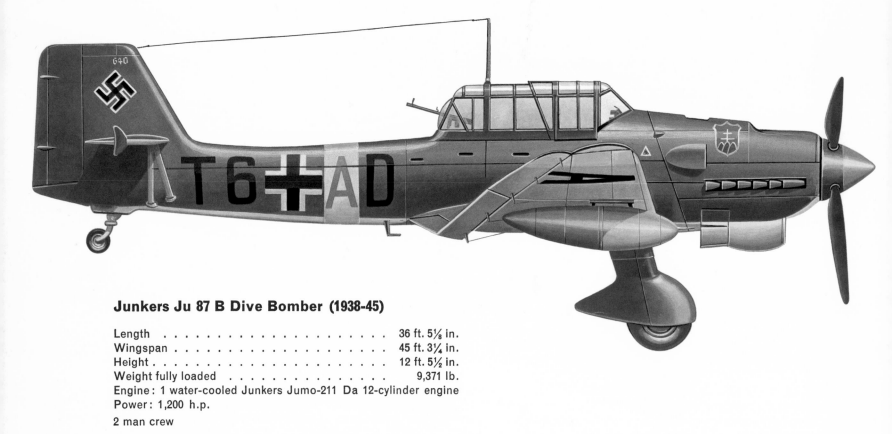

Junkers Ju 87 B Dive Bomber (1938-45)

Length	36 ft. 5⅛ in.
Wingspan	45 ft. 3¼ in.
Height	12 ft. 5½ in.
Weight fully loaded	9,371 lb.

Engine: 1 water-cooled Junkers Jumo-211 Da 12-cylinder engine
Power: 1,200 h.p.

2 man crew

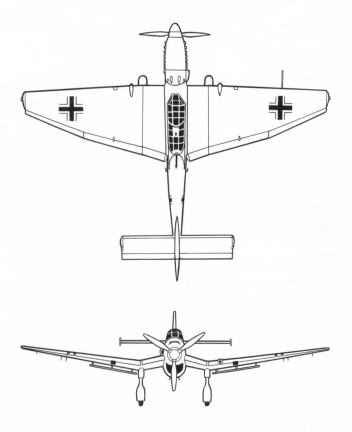

Two developments, which were to run parallel for a long time, began on June 10, 1936: Ernst Udet took over the direction of the technical department of the German Air Ministry and from that day on, he and his numerous followers advanced the legendary German dive bomber, Junkers' Ju 87 ("Stuka"), which eventually became an institution. Engineer Pohlmann von Junkers designed the gull-winged monoplane with a fixed landing gear. Even the most bitter opponent of the "Stuka" idea, Wolfram von Richthofen, became convinced after the Ju 87 made a number of practical demonstrations. A built-in siren increased the "Stuka's" psychological effectiveness. Both developments ended in disaster; Udet committed suicide, and the Junkers Ju 87 failed to forestall Germany's collapse.

When Boeing's "Flying Fortresses" went into action over German skies, they played a major role in bringing World War II to a close. The massive employment of these machines had a destructive effect not only on the enemy's war industry but almost equally so on the morale of its civilians.

with too little armor." Their performance, at first, did not come up to the Allies' expectations. Losses of up to ten per cent were inflicted on the American B-17 and the British Avro-Lancaster units by enemy flack and interceptors. But Boeing's engineers acted quickly. To protect the tail of the B-17C, two 50-caliber machine guns, operated by a tail gunner protected by reinforced armor plating, were mounted under the huge tail surfaces of the bomber.

The defensive B-17 now became "an airplane that attacked," Birdsall reported. The final type B-17G was to have a total of thirteen Browning aircraft machine guns.

Germany's Messerschmitt Me 109's and Focke-Wulf Fw 190's were not the only ones to feel the effects of the increased firepower: following its initial success in the Pacific, the Japanese Mitsubishi A6M6c "Zeros" ("Zero-Sens") fell prey to the powerful new "Flying Fortresses."

Superiority had to result in success. Allied military historians noted with satisfaction what Nazi Armaments Minister Albert Speer was later to concede at the Nuremberg Trials: "The American attacks, which followed a well-conceived system of destroying industrial targets, were by far the most dangerous. It was actually these attacks that brought about the total collapse of the German armament industry. The attacks on chemical plants alone would have been enough to make further defense of Germany impossible—even apart from our devastating military failures."

A survey published by Boeing made clear how far the actual performance of the B-17G exceeded the original specifications. It had a wingspan of 103 ft. 9½ in., was 74 ft. 4 in. long, and 19 ft. 1 in. wide. Its four Wright "Cyclone" engines developed 1,200 h.p., and the maximum speed of the bomber was more than 300 m.p.h. The plane could operate at a service ceiling of over 40,000 ft. with a total weight of more than 54,926 lb.

The unlimited means and huge expenditure of the United States resulted in proportionate production figures and great progress in the development of military aircraft. During World War II, the U.S. government appropriated 45 billion dollars for the development and production of a total of 300,000 units alone. Hitler's Germany, said Lieutenant General William S. Knudsen, Chief of the Air Technical Service Command, was overwhelmed by "a production avalanche that it had never experienced or imagined." The B-29 "Superfortress," the improved, more powerful and larger descendant of the "Flying Fortress," formed a part of this avalanche, as did the B-17 itself which was still used after the end of the war.

The B-17's flew on as cargo aircraft, as trainers, and as photo-survey machines for the French "Institut Géographique National." In 1948, the planes flew for the Israeli Air Force, and they were still serving in the U.S. Coast Guard in 1959. They went to war once again when the 3rd Air Rescue

The successful operations of Boeing's "Flying Fortresses" resulted in continual modifications and improvements based on experience. The type B-17G came into being at the end of 1943. Boeing manufactured the first 30 units, and Vega turned out the rest. B-17G's were also used as "radar jammers." Equipped with special electronic devices, they flew with regular bombing groups to cause confusion in the German warning and detection system. Hardly known, however, is the fact that a German unit—the I/K.G. 200—had a number of "Fortresses." Bearing the insignia of the German secret command, these planes flew missions to drop agents and spies behind Allied lines. Fortune favored the "Flying Fortresses," with very few exceptions. When the 8th Air Force Command lost 60 machines during an unescorted day raid on the Schweinfurt ball bearing works and the Messerschmitt factory in Regensburg on August 17, 1943, the Allies had to reconsider whether daylight missions should be flown at all. Reinforced escort and armament of the B-17's enabled the day raids to continue. The "Flying Fortresses" proved to be just that, in the literal sense of the word.

Boeing B-17G "Flying Fortress" Bomber (1944-45)

Length . . . . 74 ft. 4 in.
Wingspan . . . . 103 ft. 9½ in.
Height . . . . 19 ft. 1 in.
Weight fully loaded . . . . 54,926 lb.
Engines: 4 air-cooled Wright "Cyclone" GR-1820-97 9-cylinder radial engines with General Electric B-22 turbo-compressors (powered by exhaust)
Power: 1,200 h.p.
6–10 man crew

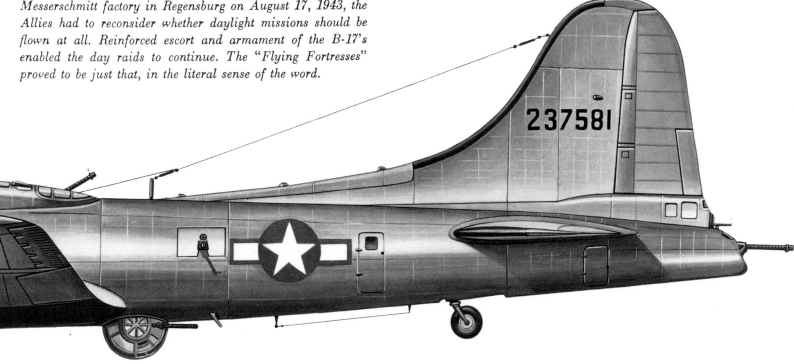

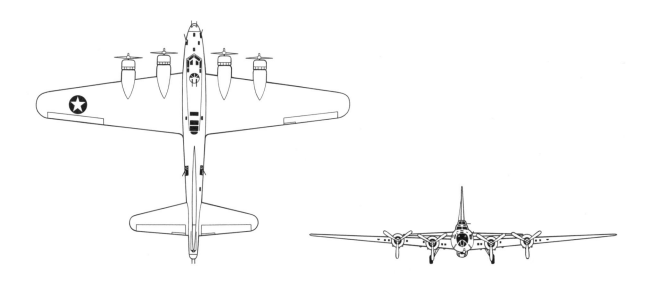

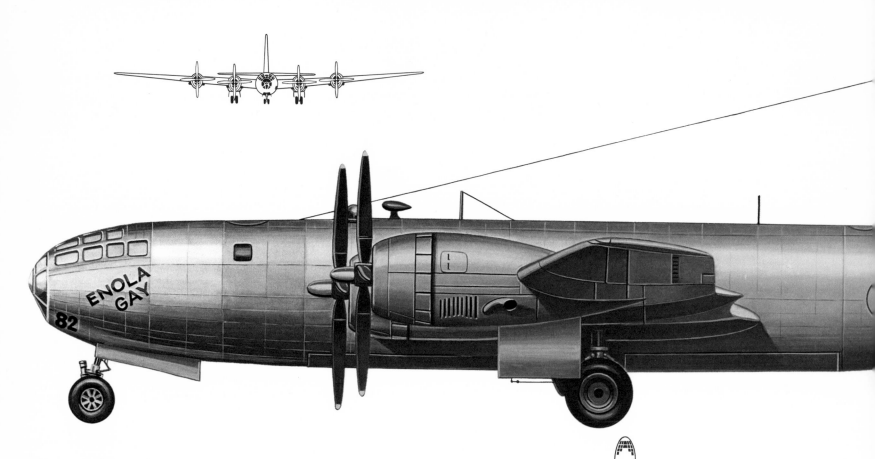

Boeing B-29 "Superfortress" Bomber (1939-45)

Length . . . . 99 ft.
Wingspan . . . . 141 ft. 3½ in.
Height . . . . 27 ft. 9 in.
Weight fully loaded . . . . 100,019 lb.
Engines : 4 air-cooled Wright "Cyclone" R-3350-23 18-cylinder
radial engines each with two General Electric turbo-compressors
Power: 2,300 h.p.

11 man crew

*Among the B-29 "Superfortresses" coming off the Boeing,
Bell and Martin production lines, one, the "Enola Gay"—
serial number 44-86292—was to play a historic role. On
August 6, 1945, the "Enola Gay" ushered in the Atomic Age
when "Little Boy," the first atomic bomb, dropped from her
bomb bay on Hiroshima. "Little Boy" leveled about 5 square
miles of the town and more than 70,000 people lost their lives.
Nevertheless, the "Superfortress" B-29 had been designed and
built for a single purpose : to bomb Japan over the vast distances
of the Pacific. A prototype of this aircraft flew for the first time
on September 21, 1942. From the 3,970 B-29's built, two were
chosen to fly on atomic bomb missions. "Enola Gay" flew
"Little Boy" to Hiroshima; "Bockscar" dropped "Fat Boy"
on Nagasaki. Japan capitulated.*

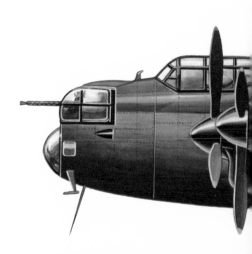

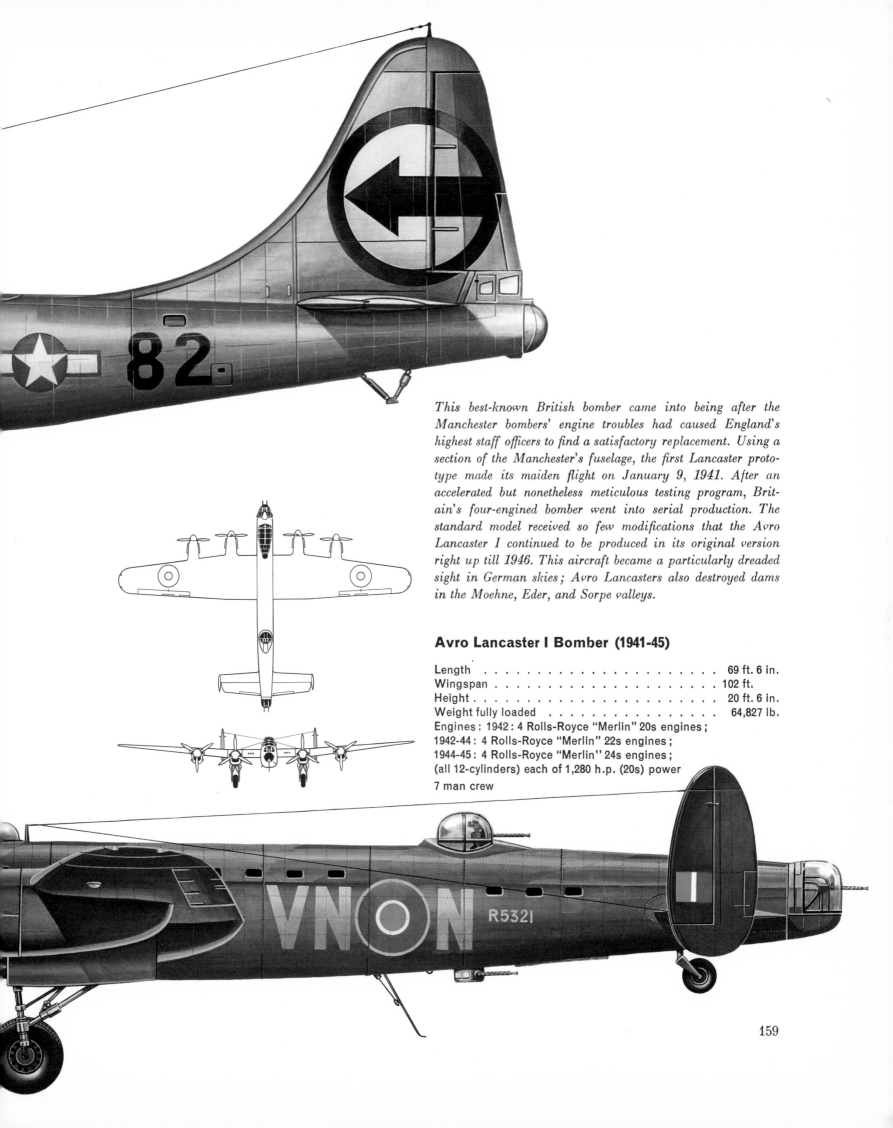

This best-known British bomber came into being after the Manchester bombers' engine troubles had caused England's highest staff officers to find a satisfactory replacement. Using a section of the Manchester's fuselage, the first Lancaster prototype made its maiden flight on January 9, 1941. After an accelerated but nonetheless meticulous testing program, Britain's four-engined bomber went into serial production. The standard model received so few modifications that the Avro Lancaster I continued to be produced in its original version right up till 1946. This aircraft became a particularly dreaded sight in German skies; Avro Lancasters also destroyed dams in the Moehne, Eder, and Sorpe valleys.

Avro Lancaster I Bomber (1941-45)

Length . . . . 69 ft. 6 in.
Wingspan . . . . 102 ft.
Height . . . . 20 ft. 6 in.
Weight fully loaded . . . . 64,827 lb.
Engines: 1942: 4 Rolls-Royce "Merlin" 20s engines;
1942-44: 4 Rolls-Royce "Merlin" 22s engines;
1944-45: 4 Rolls-Royce "Merlin'' 24s engines;
(all 12-cylinders) each of 1,280 h.p. (20s) power

7 man crew

Consolidated B-24J "Liberator" Bomber (1942-45)

Length . . . . 67 ft. 2 in.
Wingspan . . . . 110 ft.
Height . . . . 18 ft.
Weight fully loaded . . . . 55,918 lb.
Engines : 4 air-cooled Pratt & Whitney R-1830-65 14-cylinder
radial engines with General Electric B-22 turbo-compressor
(powered by exhaust)
Power : 1,200 h.p.

8–10 man crew

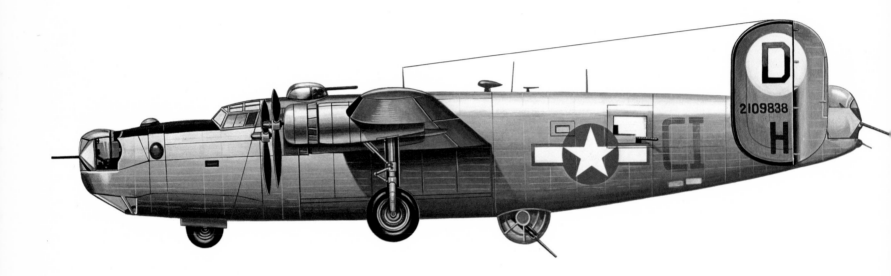

William Green, the British aviation historian, considered the Consolidated B-24J "Liberator" an "ugly duckling" compared to the Boeing "Flying Fortress." But the fact that more B-24J's were produced than any other American combat plane (a total of 18,188 were made) testifies to its successful design. This long-range bomber which, in its way, was also a "flying fortress," was developed later, and was first used by the R.A.F. in Europe. A number of essential modifications were carried out on the J types that replaced the G and H models in August 1943. Additional fuel tanks increased the four-engined bomber's range; compressors increased output of its Pratt & Whitney R-1830-65 engines; and machine guns were provided for the "Liberator's" defense. Together with the Avro Lancaster, Boeing B-17 and Boeing B-29 "Superfortress," the Consolidated B-24 J "Liberator" aircraft played the leading role in bombing attacks during World War II.

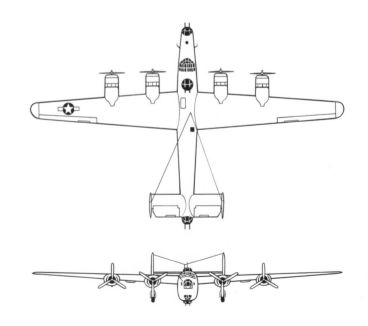

160

North American P-51D "Mustang" Fighter (1944-45)

Length . . . . 32 ft. 3 in.
Wingspan . . . . 37 ft.
Height . . . . 13 ft. 7½ in.
Weight fully loaded . . . . 10,076 lb.
Engine: 1 water-cooled Rolls-Royce-Packard "Merlin" V 1650-7
12-cylinder in-line engine with two-stage compressor
Power: 1,450 h.p.

1 man crew

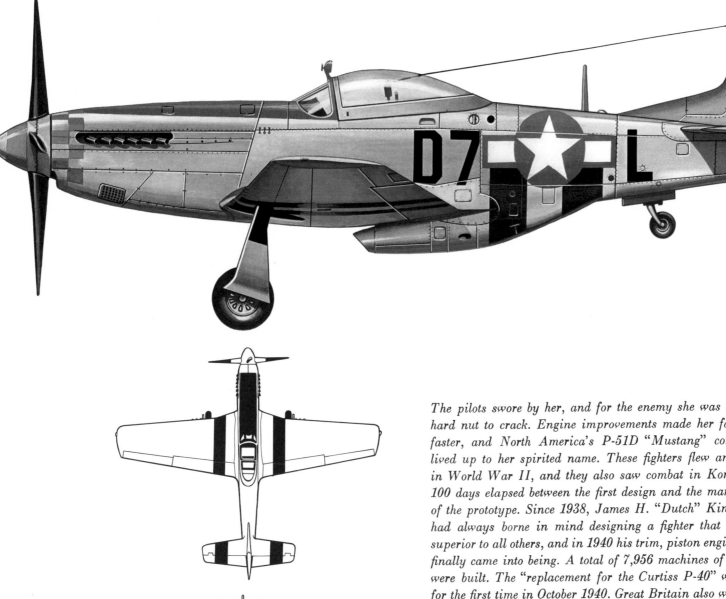

The pilots swore by her, and for the enemy she was always a hard nut to crack. Engine improvements made her faster and faster, and North America's P-51D "Mustang" continually lived up to her spirited name. These fighters flew and fought in World War II, and they also saw combat in Korea. Only 100 days elapsed between the first design and the manufacture of the prototype. Since 1938, James H. "Dutch" Kindelberger had always borne in mind designing a fighter that would be superior to all others, and in 1940 his trim, piston engine fighter finally came into being. A total of 7,956 machines of this type were built. The "replacement for the Curtiss P-40" was flown for the first time in October 1940. Great Britain also wanted the "Mustang," and when the first of 250 of the new fighter types arrived in England, R.A.F. fliers were enthusiastic. After the United States entered the war, American pilots also achieved notable successes with this tough fighter.

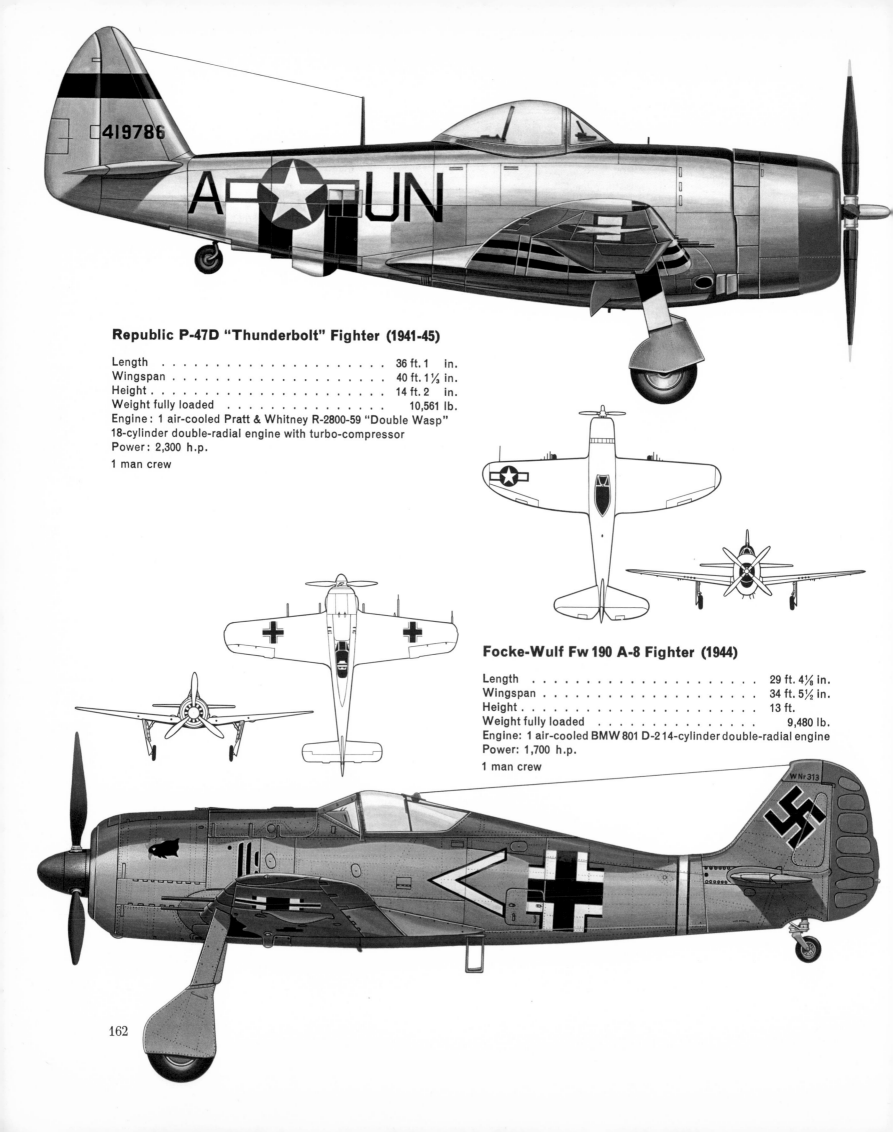

Republic P-47D "Thunderbolt" Fighter (1941-45)

Length . . . . 36 ft. 1 in.
Wingspan . . . . 40 ft. 1⅓ in.
Height . . . . 14 ft. 2 in.
Weight fully loaded . . . . 10,561 lb.
Engine: 1 air-cooled Pratt & Whitney R-2800-59 "Double Wasp"
18-cylinder double-radial engine with turbo-compressor
Power: 2,300 h.p.

1 man crew

Focke-Wulf Fw 190 A-8 Fighter (1944)

Length . . . . 29 ft. 4⅛ in.
Wingspan . . . . 34 ft. 5½ in.
Height . . . . 13 ft.
Weight fully loaded . . . . 9,480 lb.
Engine: 1 air-cooled BMW 801 D-2 14-cylinder double-radial engine
Power: 1,700 h.p.

1 man crew

Republic P-47D "Thunderbolt" Fighter (1941-45)

U.S. Air Force pilots called the streamlined Republic P-47D "Thunderbolt" a "hero maker" after many of their fighter aces in World War II had achieved notable victories in it. First Lieutenant T.S. Gabreski shot down 31 enemy planes, Captain R.S. Johnson 28, and Colonel H. Zemke 20. A total of 12,602 of these single-engined planes were built, 80 per cent of which were D types. One version of the "Thunderbolt" flew with six to eight machine guns, another could take two 1,000 lb. bombs or ten rockets. They were used as fighters and interceptors and distinguished themselves in all theaters of operation; American, British, French, and Soviet units were equipped with P-47D machines. The versatile "Thunderbolt" flew low-level missions and acted as a fighter escort for long-range bombers. As a flying weapon, the "Thunderbolt" record remains outstanding today. In 1,934,000 flying hours, the Republic fighters dropped 132,000 tons of explosives and fired 60,000 rockets—a remarkable achievement for a one-seater fighter. Republic's chief designer, Alexander Kartveli (an exiled Russian, like his former superior, Alexander P. Seversky), wrote another page in aviation history with his "Thunderbolt."

Focke-Wulf Fw 190 A-8 Fighter (1944)

Chief pilot Sander, who was entrusted with Focke-Wulf's new creations, made the first flight of the Fw 190 V-1 on June 1, 1939. The engineers under Professor Tank's direction had designed an addition to the standard Me 109 fighters within ten months. When the prototype was tested it was found capable of achieving 373 m.p.h., and, along with the Me 109, it soon enjoyed great popularity among combat fliers. The A-8 type went into production in 1943 with a modified fuselage containing an auxiliary tank. The plane was armed with two 13 mm. machine guns and four 20 mm. machine guns.

Squadron flew "Flying Fortresses" in Korea, and Lieutenant General Matthew B. Ridgway traveled around the Far East theater of operations in a veteran B-17.

Wartime U.S.A.F. pilots wistfully recall "our Fortress," to which they gave such imaginative names as: "Memphis Belle", "Millie, the Vicious Virgin", "Lassie come Home", "Headache for Hitler", "Lady Satan", "Satan's Workshop," or "Hell's Angels," as well as other graphic, unequivocal or double-meaning pet names, some of which could hardly be repeated in their original inscription on the fuselage without indiscretion. After all, the war was hard, the joys of life distant, and names such as "Daddy's Delight," inscribed under a voluptuous, larger-than-life naked beauty, reflected a certain nostalgia.

The fact that "Daddy's Delight" was able to return to home base so often was one of the B-17's merits. Both friend and foe of the "Flying Fortresses" were right when they said that the machines often flew back as virtual wrecks—but they made it.

"We saw such planes return every day. One B-17 landed with half its tail shot away, another with riddled wings. Soon one with its plexiglass nose shot off, then another with both port engines missing. But they came back," said Robert Morgan, Flight Captain of the famed "Memphis Belle" of the U.S. 8th Air Force. And he was not exaggerating. Countless eyewitness reports confirmed the legendary indestructibility, and the glory that surrounded Boeing's "Flying Fortresses." The crews were worthy of the machines; Birdsall reports the incident of a flight engineer who flew his B-17E home after an attack from a Focke-Wulf Fw 190 had seriously wounded the pilot and killed the copilot.

An outlandish joke circulated among the B-17 crews, which, even if untrue, stemmed from the unlimited trust the men had in the "Flying Fortress." "The ground crew looked up. What circled over them was no B-17. A single engine was making an approach, a sergeant straddling it, his machine gun across his knee. He made a clean landing, taxied right up to the astonished mechanics, and jumped down. 'Boy oh boy,' he said, 'that was some mission!'"

The German Me 109 fighter flew on all the World War II fronts and also against the Soviet Union. The aircraft showed its superiority particularly against the Russian "Rata." The great progress made by German designers was clearly borne out by the Me 109's flying qualities; it was fast, tough in combat, and easy to fly.

MITSUBISHI A6M6C "ZERO-SEN"

The Emperor's new bird of prey

Japan's most famous hunter of World War II

Japan was adequately armed in 1923; her Air Force consisted of 548 aircraft, mostly of foreign origin, and 6,156 soldiers. Nevertheless, in 1941 when Japan entered the Second World War, she invested two billion dollars in armament production alone. A large share of this went for the manufacture of bombers and fighter-interceptors. By then, Japan's designers had long been at work developing their own airplane models. Aitshi and Ishikawajima built reconnaissance planes, and the machines manufactured by Kawanishi, Kawasaki and Nakajima flew from 1937 to 1941 in the Sino-Japanese War. But Japan's best-known combat planes were produced by the Mitsubishi Company, and their A6M "Zeros" ("Zero-Sens") were standard fighters of exceptional quality. On December 7, 1941, the first surprise attacks on the U.S. fleet base at Pearl Harbor involved 54 Japanese dive bombers, 40 torpedo bombers, 50 horizontal bombers and 45 "Zeros" taking off from aircraft carriers. Japan had effectively proved her strength.

"An erroneous idea cropped up in China that the Japanese were unsuited for flying, that they could imitate certain foreign designs, but that it was not necessary to take the Japanese Air Force seriously or fear its attacks," a Shanghai correspondent reported in 1938, at the time China was defending herself against Japanese expansion.

American machines flew for China, and so did the Soviet's Polikarpov I-15's and I-16's. Japan's pilots fought with the type 96 A5M, with Mitsubishi's "Oktori," a three-seater, twin-engined, multi-purpose aircraft which served as a fighter, reconnaissance plane, or bomber, and with Nakajima's AN-1 one-seater, single-engined monoplane fighter.

In April 1938, Japanese Navy pilots suffered several major defeats; and in a one day raid on Hankow they lost 36 machines out of a total of 40, flying without fighter escort. Nevertheless, Chiang Kai-shek's soldiers slowly gave way. One German reporter in Shanghai suggested that the growing inferiority of the Chinese forces may have been due to Madame Chiang Kai-shek acting as General Secretary for the Aviation Commission. This she continued to do until the end of February 1938, after the fronts began to stiffen.

The bombers of the Imperial Japanese Air Force continued to attack—now with fighter cover. Meanwhile, the Mitsubishi Company's designers had developed more advanced aircraft, including the Emperor's new eagle: the Mitsubishi

A6M2 (type 0) "Zero." For five years, this maneuverable fighter remained the crowning achievement of Japanese design.

When Japan started her air force, she employed a method which has been traditionally ascribed to her—sometimes with and sometimes without justification—copying. At first she copied what had been developed by aircraft designers in America and Europe. Her aviation industry acquired licenses for engine construction from Hispano-Suiza, Piaggio, Lorraine and B.M.W. (B.M.W. "Kawasaki"). Mitsubishi made the "Jaguar" double-row radial engine, and Nakajima made the "Jupiter" radial engine. Then the engineers began developing their own ideas out of the experience they had gained from building foreign models and through the study of foreign engines and machines.

Japan was an island empire, and she saw that her future must lie on the water. Consequently, carrier aircraft took precedence.

"The number of Japanese aircraft carriers is not known exactly," Clarence Winchester wrote in his "Wonders of World Aviation" published in 1938, "but it is probably more than 300, and therefore the Japanese Navy Air Force must be counted among the strongest at present."

Like Heinkel in Germany, the Japanese were devoting great attention to the catapult takeoff, and this installation was to become so far advanced that fighters, torpedo aircraft, bombers and reconnaissance planes could all be launched from the flight deck of an aircraft carrier.

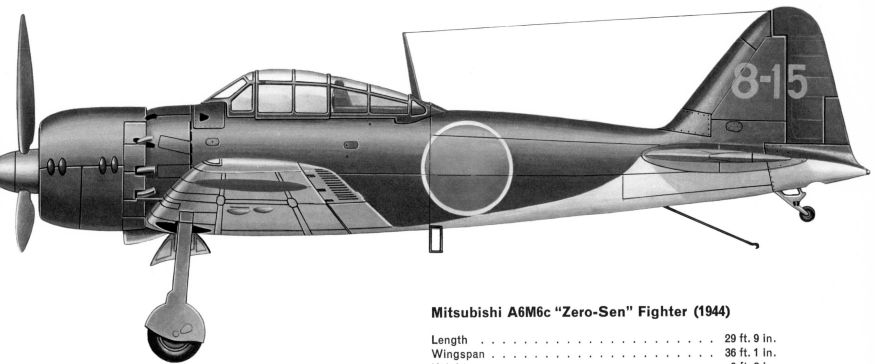

Mitsubishi A6M6c "Zero-Sen" Fighter (1944)

Length . . . . 29 ft. 9 in.
Wingspan . . . . 36 ft. 1 in.
Height . . . . 9 ft. 2 in.
Weight fully loaded . . . . 5,997 lb.
Engine: 1 air-cooled Nakajima NK1P "Sakai" 31 14-cylinder double-radial engine
Power: 1,120 h.p.

1 man crew

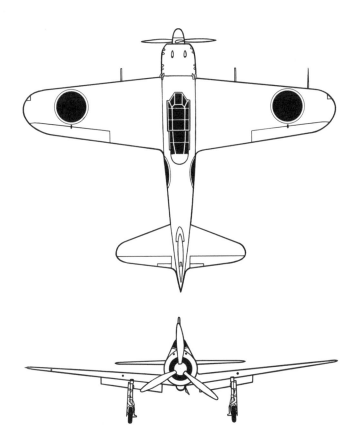

In 1938, during her conflict with China, Japan was still flying Nakajima's obsolete one-seater, single-engined AN-1. But a year earlier, on October 5, 1937, the Imperial Japanese Navy Air Force Technical Department had begun to make plans for a new fighter. On April 1, 1939, a prototype of the "Zero" A6M6c fighter made its maiden flight. Bugs were quickly eliminated, and the plane gave an excellent performance. The Mitsubishi "Zeros" are still held in esteem today for their balanced construction. They were Japan's most successful fighting machines in World War II, operating mostly in the Pacific theater.

165

The Mitsubishi Company seemed best adapted to develop an aerial armada stationed on ships; while Nakajima, its competitor, had the most experience in constructing seaplanes. But Mitsubishi developed carrier fighters, and a subsidiary of the company had emerged from the Mitsubishi Shipbuilding and Engineering Company to become engaged in aircraft production. Their yards were known for the high quality of the ships, an image which soon applied to their airplanes as well. In time, Mitsubishi also gained a reputation for progress in the field of light construction.

Japan won her first international laurels when pilots Masaaki Iinuma and Kenji Tsukagoshi set a long-distance record with their single-engined "Kamikaze" or "Divine Wind." They took off from Tokyo on April 5, 1937, and landed in Croydon, England on April 9, with a flight time of three days, 22 hours, and eighteen minutes. But apart from this achievement, Japan's aviation industry received further recognition. The great air nations, America, Britain, and France, found it worth their while even to study the sparse information contained in Japanese publications on that country's discoveries in air flow and fuselage design.

Regarding Japan's pilots, whose reputation was none too great abroad at this time, Winchester wrote in 1938: "It is clear that they are keeping close to the British in their training methods and there are indications that the Japanese are thoroughly capable of learning to fly."

They learned it so well, that U.S. veterans of the air war in the Pacific still speak of the flying skill of their one-time opponents with utmost respect. In the hands of the Japanese pilots, Mitsubishi's "Zero" became a dreaded instrument of war, a weapon that always represented a threat to the Grumman F6F "Hellcats" and the Brewster "Buffaloes."

The Mitsubishi A6M was conceived as a replacement for its predecessor, the A5M type 96, which was also a one-seater, single-engined fighter. But the Japanese Imperial Navy Air Force wanted something even better, and on October 5, 1937, the Mitsubishi and Nakajima companies received orders to design a new fighter with a maximum speed of up to 310 m.p.h., a climb rate of approximately 9,840 ft. in 3.5 minutes, greater range and maneuverability than any other known fighter, and an armament of two cannons and two machine guns.

Nakajima considered the project impracticable, but Mitsubishi's chief designer, Jiro Horikoshi, rolled up his sleeves and went to work. For his first prototype Horikoshi planned to use a 780 h.p. MK2 Zuisei 13 engine, a 14-cylinder double-row radial engine made by Mitsubishi. The engine was chosen for its light weight, which the Japanese considered of utmost importance in aircraft design. To meet the maneuverability demands, an "extra super" Duralumin, developed in Japan especially for aircraft construction, was used for the broad wing surfaces.

On April 1, 1939, test pilot Katsuzo Shima took off from Kasumigaura airfield for the maiden flight of the new "Zero." This Horikoshi and Mitsubishi fighter was a success; defects were only apparent in the oil system and the landing gear, and excess vibration was removed after a bigger, three-bladed prop replaced the double-bladed propeller on the prototype.

A year later, in July 1940, the first fifteen "Zero" type A6M2 fighters went into action in China, where the Mitsubishi type A5M (96) was barely holding its own. The "Zero's" success moved U.S. Air Force General Claire Chennault to warn of the surprising combat ability of this new Japanese fighter. "It would bear watching in future," Chennault said: but his warning fell on deaf ears. Then came Pearl Harbor.

In December 1941, Japan's "Zero" units had more than 400 fighter aircraft of the A6M2 (21) type, and before the end of the war, Mitsubishi had built a total of 740 model 21 machines.

When the "Zero" fighters appeared over Hawaii, the performance of the new eagles had markedly increased. The A6M2 (21) could attain 314 m.p.h. at an altitude of 13,008 ft., and could climb to 19,680 ft. in a mere 7 minutes 27 seconds. In November 1941, a month before Pearl Harbor, Nakajima, under license, began production of this "Zero" model at its factory near Koizuma.

After recovering from the shock of Pearl Harbor, the U.S. was at first hard put to it to find a good match for the speedy and versatile "Zero" fighter. Another unpleasant surprise occurred in September 1942, when, over New Guinea, they spotted more powerful and faster Japanese fighter planes that for a time were not identified as the "Zero". Armed with two 7.7 mm. machine guns in the fuselage, the diving properties of the new A6M3 (32) had been considerably improved. A supercharged 1,130 h.p. Sakai 21 engine had increased the speed of the new type to about 339 m.p.h., and wing tanks had lengthened its operational range. Mitsubishi constructed a total of 560 machines of this aircraft carrier type, which was finally designated the standard fighter for aircraft carriers.

However, Mitsubishi's new A6M3 (32) had arrived on the scene too late. Two months earlier, in June 1942, Japan had already lost out in the Battle of Midway. Before the Japanese attacked the U.S. base on the island, Admiral Isoroku Yamamoto had set sail with a task force of 150 ships and more than 700 aircraft, determined to swing the war over in Japan's favor. The battle opened on June 4, with an attack by 108 Japanese combat planes. A U.S. Marine squadron of Brewster "Buffaloes" was destroyed on the ground; and only six out of 41 Douglas TBD "Devastators" which attacked the Japanese aircraft carriers returned. The "Zeros" and the suicidal determination of the Japanese pilots provided stiff competition. But the American Douglas SBD "Dauntless" dive bombers dealt the first decisive blow against Japan. Within five minutes after going into action, they sank the Japanese aircraft carriers "Akagi", "Soryu", and "Kaga."

Attacking from an altitude of 16,404 ft., the "Dauntlesses" bore in at a 70 degree angle to within 2,600 ft. of the Japanese carriers. 322 Japanese airplanes went down with their ships, and more than 2,500 airmen and soldiers lost their lives.

Although Japan had an excellent fighter in her "Zero," and an even faster weapon in her Kawasaki-Hien and Kawanishi-Shi fighters, the U.S. had its "Dauntless," and, at the same time, had the advantages of greater reserves and higher production figures. Douglas alone produced about 5,000 "Dauntless" dive bombers which had played such an important role in the Battle of Midway.

In the next three years, Japan's aircraft industry made desperate all-out efforts to improve its production figures, as again and again the Mitsubishi "Zero" fighters attempted to bring about a turning point in the war. The A6M5 (52) made its appearance in 1943, and was flown at 354 m.p.h. But Japan's war against the Allies continued to be defensive. Although 747 "Zero" fighters of the A6M5 type rolled off Mitsubishi's assembly lines, in addition to those produced by Nakajima, Japan was no longer capable of changing the course of the war.

In 1944, the A6M designers finally cast their last dice. They completed their prototype of the A6M6c, and Nakajima took over its production. The Sakai 31 engine with water-methanol injection systems was used to hike immediate performance. The wing tanks were self-sealing to prevent loss of fuel through bullet holes, and rocket racks were installed under both wings. The 53c model of Mitsubishi's "Zero" A6M6c had a wingspan of 36 ft. 1 in., a length of 29 ft. 9 in., and a height of 9 ft. 2 in. With a normal load, takeoff weight

was 5,997 lb. Its maximum speed was 343 m.p.h. at an altitude of 19,626 ft. The A6M6c (53c) had a cruising speed of 199 m.p.h. at 75 per cent power output. This "Zero" type had a range of 1,300 nautical miles with a maximum service ceiling of 35,006 ft.

But the "Zero" fighters had now become too heavy, and had to be modified again to enable takeoff from a carrier flight deck. The designers eliminated the fuselage tank for a single bomb. Range became limited. The bomb racks frequently malfunctioned, forcing the pilots to fly home with a bomb still fastened to the belly of their "Zero."

Of necessity, the Japanese combat pilots had to exploit every virtue of their "Divine Wind." The first suicide pilots came from the 201st squadron, which was formed from volunteers of the 206th. Wrapped in "Sun" flags, they crashed their explosive-filled "Zeros" on enemy ships. During the Okinawa campaign, Kamikaze pilots flew 1,900 sorties, inflicting heavy losses on the U.S. Navy, but their suicidal tactics failed to save their country from defeat. The 13th century fable, according to which a Kamikaze (Divine Wind) in the form of a storm drove back a Mongolian invasion fleet off Japan's shores, failed to reappear in the 20th century.

Those who sacrificed themselves and those who survived, like Saburo Sakai, Japan's greatest fighter ace in World War II (he is accredited with 64 air victories); those who flew them and those who fought against them—all considered the "Zero" a milestone.

The Mitsubishi myth was great in the Far Eastern theater of operations, and the U.S. was delighted when the first nearly intact A6M2 was captured, making it possible to study first hand its most vulnerable points. In his "Famous Fighters of the Second World War," William Green said: "This single fighter was probably one of the greatest prizes of the Pacific war."

Japan's prize: 10,938 "Zeros" and a lost war.

ROCKET AND JET ENGINES

Faster with thrust

New engines open up an era in aviation

Aviation began with the first engine-propelled flight of a heavier-than-air machine made by Orville Wright on December 17, 1903, and it culminated on October 14, 1947, when another American, pilot Charles "Chuck" Yeager, broke the sound barrier for the first time in his Bell XS 1. (Because the Me 163, the first really high-performance fighter, and the Bell XS 1, the first supersonic airplane, were both rocket-powered, there is often confusion as to the differences between rocket and jet propulsion systems. The rocket engine is completely self-contained and needs no air in its operation, whereas the jet engine cannot burn its fuel without air taken from the surrounding atmosphere. This difference has led to the use of rockets for long-range missiles such as the V-2's, and the rejection of rockets for aircraft after the German experience with the Me 163.) Along the way to rocketry and jet-propelled aircraft were many successful pioneers: among the most noted were Robert H. Goddard, Wernher von Braun, Geoffrey De Havilland, Hermann Oberth, Pabst von Ohain, Hellmuth Walter, and Frank Whittle. The way was also marked by highly advanced piston, rocket, and jet engines with which aerodynamics and frame construction could scarcely keep pace; and by futile attempts to extend the limits of flight through other means of propulsion. When rockets and jets reach their peak velocity, their speed is usually expressed in terms of Mach number instead of miles per hour. Ernst Mach (1838-1916), philosopher and physicist, gave his name to this advanced measurement of speed. The Mach number indicates the ratio of the speed of a body to the speed of sound in the surrounding medium. Mach 0.5 in air near the ground corresponds to about 370 m.p.h.; Mach 1 is about 750 m.p.h. The first step toward the current high-speed aircraft was taken in Paris. Henri Coanda built the first jet aircraft there, in 1910!

One afternoon in December 1910, a group of spectators stared in amazement at an airplane on a meadow at Issy-les-Moulineaux. They had never seen anything like it before. The biplane was unbraced, and it had no propeller. Henri Coanda, a student of the Paris "Ecole Nationale Supérieure de l'Aéronautique," was determined to fly this strange contraption. The 24 year-old Rumanian started up the engine, and to the spectators' increased amazement the clatter of the piston engine was accompanied by an unearthly whine: Coanda's jet unit was working.

Pierre Clerget, a friend of the Bucharest-born Coanda, had built the machine according to the plans he had been given, while Ernest Archdeacon, the uncrowned flight king of Paris, gave the two men his continued encouragement. The plane's 4-cylinder engine drove a radial compressor mounted in front of it, and the exhaust gases were directed into the compressor inlet where fuel was injected for combustion. Coanda had installed protective metal plating on both sides, behind the outlet of the gas jets, but this plating directed the flames against the wooden fuselage and threat-ened to set the plane on fire. At first, Coanda was chiefly concerned about this danger, but then as his plane began to take off, he saw that he was heading, at a low level, straight for the houses bordering the meadow. While attempting to gain sufficient altitude to miss hitting the buildings, Coanda stalled the machine. He crashed. The biplane burned up, but Coanda was pulled out in time and survived. The painful experience taught him a valuable lesson: he learned to fly and acquired a pilot license number 11 of the "Fédération Aéronautique Internationale."

Coanda continued to make airplanes, but his experiments ruined him financially. Then Sir George White of the English Bristol Airplane Company hired him as chief designer. In World War I, Coanda flew for France in the 22nd Artillery Regiment, but was soon recalled to construct reconnaissance planes. When the war ended, Coanda and the English Channel flier, Louis Blériot, built steel and concrete houses with prefabricated parts. Finally, Coanda settled in the United States, and as an inventor this one-time pupil of the sculptor Auguste Rodin became holder of over 30 patents.

Coanda's influence on the history of jet aircraft is limited to his one unique experiment. But his friend Gianni Caproni, with whom he had studied and who had built his first glider model, made the second jet machine in aviation history—after Heinkel. His Caproni-Campini N.1 took off on its maiden flight from Taliedo near Milan on August 27, 1940.

For many years after Coanda, piston engines and propellers were to remain unchallenged. Coanda's attempt at jet propulsion was premature even had his flight been successful. The efficiency of jet propulsion is extremely low at the low maximum speeds of aircraft at the time. The propeller, on the other hand, is very efficient at low speeds but suffers a drastic loss of efficiency as the speed of sound (about 750 m.p.h. at Mach 1) is approached. Thus when Flight Captain Fritz Wendel raised the absolute speed record to 468.9 m.p.h., a Mach number of over 0.60, on April 26, 1939, with the Messerschmitt Me 209 V-1, all far-sighted aircraft designers agreed that the limit for reciprocating engine propeller propulsion systems had now been reached. Yet, at the same time, anyone who seriously proposed jets as a practical possibility for future aircraft propulsion was laughed at by the uninitiated.

In his book, "The Wonders of Flying," published in 1938, aviator Franz Ludwig Neher devoted a curious chapter to pioneers whom he called "pseudo-inventors." For Neher, pseudo-inventors were outsiders who "cockily approached this problem [of rocket technique] without having the necessary physical-technical preparation, indeed, sometimes with knowledge on a level not even reaching that of a good senior in high school."

The basis for such skepticism is baffling, and it appeared to extend to the highest echelons of the German Air Ministry. For when Erich Warsitz returned to the Heinkel works near Marienehe after reporting to the Ministry on his He 176 jet flight, he told his boss: "I have gained the impression in Berlin that the matter is considered an impressive plaything. No one believes that anything practical will come of it within the foreseeable future."

Serious scientists and designers had long since attached real importance to discussions about the future of jet aircraft. But any real efforts in that direction were tripped up again and again by government authorities. Even after rockets became detached from the mere visionary, Nazi officials during the mid-thirties were still speaking of them as "playthings"; research in rockets remained a sort of recondite science.

Only diehards like Robert H. Goddard in America, and Wernher von Braun and Hermann Oberth in Germany continued to experiment. For a while England, open-minded and unfettered by ideology in her technical approach, appeared to be the furthest along. Her research, uncontrolled by the state, sought new methods everywhere

—even with long-since forgotten steam. It is reported that the Aero Turbines Company was established in London to develop steam jets for aircraft. The company hoped to reach the best possible utilization of fuel through a rotating boiler, steam turbine, condenser and starter, combined in one unit. In addition, there were fuel tanks, water containers and a starter battery.

Though aviation was spared the flying steam machine, rockets as engines were regarded as basically realistic in Great Britain, France and the United States. An excerpt from the British "Wonders of World Aviation" pointed out in 1938 that scientists and engineers throughout the world were devoting attention to other systems besides propeller: the "propulsion through thrust independent of the surrounding medium." And when the Aero Turbines Company began its work on full steam in England, Frank Whittle had long been brooding over his first jet turbine.

As early as 1907, Robert Esnault-Pelterie had worked out theoretical considerations on a reaction principle, and in 1912 he presented his findings to the "Société Française de Physique." In the United States Robert H. Goddard began his work on the development of rockets around 1909, and he carried out his first practical tests at Clark University in Worcester, Massachusetts, in 1915 and 1916. Goddard launched the world's first liquid-propellant rocket at Auburn, Massachusetts, on March 16, 1926.

Despite state mistrust and official disapproval, Germany's researchers did not intend to be left behind. They were familiar with Goddard's patents and with his first Smithsonian report of 1919. Hermann Oberth, Max Valier, Otto Wilhelm Gail and Fritz von Opel tested a rocket car on the test track at the Opel works in Rüsselheim. The vehicle hit 130 m.p.h. straight off. Opel then built three more test vehicles. When the fourth car exploded, the authorities intervened and expressed "utmost distrust" of the project. Opel suspended further testing. Max Valier continued to experiment alone. His rocket-propelled sled attained a speed of 229 m.p.h. on the ice of Lake Starnberg.

But Fritz Opel did not let the matter drop for long, and on September 30, 1929, he flew a rocket-powered vehicle over a short stretch at a 50 ft. altitude. Max Valier congratulated him. Shortly afterwards, Valier was killed when his stationary test car exploded.

Hermann Oberth continued to press for official approval of rocketry, and a semi-official "Rocket Air Base Berlin" was inaugurated for future experiments—with moderate backing. Also permitted to experiment there was a young man who had rigged up rockets more or less successfully when he was still a high school student: Wernher von Braun.

The youthful rocket designer first met Ernst Heinkel in November 1935. "That gentleman," von Braun complained of the famed air pioneer, "isn't interested in my experiments.

Neither does the Air Ministry show any interest. They even doubt that an aircraft can be propelled by an explosive drive unit mounted in the end of the fuselage. They think that the plane would overturn instead of moving forward. I intend to prove the opposite." And he did.

Ernst Heinkel placed the fuselage of an He 112 at von Braun's disposal. Test pilot Erich Warsitz joined the von Braun team. Years later Heinkel related details of the experiment with considerable enthusiasm:

"Braun's engine was mounted in the fuselage of the He 112 so that an oxygen tank was in front of the cockpit and a spirit tank in its rear. The contents of both tanks were under pressure and thus were directed to the combustion chamber, also known as the 'oven,' at the end of the fuselage. Here the fuels mixed and caused a series of explosions, whose pressure waves and a monstrous tail of fire were driven out of the end of the plane. Braun anchored the undercarriage of the He 112 in the ground. The end of the body was propped up so that the explosive thrust would shoot out horizontally rather than at the ground. The engine functioned only as long as the spirit and liquid oxygen lasted. There was no way to stop the process once the oxygen and spirit had begun flowing into the combustion chamber.

"At the beginning of February 1936, I went for the second or third time to Kummersdorf on the sly. I also met Warsitz then. Up until this visit, all tests of the He 112's engine had been ignited by 'remote control' from an observer's platform behind a protective concrete wall—the 'pot' had burst and flown into the air a number of times—but now Braun and Warsitz intended to show the progress and safety of the engine on a 'manned' fuselage, so to speak. A lever, necessary to mix the fuels and set off the explosions, was mounted on the He 112's instrument panel. When the test began, von Braun and Warsitz were standing on either side of the cabin on the roots, to which wings were attached in a fully assembled plane. The rest of us waited behind the concrete wall. A few seconds later a weird red-white blaze shot out of the end of the plane's fuselage. It developed into a dazzling stream of flame some 30 ft. long. The air shocks and noise forced us involuntarily to our knees. About 130 ft. behind the aircraft, some heavy steel plates—30 square inches large—resting on a sand wall were tossed into the air and whirled around.

"In just 30 seconds, everything was still again. Von Braun and Warsitz, though a little dizzy, were standing on the machine unharmed, and the plane itself was undamaged. From this moment on, when the huge force of the rocket had developed before my eyes, I was convinced that the rocket airplane would become an inevitable reality."

Heinkel's conviction was confirmed in the summer of 1937, when Erich Warsitz, who had started up the rocket unit several times in the air after having taken off by propellers,

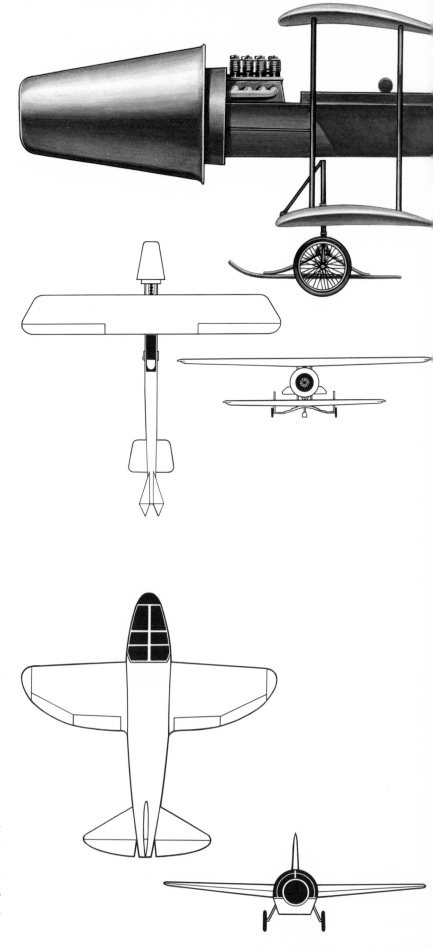

Henri Coanda, the Rumanian-born inventor working in Paris after the turn of the century, can claim to have been the first to have produced a "jet effect." He linked a propeller to a large tube which narrowed toward the rear. Behind the propeller a fuel mixture was injected and ignited by magnetos. Coanda gave up practical flight experiments after a crash landing, but his reputation as a designer continued. Apart from almost countless patents in other technical fields—among them a useful invention in the field of seawater distillation—he devoted himself to a kind of early flying saucer, the so-called circular aircraft. Anyone who studies flight properties, aerodynamics or the behavior of jet flow from jet machines, sooner or later is bound to come across the concept of the "Coanda effect."

Coanda Jet Aircraft (1910)

Length . . . . 40 ft.
Wingspan . . . . 38 ft. 6 in.
Height . . . . 8 ft. 10 in.
Engine: 1 water-cooled Clerget 4-cylinder in-line engine with jet engine and post combustion
Power: 484 lb. thrust
1 man crew

Under the heading "Flier Humor," a German aviation magazine published a rumor that Ernst Heinkel had an airplane that would go faster than 621 m.p.h. On June 20, 1939, the first rocket plane, He 176, made its initial flight under strict secrecy. The power unit, a HWK-RI engine, designed by Hellmuth Walter, developed a paltry 690 kilopond thrust—sufficient for about 466 m.p.h. "Those aren't wings," Ernst Udet sneered when he was confronted by Heinkel's new creation for the first time, "they're rails." Udet was told that Lippisch had already done considerable work on flying wings and delta wings, but the veteran airman thought more of rattly piston engines and sturdy conventional wings. The project of the He 176 came up against the world's first jet, the He 178, and fell into oblivion.

Heinkel He 176 Rocket Aircraft (1939)

Length . . . . 17 ft. 1 in.
Wingspan . . . . 16 ft. 5 in.
Height . . . . 4 ft. 9 in.
Weight fully loaded . . . . 3,572 lb.
Engine: 1 Walter HWK-R-I rocket engine
Power: 690 kp. thrust
1 man crew

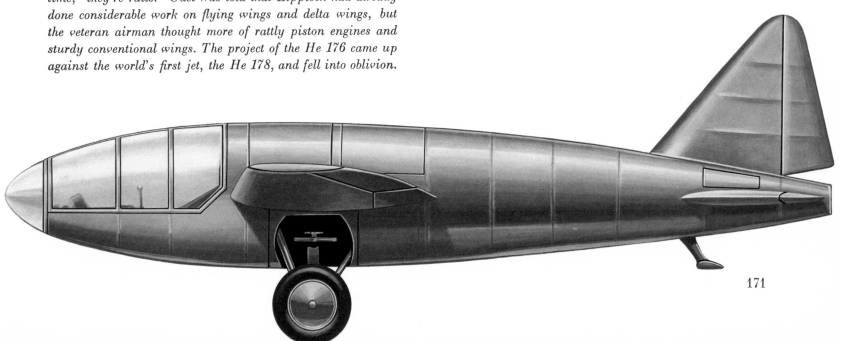

flew for the first time without props. On June 20, 1939, Warsitz finally succeeded in making the first pure rocket flight in an He 176, whose water propulsion unit developed 690 kiloponds of thrust. The next most important advance after Opel's rocket test had been made.

Duration and range limited the military possibilities of rocket aircraft. Nevertheless, an undisputed milestone in the history of aviation emerged with the development of the German rocket fighter Me 163 after prolonged aerodynamic studies and glider tests. The Me 163 was to become the greatest triumph of its designer, Alexander Lippisch.

Lippisch was enthusiastic about flying and loved airplanes. But he wanted to make special aircraft: delta-shaped, tailless, flying wings. He had been gaining practical experience by flying wing machines with gliders in the Rhön Hills since 1927. He stuck to his ideas, though only limited means were available for his experiments. So he was all the more impressed when the flier Hermann Köhl gave his encouragement and a donation of 4,200 marks.

In 1936 Lippisch began construction on a tailless rocket aircraft designated DFS 194 at the German Research Institute for Gliders in Darmstadt-Griesheim. The proposed propulsion unit was a liquid rocket engine designed by Hellmuth Walter. Lippisch's work soon became too extensive for the Institute, and on January 1, 1939, the designer took his team to Messerschmitt in Augsburg. From then on the baby had a new name: Me 163, the world's first genuine rocket interceptor and the first rocket plane to go into aerial combat.

Heini Dittmar, who knew Lippisch from their flying days in the Rhön Hills, tested the Me 163 as a glider without engine at Lechfeld near Augsburg in the summer of 1941. He hit speeds approaching 560 m.p.h. several times during nose dives. He broke the world speed record on his fourth flight on October 2, 1941, reaching 622.6 m.p.h. in his Me 163 V-1. The plane's fantastic properties put the final seal on the Air Ministry's decision to develop the famed "Kraftei" or "Power Egg" from this Me 163, the Me 163 B and C.

Walter designed still another rocket engine for this Me 163 B: the HWK 109-105 unit, from which Lippisch and the Air Ministry expected even greater things. Unlike the earlier Walter rockets, which ran "cold" (burning hydrogen-per-oxide with calcium-permanganate as a catalyst), the new propulsion unit was to operate "hot" with hydrogen-per-oxide, hydrazine-hydrate and methyl alcohol. The engine, installed in an Me 163 V-3 in Peenemünde in May 1943, actually did develop a thrust of 2,000 kiloponds.

Messerschmitt constructed only 70 of the new interceptors, with Hans Klemm in Böblingen producing the remainder in the series of this design.

The first experimental combat group under the command of Major Späte went into action at the end of 1944 with an assignment to defend the Leuna synthetic oil plant near Leipzig. The world's first rocket fighter displayed:

- a climb rate second to none: the Me 163 B climbed to 11,483 ft. in one minute, and needed only 2.6 minutes to reach 29,528 ft.;
- a service ceiling of 49,210 ft.;
- a maximum speed of 547 m.p.h., which put the fighter practically out of enemy reach (two 30 mm. machine guns MK 108, each with 60 rounds, were mounted in the wing roots).

There were disadvantages. The 620 mile range was small; the fuel lasted only two and a half minutes after the maximum altitude was reached, and the return flight to base had to be made in a glide. Furthermore, the landing, using a skid (the undercarriage was detached after takeoff), had to be made at such a high speed that apparently more Me 163's were lost in coming down than on missions against the Allies.

As one of the first high-speed flying wings, the Me 163 is still considered especially revolutionary. Hugo Junkers, who had applied for the first patent on a flying wing aircraft in 1910, did not live to see this realization of his dream.

Mano Ziegler, in his book "Rocket Fighter Me 163," described just how functional the "Power Egg" was. Ziegler, a member of the new fighter's test command since 1943, flew the delta mid-wing Me 163 B-la at Brandis. It was 19 ft. 5 in. long and 9 ft. 1 in. high, with a wingspan of 30 ft. 6 in. The author, who remained with the Messerschmitt company after the war, described a typical Me 163 blitz attack following an alert: "It was just before sundown and high time if anything was to be done at all. A few minutes after the report [of an approach of a number of Lockheed 'Lightnings'] a fine vapor trail, golden in the waning sunlight, appeared high above at an altitude of 25 to 30 thousand ft.

"Hans Bott and Franz Rösle received orders to take off. Rösle took off first, followed closely behind by Bott, both dead set on catching up with the reconnaissance plane as fast as possible. Both engines functioned flawlessly, the machines rose normally, the undercarriages danced over the field as Rösle and Bott shot upwards. Meanwhile, the vapor trail had become four trails, and they stood out against the background of the violet evening sky.

"Rösle, eyes fixed only on the enemy machines, was leveling off at 26,250 ft. to get the first 'Lightning' in his sights when his Me 163 suddenly reared almost vertically, began to shake itself angrily and went so hard on its nose that it tore the stick from Franz's hand. Then he saw that the needle of the air speed indicator was at 652.4 m.p.h. and knew that he had flown into the edge of the sound barrier. Bott, behind him, experienced the same thing.

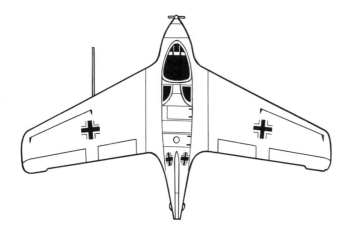

Messerschmitt Me 163 B-Ia "Comet" Rocket Fighter (1944-45)

Length	19 ft. 5 in.
Wingspan	30 ft. 6 in.
Height	9 ft. 1 in.
Weight fully loaded	9,503 lb.

Engine: 1 Walter HWK 109-509A-2 fluid-cooled rocket engine
Power: 1,700 Kp. thrust

1 man crew

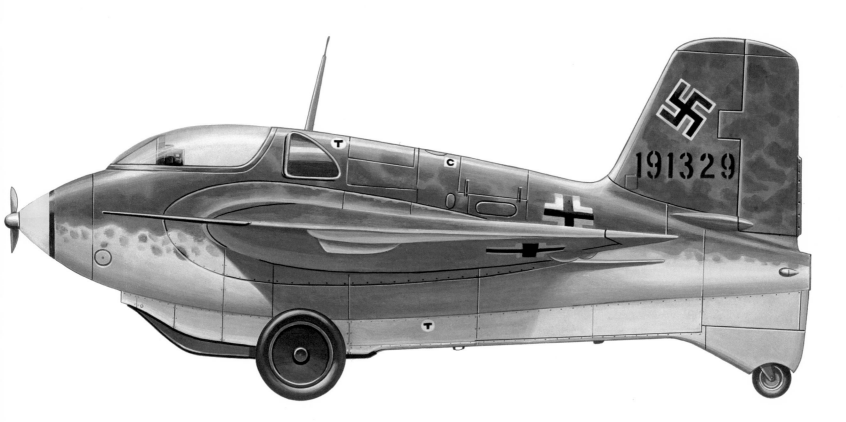

The Americans and Russians, as well as the Germans, kept working on the developments of rocket-powered planes. In the Soviet Union, Beresniak, Isayev, Tichonravov, and no less than Polikarpov himself, made experiments; and in the United States Northrop's experiments and testing resulted in the MX-324. Germany, however, claims to have been the first to have succeeded in actually manufacturing and making operational a rocket fighter with satisfactory flight properties. The Me 163 interceptor had a Walter liquid rocket developing 1,700 kilopond thrust. Alexander Lippisch's flying wing idea had turned out to be a great success.

173

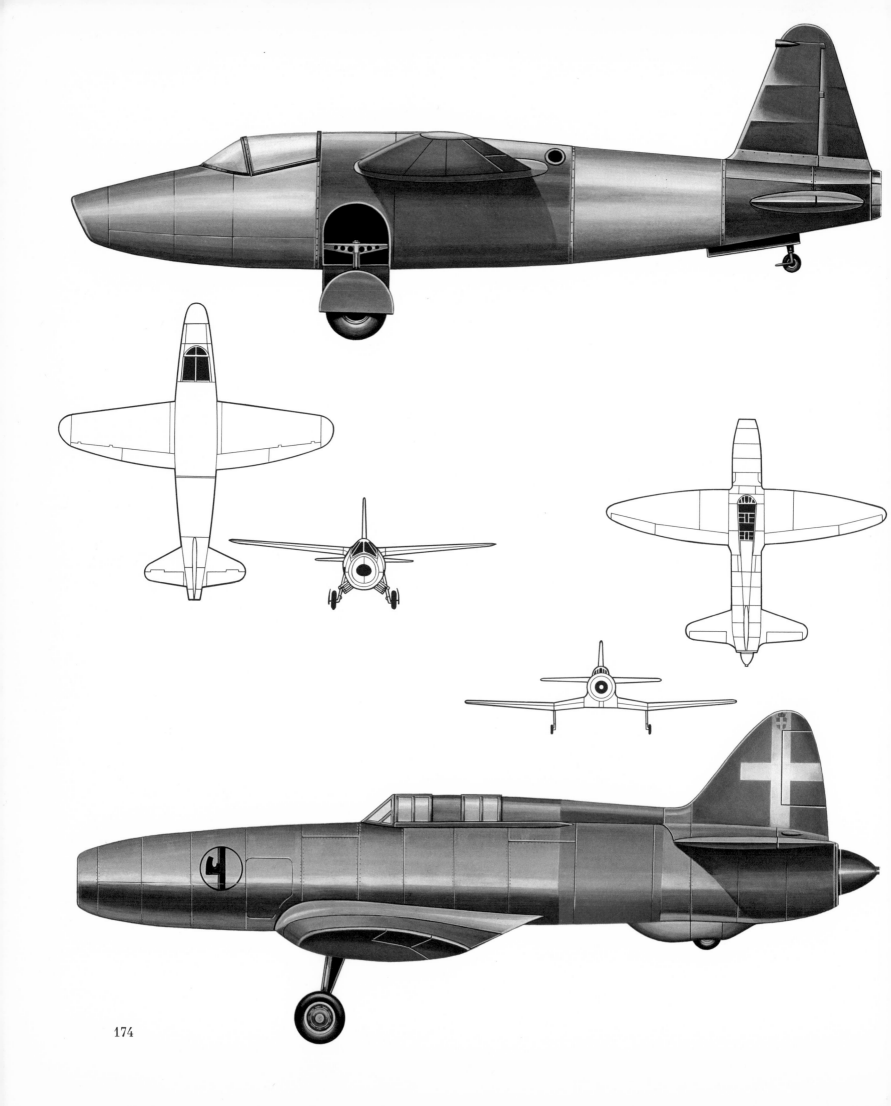

Heinkel He 178 Jet Aircraft (1939)

Length . . . . 24 ft. 6 in.
Wingspan . . . . 23 ft. 7 in.
Height . . . . 6 ft. 10½ in.
Weight fully loaded . . . . 4,387 lb.
Engine: 1 He S 3-B Heinkel jet engine
Power: 500 kp. thrust at 13,000 r.p.m.
1 man crew

On August 24, 1939, two months after the success of Heinkel's He 176, the indefatigable pioneer surprised designers with the first jet to make a brief flight. On August 27, 1939, the plane (powered by an He S 3-B turbine) passed its first real test. Flight Captain Erich Warsitz took off in the jet and circled overhead as the engineers and mechanics cheered. But the He 178 suffered the same fate as Heinkel's rocket plane; further development gave way to more urgent projects. Only the initiative and persistence of Heinkel and his team enabled the Heinkel works to bring out the He 280 later on.

Caproni-Campini N.1 Jet Aircraft (1940)

Length . . . . : . . . . 43 ft.
Wingspan . . . . 52 ft.
Weight fully loaded . . . . 9,239 lb.
Engine: 1 Isotta-Fraschini piston engine and three-stage jet engine with post combustion
Power: 900 h.p.
2 man crew

Speed and enthusiasm go hand in hand, especially in Italy; and to that country goes the credit for having made the second successful test of a jet-powered aircraft. The N.1 was designed by Secondo Campini and built by the "Società Italiana Caproni." This was a "mixed" jet whose propulsion unit was kept going by an Isotta-Fraschini piston engine. The machine was tested and flown for months, but to Campini's dismay the jet only achieved a limited success. The output of the turbine failed to meet expectations, and development of this type, which made its first flight on August 27, 1940, was discontinued.

"His machine also reared up, made a number of hefty undulations and then went immediately towards the right on its nose, since he had held to Rösle's speed. Both pulled back on the thrust lever immediately, but they lost so much time and altitude during this maneuver that the 'Lightnings' had long since gone."

Familiar reasons had made pursuit of the "Lightnings" impossible; limited range, shortage of fuel reserves, and brief flight duration hindered the Me 163 pilots. Even before the "Power Egg" went into serial production, these three main disadvantages led the airplane to the jet engine plant where the defects were to be offset.

Again it is Ernst Heinkel, whose pioneer enthusiasm—coupled with the financial resources of his own large aircraft works—who is to be credited for the first successful advance in the development of jet aircraft, a step that led to the jet-propelled Heinkel 178.

Wernher von Braun was devoting himself entirely to rockets. But Heinkel and his designers, Günter and Schwärzler, as well as test pilot Warsitz, wanted to get ahead with the newest developments. Professor Pohl, Director of the Physical Institute at the University of Göttingen, had recommended to Heinkel one of his junior assistants, Dr. Pabst von Ohain, and this 25 year-old scientist dedicated himself to the problem of an operational jet engine with the same zeal as had Wernher von Braun with his rockets.

However, funds at the Göttingen Institute were tight. Ohain's salary and pocket money were like mere drops of water on a hot stone. Even as a student, Pohl's assistant had shown enthusiasm for the ideas of the genial French physicist, René Lorin, who wanted to convert the gas explosions of a piston engine directly into kinetic energy in the form of thrust. Lorin tried to avoid the complicated power transmission. The prophetic Frenchman envisaged direct, intensive and efficient use of energy—propulsion through jets.

Pabst von Ohain was thinking of the same thing. He was also familiar with the ideas of Lorin's compatriot, Marconnet, who had taken out a patent on a thrust device as early as 1909—which Lorin was again trying to perfect. Another Frenchman, the physicist Charles Guillaume, patented a gas turbine in 1921; its principle scarcely differs from that of a modern radial jet turbine.

In 1936 Heinkel established a secret department for jet engines at his Marienehe factory. Von Ohain and Hahn, his assistant, at last were able to carry on in industrial research style without worrying about money. In 1937, they succeeded in starting their first air jet turbine, the hydrogen-heated He S 1 with a 130 kilopond thrust. For the first time, that typical roar was heard from secret production halls. A year later, the considerably more powerful He S 3-A turbines were running regularly and above all could be regulated. Their output was about 450 kiloponds.

The Me 262 was the first aircraft in which conventional propellers and piston engines were replaced by jet propulsion. In the later years of World War II, as night fighters, these machines scored spectacular successes against Allied bombers and fighter escorts.

The experimenters were itching for flight tests. Heinkel, who was financing the entire project out of his own pocket—following the disappointing reaction from Udet and the Nazi officials to his rocket plane—went ahead at first without the knowledge of the Air Ministry. He, Schwärzler and the designer brothers Günter agreed to use the air frame of an He 118 for the purpose.

The He 118 had resulted from a design competition for a single engine dive bomber and had been rejected by the Technical Office in Berlin. It appeared to be ideally suited for the new project. The internally-braced, mid-wing monoplane had an all-metal stressed skin, and oval cross-cut fuselage. Its main advantage was the relatively high (retractable) landing gear, which allowed an He S 3-B engine to be mounted under the fuselage. Flight Captain Künzel, who was working with Warsitz on the testing program, started up the turbine at an altitude of 1,312 ft.; the machine surged forward with a noticeable jolt and disappeared from view. The landing was also made by propeller; nevertheless, the He 118 had flown with a jet engine.

All of the test flights made by Warsitz and Künzel were successful—except for one. Künzel had a narrow escape when the engine suddenly caught fire and burned up after the plane had already taxied to a standstill. Künzel managed to leap out of the cabin in time to save himself.

The great moment for Heinkel, von Ohain, the designers—and for Erich Warsitz—came in the early morning hours of August 24, 1939. The He 178 took off under its own power, made a straight flight, turned and landed. There was only one fault: the landing gear jammed, forcing Warsitz to remain under the planned speed. A new milestone had been laid, and in great excitement Heinkel, at 4:30 that morning, telephoned his friend Ernst Udet in Berlin.

"It was some time before Udet, drowsy and cross, answered," Heinkel said in his autobiography, "A Stormy Life." "'Good morning, Heinkel here. I just wanted to report that Flight Captain Warsitz has successfully flown the world's first jet plane, the He 178, with the world's first jet engine, the He S 3-B, and landed safely after the flight.'

"There was silence at the other end of the line. Then Udet growled back: 'Well then, fine. I congratulate you. And Warsitz too. But now let me get some sleep!'"

Germany's top officials slept all too well during this period. It was not until the report slipped out of England through devious channels that Great Britain was about to test her first jet aircraft—the Gloster Whittle E 28/39—that it dawned on them what scientists and designers had long believed: a revolution in aviation was at hand.

No narrow-mindedness on the part of the government curbed the aircraft industry's search for progress either in England or in the United States. Even Italy got into the act independent of German developments. And on August 27,

1940, nearly a year to the day after the first flight of the He 178, the Caproni-Campini N.1 (often erroneously designated as the C.C. 2) took off from Taliedo Airfield near Milan. It had an Isotta-Fraschini piston engine driving a three-stage fan with after burner. Secondo Campini's plane, designed by him and made by the "Società Italiana Caproni," did not come up to expectations. After a series of test flights and improvements, the machine was flown from Taliedo to the Guidonia testing station near Rome. The plane made a stopover in Pisa to refuel. The average speed on this overland flight of the "mixed" Caproni jet was 130 m.p.h. In Guidonia, the N.1 was tested for eight months. Unsatisfactory results led to a suspension of further practical testing. Nevertheless, Campini still pressed for construction of a combat version of the model, with the idea of retaining the mixed propulsion unit which somewhat resembled the earlier Coanda.

Meanwhile, in England Frank Whittle was readying his Gloster E 28/39 for his country's leap into the jet age. This machine was the predecessor of the Gloster G. 41 "Meteor," which was used with such telling effect against German V-1 "Buzz Bomb" rockets during the second half of 1944. "Meteors" destroyed thirteen of the flying bombs that were released over England. After the Allied invasion in Europe, a fighter unit equipped with Gloster "Meteors" was transferred to France, but they never went into combat on the continent.

Geoffrey De Havilland was also working with jets, but his DH 100 "Vampire" never saw action. At the start of World War II the U.S. was about three years behind in the development of jet engines, and did not fly her first jet machine, the Bell XP "Airacomet," until October 1942. General Electric had built the engines according to Frank Whittle's plans. The first truly American jet airplane, the Lockheed P-80 "Shooting Star"—first tested in 1944—did not come into its own until it went into operation in the Korean War.

France, the grand nation during the early era of flight, entered the jet competition rather late, when Dassault began making the "Mirage" types, and the Soviet Union's first jet-propelled plane was also built after the war. The engine of the Yakolev Yak-9 was similar to German axial compressor jet engines which the Russians were able to study from fighter jets they had captured. Germany became the first country to mass produce rocket and jet fighters, which was a considerable achievement in view of the desperate situation the country's armament industry was in after the war.

At first, Heinkel had thought that he might have to give up on Ernst Udet, but the gruff Bavarian, whose office worked closely with Heinkel and Messerschmitt, finally secured the German Air Ministry's word for unconditional support of two projects: the Heinkel He 280 and the Messerschmitt Me 262, both twin jet fighters. The twin jet version came about through experience with the He 178. A single engine, with its extended inlet and outlet tubing within the fuselage, appeared to have little promise. And Udet, with his vast experience in aircraft, was well aware that the engines were still too weak.

In the meantime, von Ohain had developed his He S 8 engine for the Heinkel project, which called for it to be suspended in the free air stream under the wings. A three-wheel undercarriage with nose wheel was to prevent the blast of both engines from hitting the ground on takeoff. Another innovation: the Heinkel men, who despite their experimental zeal always thought of pilot safety first, installed a compressed-air ejection seat.

The twin jet one-seater fighter, an internally-braced mid-wing monoplane with a twin elevator unit and two He S 8-A engines which each developed 700 kiloponds, was first flown by Flight Captain Schäfer on April 2, 1941. Udet was impressed by the new fighter—but he wanted to make comparisons. The He 280 promptly flew rings around a Focke-Wulf Fw 190 in a sham air battle. Udet was no longer merely impressed, he was enthusiastic.

Heinkel's factory came up with two 1,300 kilopond He S 011 engines for the improved He 280 version. Then on September 15, 1942, the Air Ministry ordered further work suspended. The command came from Field Marshal General Milch, who gave as his reason the use of the "American" nose wheel. This threw a monkey wrench into the entire program for the first jet fighter to be mass-produced. The mistake was conveniently forgotten when the nose wheel was eventually ordered to be installed in the later Messerschmitt Me 262. Despite the loss of time incurred, few believe that the forced construction of fast fighter planes in 1941 and 1942 would have done much to change the course of the war.

As the Heinkel He 280 project died, priority and interest was concentrated on Messerschmitt's parallel development, the Me 262. But, as the ex-pilot Mano Ziegler was to write later: "Even Adolf Hitler and Hermann Göring slowly and reluctantly began to see in the autumn of 1942 that construction of faster fighter planes had been forgotten in the wishful thinking about a retaliation bomber."

Historians and designers alike have suscribed to the opinion expressed by General Spaatz on September 1, 1944, in a frequently cited report. It was clear to both him and General Eisenhower, Spaatz said, that the "deadly German jet fighters were capable within a foreseeable time of making the Allied losses in air operations against Germany unendurable."

Karlheinz Kens and Heinz J. Nowarra gave their reasons in the handbook on German aircraft from 1933 to 1945 as to why the "deadly German jet fighter" Me 262 could no longer bring about a turning point in the war. Its "development and construction history resulted in the greatest tragedy in

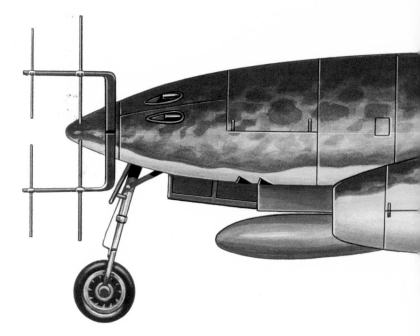

German aviation strategy, and the two year delay in mass construction caused by the pigheaded, unimaginative and unrealistic leadership was the biggest folly in German air war planning, which was not lacking in tragedies."

In April 1941, three air frames of the Me 262 were completed, but engines were still unavailable. When B.M.W. delivered the first jet turbines in November, they turned out badly, suffering ruptured turbine blades on the initial take-offs. Nor could Junkers' Jumo 004 aggregate, whose development began in summer 1939, be reported ready for operation before July 1942. The eight-stage axial construction with six single combustion chambers put out 1,000 kiloponds (overloaded) in December 1942.

The Me 262 pilots faced the same old trouble that had killed the He 280; the Air Ministry decreed that "the American invention" of the nose wheel could not be used. During taxiing and the start of the takeoff, the older tail wheel obscured pilot visibility ahead. The rear wheel could be raised only at high speeds because there was no propeller slip-stream on the elevators; this also unduly lengthened the run on takeoff.

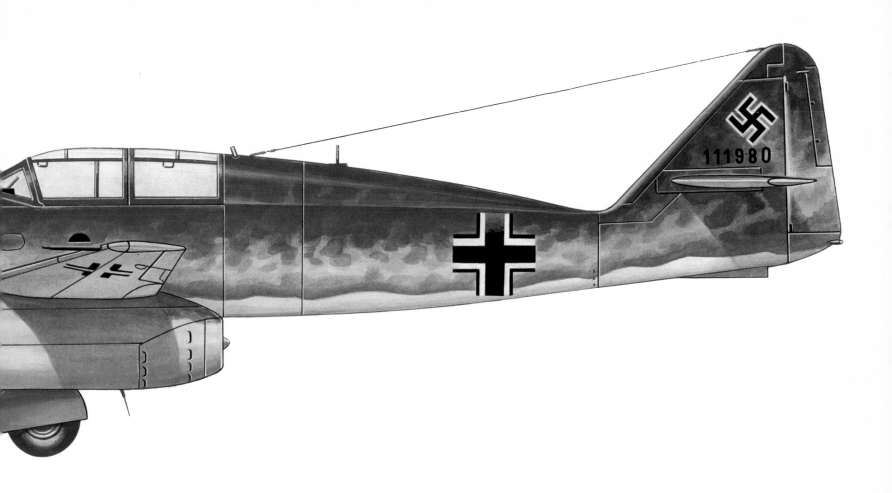

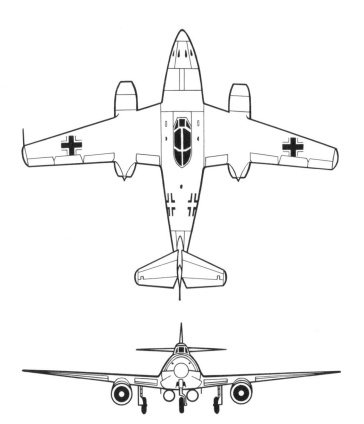

Messerschmitt Me 262 A Fighter (1942-45)

Length . . . . 34 ft. 9½ in.
Wingspan . . . . 41 ft. ²/₅ in.
Height . . . . 12 ft. 7 in.
Weight fully loaded . . . . 15,435 lb.
Engines : 2 Junkers Jumo 004 B-1 jet engines
Power : 900 kp. each
1–2 man crew

*In World War II, progress of Germany's jet aircraft encoun-
tered a setback when Heinkel's He 280 was rejected. This
followed the appearance of the new "American invention," the
nose wheel. Hitler wished to transform Messerschmitt's Me 262
(likewise equipped with two landing gears) into a bomber. After
years of wrangling, the first fully operational jet fighter was
finally launched. In February 1945, First Lieutenant Walter
was so successful with the Me 262 as a night fighter—using the
"wild sow" method of visual flying with searchlights—that two-
seater Me 262 trainers, equipped with FuG-218 radar devices,
went into action as the Me 262 A on night missions.*

According to Karlheinz Kens the pilots resented the all-too dangerous stunt. "The trick of making an early takeoff through short braking did not find approval."

The folly mentioned earlier by author Kens took place on December 2, 1942, when a decree was issued that "production was not to follow until 1944, when 20 machines were to ensue, but only with the stipulation that the prescribed output of piston aircraft engines continued unrestricted."

Fighter pilot General Galland made vain appeals to Milch and Göring after flying the Me 262 himself on May 22, 1943. Galland declared in April 1944, that he preferred one machine of this type to five Me 109's. And Colonel Steinhoff, today Commander of the Air Force in the Federal Republic of Germany, came out in favor of the Me 262 when Hitler made him a "Knight of the Order of the Swords." Nevertheless, Hitler issued a typical command: "Effective immediately: I hereby refuse to discuss the Me 262 jet airplane in any other connection except as a fast or lightning bomber."

By the end of 1944 production of the Me 262 bomber version had risen to 568, and the 6th, 27th, 51st and 54th combat squadrons were equipped with it. Major Walter Nowotny was provisionally permitted to operate a special command unit with fighter machines of this type from a base near Osnabrück. Nowotny, described by American air war historians Edward Maloney and Frank Ryan as "popular with his comrades, respected as a 'crack shot' and 'top German fighter ace' by the pilots of the U.S. Air Force and the Royal Air Force," failed to return from an attack on a formation of Boeing B-17's. Lieutenant Unhan L. Drew of the U.S. 8th Air Force's 361st Fighter Group reported shooting down the most successful German jet fighter pilot.

Early in 1945, a fresh order from the "Führer" permitted establishment of the 44th Fighter Squadron under Lieutenant General Gallands's command and the 7th Fighter Squadron under Major Steinhoff.

The Me 262 A-la "Schwalbe" or "Swallow" standard one-seater fighter with four 30 mm. machine cannons MK 108 fixed in the nose, had a wingspan of 41 ft. $^2/_5$ in. (an automatic slat extended the entire length of the span), and a length of 34 ft. 9½ in. and was 12 ft. 7 in. high. The flight weight was 15,435 lb. and the maximum speed at 19,685 ft. altitude was 543 m.p.h. The service ceiling of this type was said to be 3,608 ft.; the range was 622 miles, ten times that of the Me 163. The climb rate, however, lay considerably under the 11,483 ft. to which an Me 163 could ascend in a minute: the Me 262 could climb 3,936 ft. in that time.

At last the speedy fighter had won out. And in the end it was to give the German night fighters a boost. The remarkable success with the "wild sow" night fighter tactics (without radar) against British "Mosquitoes" led to the development of the Me 262 B-la models, which were equipped under the new designation Me 262 B-1a/U as a two-seater auxiliary

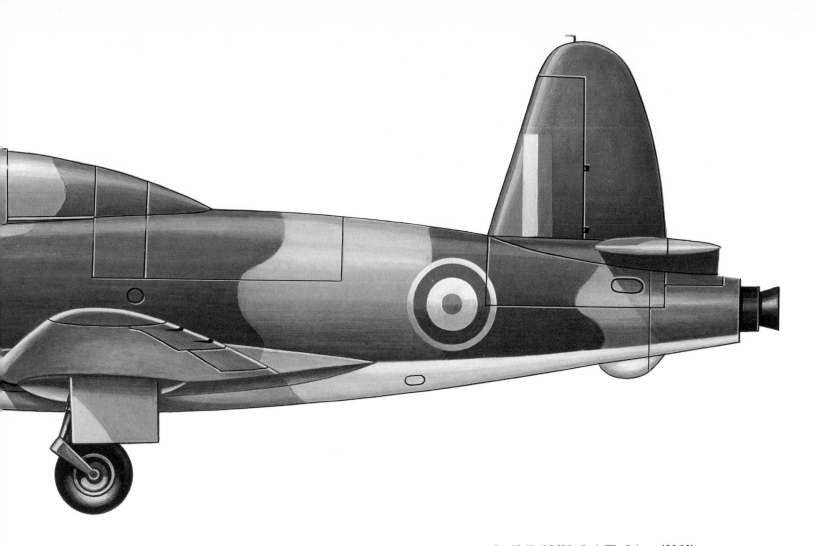

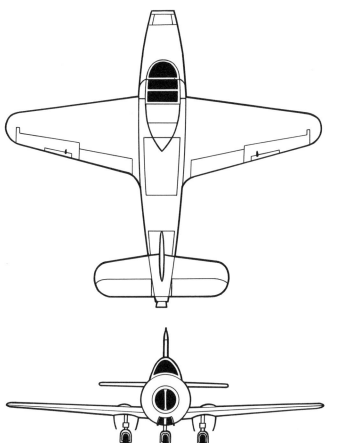

Gloster G. 40 E. 28/39 Jet Fighter (1941)

Length	25 ft. 2 in.
Wingspan	29 ft.
Height	9 ft. 3 in.
Weight fully loaded	3,900 lb.

Engine: 1 W.1 or 1 W.1A or 1 W.2/500 (Whittle) engine
Power: 850 kp. (W.1); 860 kp. (W.1A); 1,700 kp. (W.2/500) thrust
1 man crew

Unlike the conservative and rather backward officials of the German Air Ministry, the British Air Ministry approached the nation's designers with a project to develop a jet machine. And on May 15, 1941, the Gloster G.40 took to the air for a first performance in jet aircraft aviation. After an intense ten-hour testing program, during which the plane climbed to 25,000 ft. and attained a speed of 300 m.p.h., the designers obtained the ministry's approval to go ahead with the construction of a second machine with a more powerful engine. Britain had taken her first step toward her dominant position in the field of aircraft jet propulsion.

night fighter. A Lichtenstein SN-2 radar device with antler-type antennae in the nose was employed on this model.

Armament Minister Speer succeeded in bringing off the trick of manufacturing 865 jet fighters during the first four months of 1945 (the total number produced in the series was 1,433 Me 262's). Then the war, cause of all these jet devices, finally came to an end.

The Allies were so impressed by the Me 262's that General Carl Spaatz appointed an "Air Technical Intelligence Team" in 1944 under the direction of Colonel H.E. Watson. It was the colonel's task to occupy himself with German fighter aircraft developments, and particularly with the Me 262.

In May 1945, Watson asked Professor Messerschmitt if he was willing to supply him with an Me 262 for test flights. Messerschmitt hesitated, then Watson promised him a trip to America. Messerschmitt placed a list of names and addresses at the colonel's disposal. Watson arranged to bring together a number of technicians named on the list.

Karl Baur, who was in a crew of the 20 men on Watson's team, reported that six weeks later ten Me 262's had been cleared for takeoff—among them two-seater trainer versions. Baur himself instructed Watson and his pilots, and for weeks the enthusiastic U.S. fliers romped with the jet fighter, thoroughly enjoying the new flight sensation.

In his summary, Watson said: "The Me 262 is at present the best jet fighter in the world—better even than the Lockheed 'Shooting Star,' or the British Gloster 'Meteor.'"

German technicians and pilots had never succeeded in breaking the sound barrier, and British designers had racked their brains for a further two years before they mastered the phenomenon observed earlier by the Messerschmitt pilots.

Recalling Germany's struggles, Mano Ziegler, Me 163 pilot, says: "Everything went normally up to the speed of Mach 0.8. Then things began to happen to the Me 163 at that confounded Mach number: the machine reared up, went on its nose, fell out of control into the depths. In short, it behaved like a skittish horse that responded neither to the reins nor to the command of the rider. It no longer concerns the engine. It concerns aerodynamics, ruggedness, weakness of fuselage and the inability to find an aerodynamic shape suited for transsonic speeds."

During the latter days of the war the aircraft of all the warring nations were exhibiting behavior at high speeds similar to that described by Ziegler. In order to investigate the causes the U.S. constructed the rugged Bell XS-1. This aircraft was first glided in the spring of 1946 and flown with rocket power at the end of the same year.

On September 27, 1946, Geoffrey De Havilland's son became the first prominent victim of this weakness: shortly before reaching the speed of sound, huge shock waves disintegrated his DH 108.

Then, a full year later, on October 14, 1947, U.S. test pilot Charles "Chuck" Yeager went up in his Bell XS 1 attached to the fuselage of a Boeing B-29 to an altitude of 19,685 ft. Cut loose, he turned on the four-chamber rocket engine of his machine over Muroc Dry Lake in California. Yeager ascended to an altitude of 36,089 ft. At Mach 0.96 he felt the familiar shaking. A fraction of a second later he had the feeling as if the Bell were without elevator resistance. Then suddenly the needle on his meter clambered over the Mach 1 mark.

"I was almost disappointed that nothing happened." Yeager wrote in his diary that historic evening. Ernst Mach could have consoled him: "Things are mere complexes of sensation," was one of his maxims. For Charles Yeager, Mach 1, fast as sound, was a thoroughly complex sensation.

In 1938 Heinkel's revolutionary He S 3-B engine was perfected. Built into this He 178, it powered the world's first jet aircraft.

PRINCIPAL WORLD AIR SPEED RECORDS

Year	Pilot	Aircraft	Country	Speed in m.p.h.
1906	Santos-Dumont	Santos-Dumont	France	24
1913	Prévost	Deperdussin	France	128
1925	Biard	Supermarine	England	227
1927	di Bernardi	Macchi MC-52	Italy	298
1929	Stainforth	Gloster	England	336
1931	Stainforth	Supermarine S-6	England	407
1933	Agello	Macchi-Castoldi MC-72	Italy	421
1934	Agello	Macchi-Castoldi MC-72	Italy	441
1939	Wendel	Messerschmitt Me 209 V-1	Germany	469
1941	Dittmar	Messerschmitt Me 163 V-1	Germany	623

METRIC EQUIVALENTS

1 foot = 0.305 meter   1 meter = 3.281 feet

10,000 feet = 3,048 meters   1 kilometer = 3,281 feet

1 mile = 1.609 kilometers

1 nautical mile = 1.853 kilometers

1 knot (imp.) = 1.853 kilometers per hour   1 knot (U.S.) = 1.855 kilometers per hour

SCALE DRAWINGS
OF
ILLUSTRATED AIRCRAFT

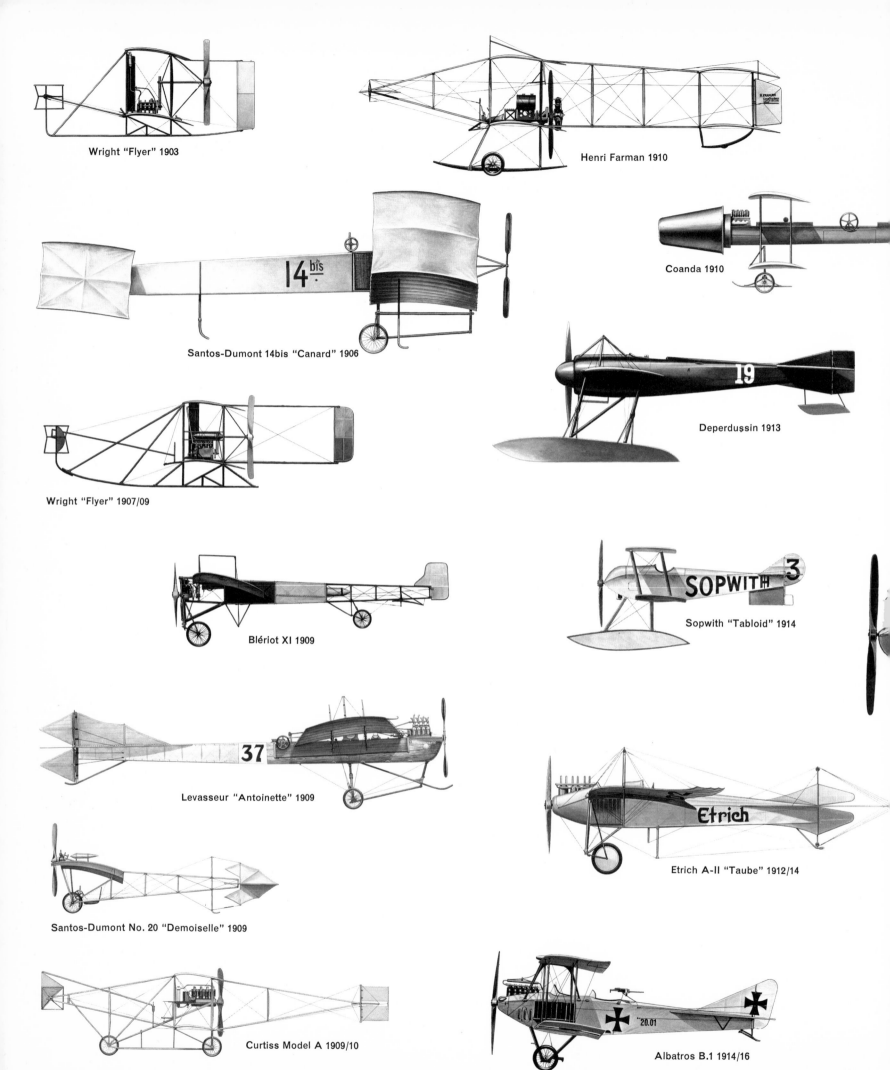

Wright "Flyer" 1903

Henri Farman 1910

Santos-Dumont 14bis "Canard" 1906

Coanda 1910

Deperdussin 1913

Wright "Flyer" 1907/09

Blériot XI 1909

Sopwith "Tabloid" 1914

Levasseur "Antoinette" 1909

Etrich A-II "Taube" 1912/14

Santos-Dumont No. 20 "Demoiselle" 1909

Curtiss Model A 1909/10

Albatros B.1 1914/16

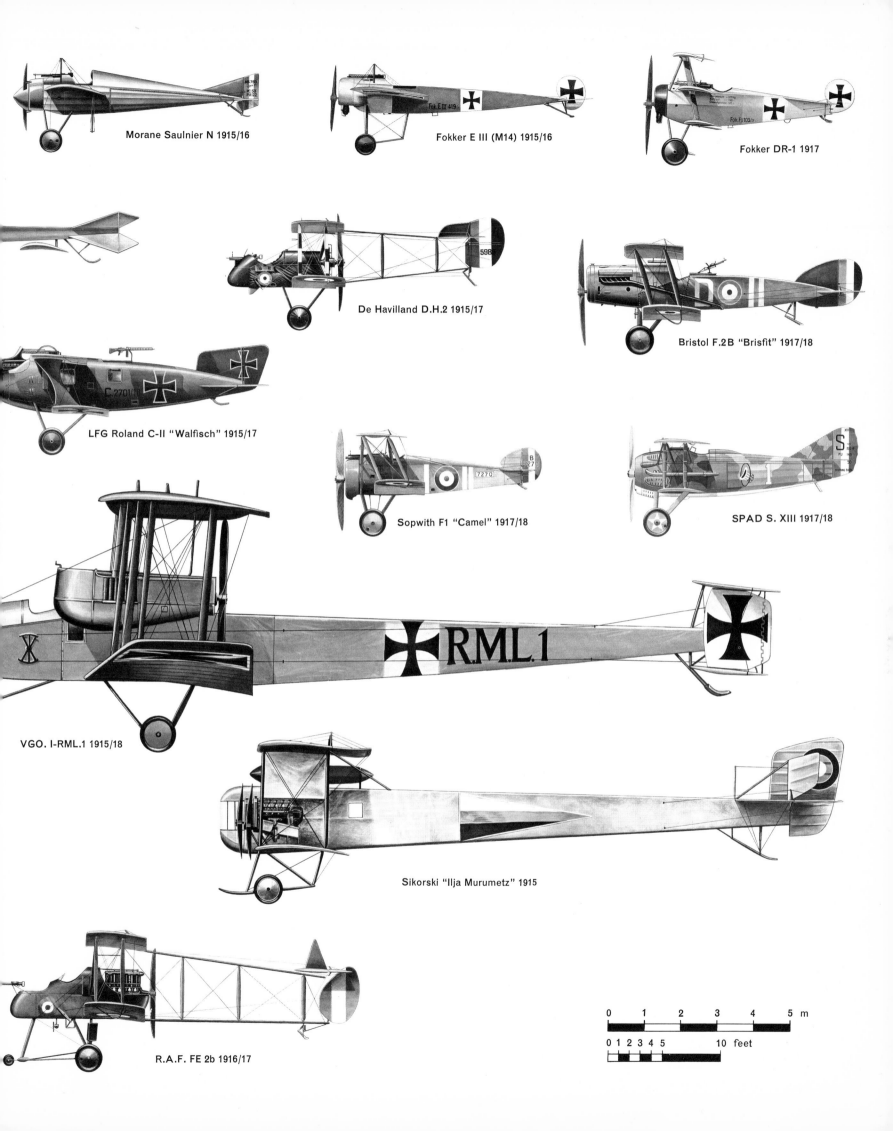

Morane Saulnier N 1915/16

Fokker E III (M14) 1915/16

Fokker DR-1 1917

De Havilland D.H.2 1915/17

Bristol F.2B "Brisfit" 1917/18

LFG Roland C-II "Walfisch" 1915/17

Sopwith F1 "Camel" 1917/18

SPAD S. XIII 1917/18

✠ RML.1

VGO. I-RML.1 1915/18

Sikorski "Ilja Murumetz" 1915

R.A.F. FE 2b 1916/17

0 1 2 3 4 5 m

0 1 2 3 4 5   10 feet

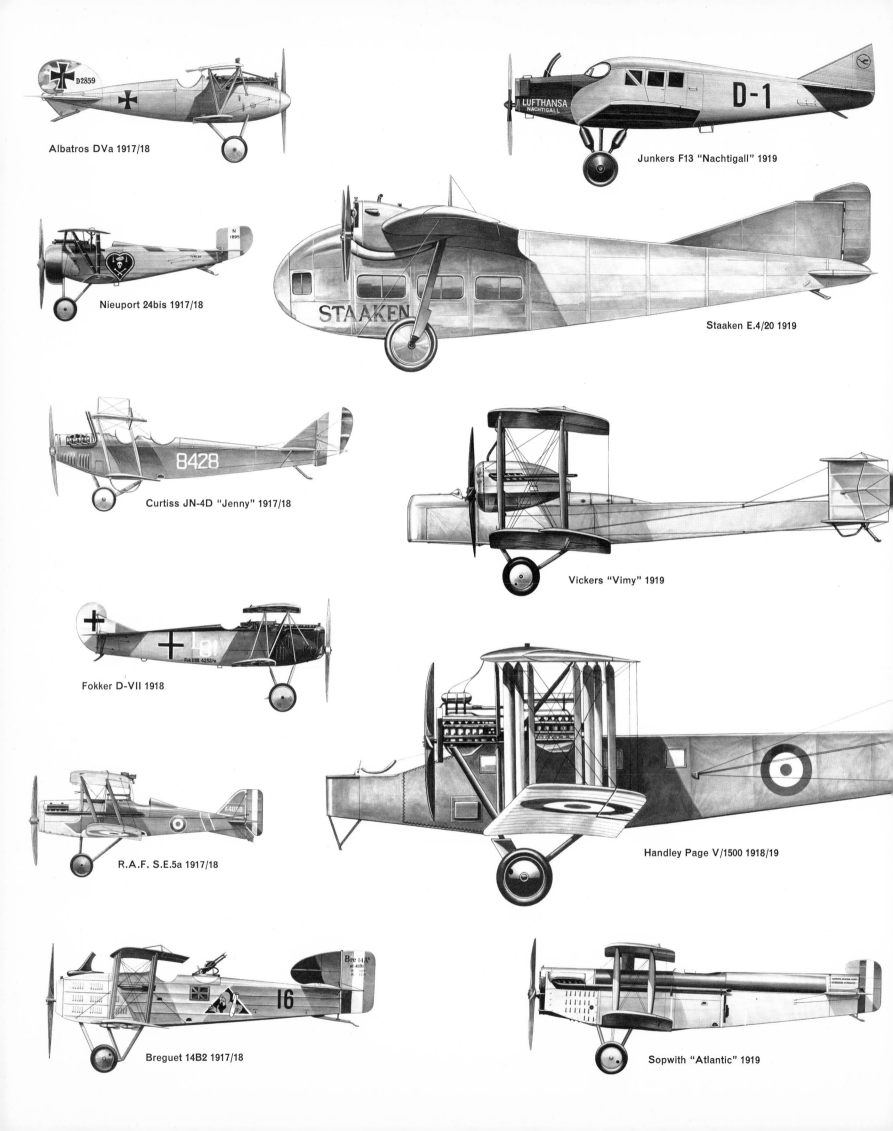

Albatros DVa 1917/18

Junkers F13 "Nachtigall" 1919

Nieuport 24bis 1917/18

Staaken E.4/20 1919

Curtiss JN-4D "Jenny" 1917/18

Vickers "Vimy" 1919

Fokker D-VII 1918

R.A.F. S.E.5a 1917/18

Handley Page V/1500 1918/19

Breguet 14B2 1917/18

Sopwith "Atlantic" 1919

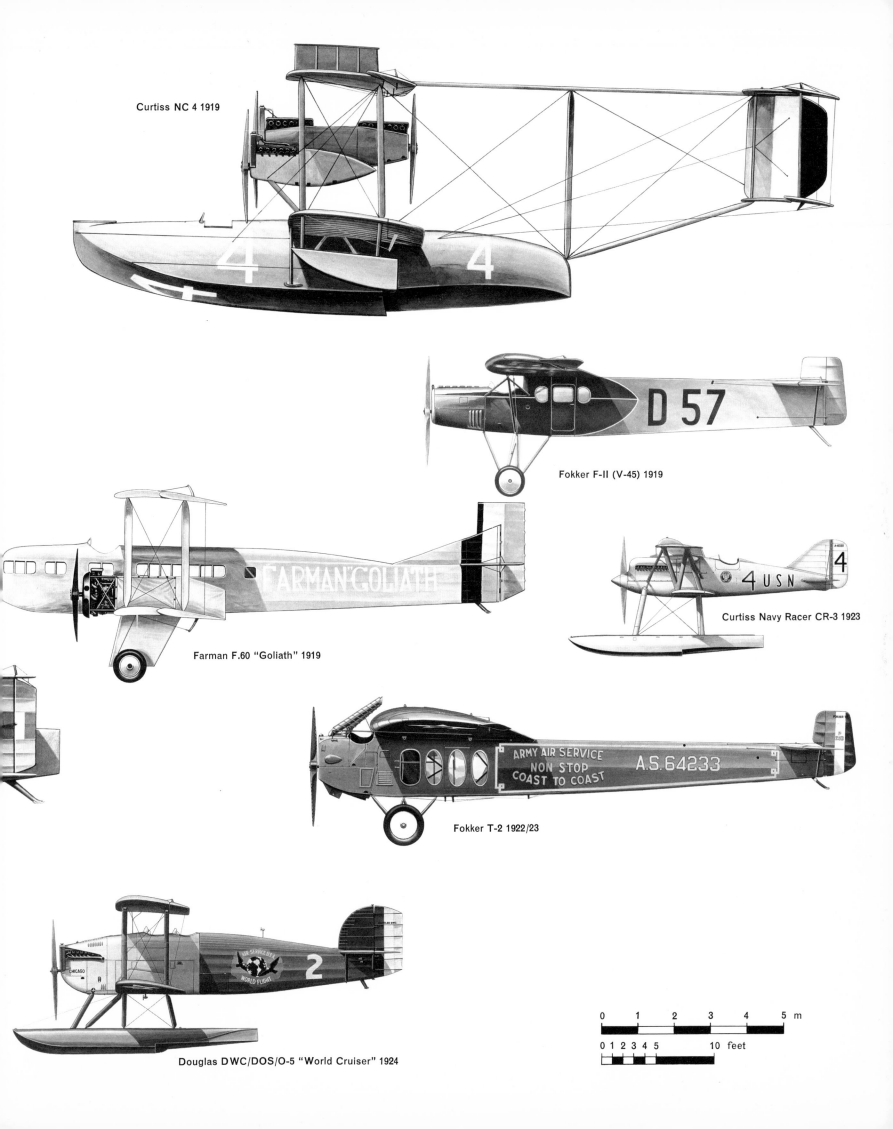

Curtiss NC 4 1919

Fokker F-II (V-45) 1919

FARMAN GOLIATH

Farman F.60 "Goliath" 1919

Curtiss Navy Racer CR-3 1923

ARMY AIR SERVICE
NON STOP
COAST TO COAST   A.S.64233

Fokker T-2 1922/23

CHICAGO   AIR SERVICE U.S.A.
WORLD FLIGHT

Douglas DWC/DOS/O-5 "World Cruiser" 1924

0   1   2   3   4   5 m

0 1 2 3 4 5   10 feet

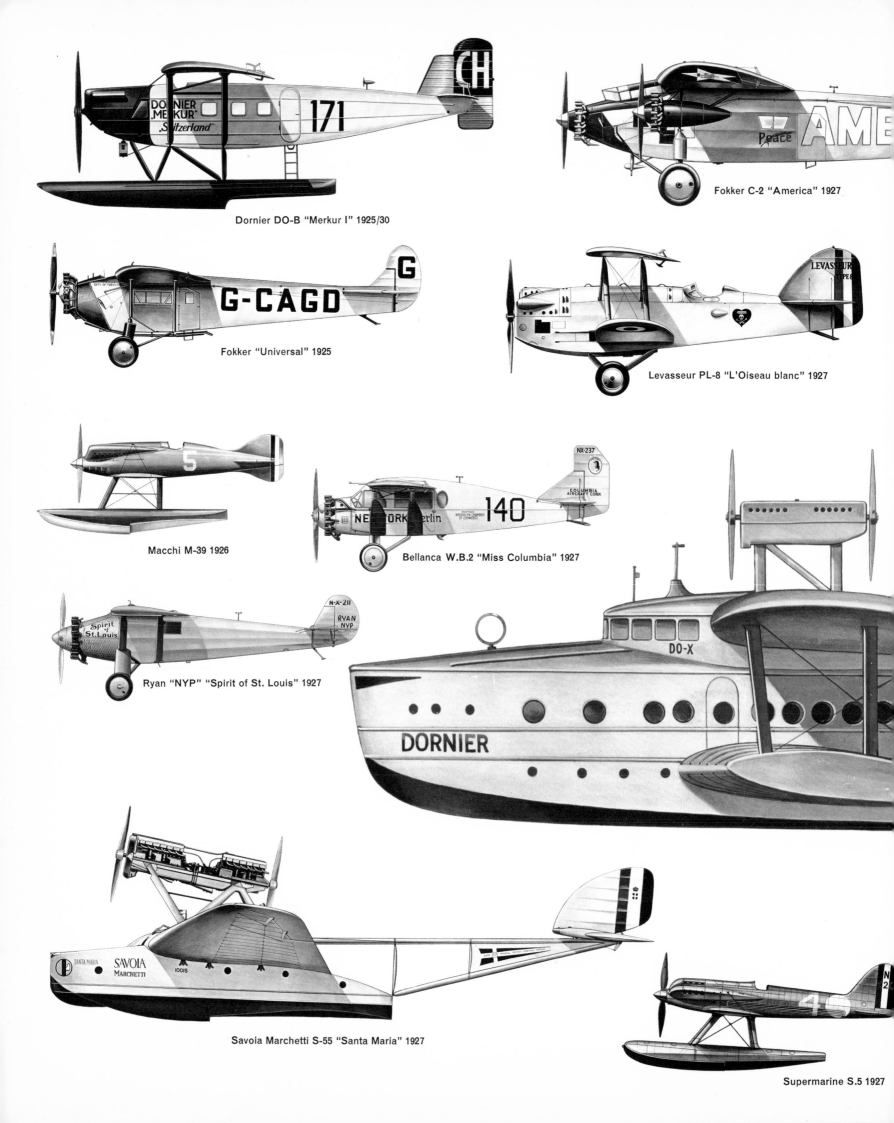

Dornier DO-B "Merkur I" 1925/30

Fokker C-2 "America" 1927

Fokker "Universal" 1925

Levasseur PL-8 "L'Oiseau blanc" 1927

Macchi M-39 1926

Bellanca W.B.2 "Miss Columbia" 1927

Ryan "NYP" "Spirit of St. Louis" 1927

Savoia Marchetti S-55 "Santa Maria" 1927

Supermarine S.5 1927

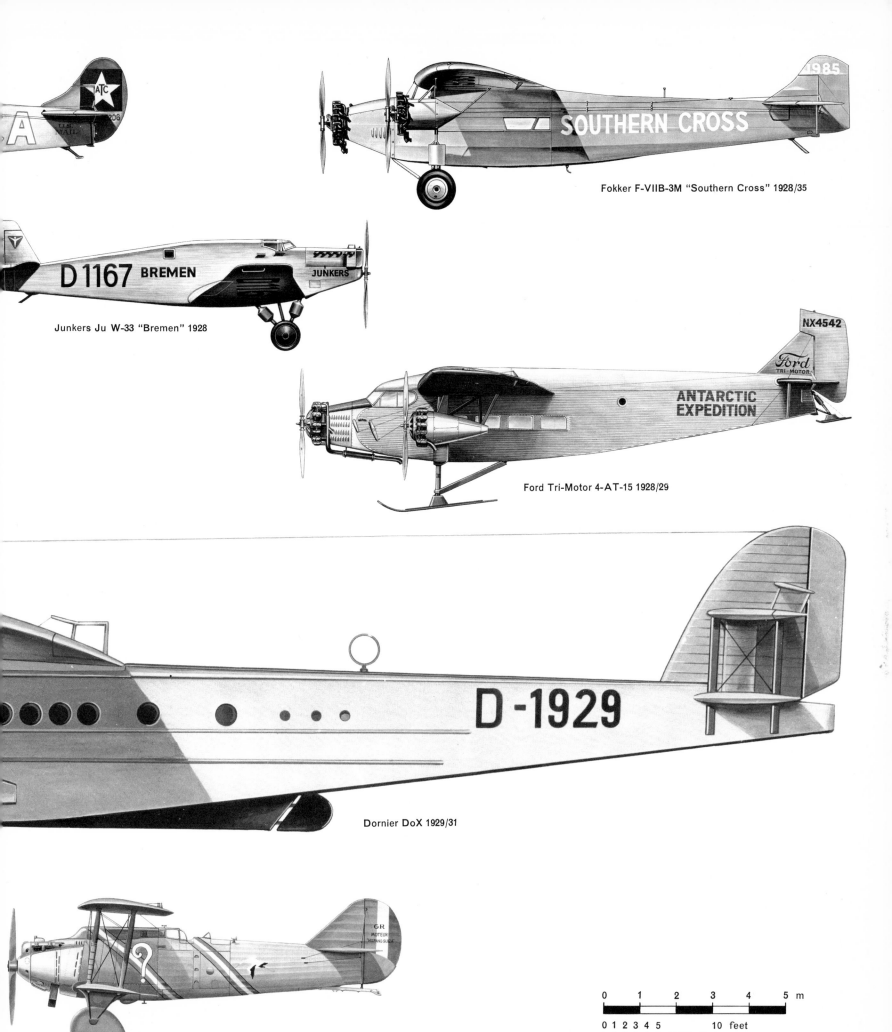

Fokker F-VIIB-3M "Southern Cross" 1928/35

Junkers Ju W-33 "Bremen" 1928

Ford Tri-Motor 4-AT-15 1928/29

Dornier DoX 1929/31

Breguet XIX "Super-TR" "Point d'Interrogation" 1929

0 1 2 3 4 5 m

0 1 2 3 4 5   10 feet

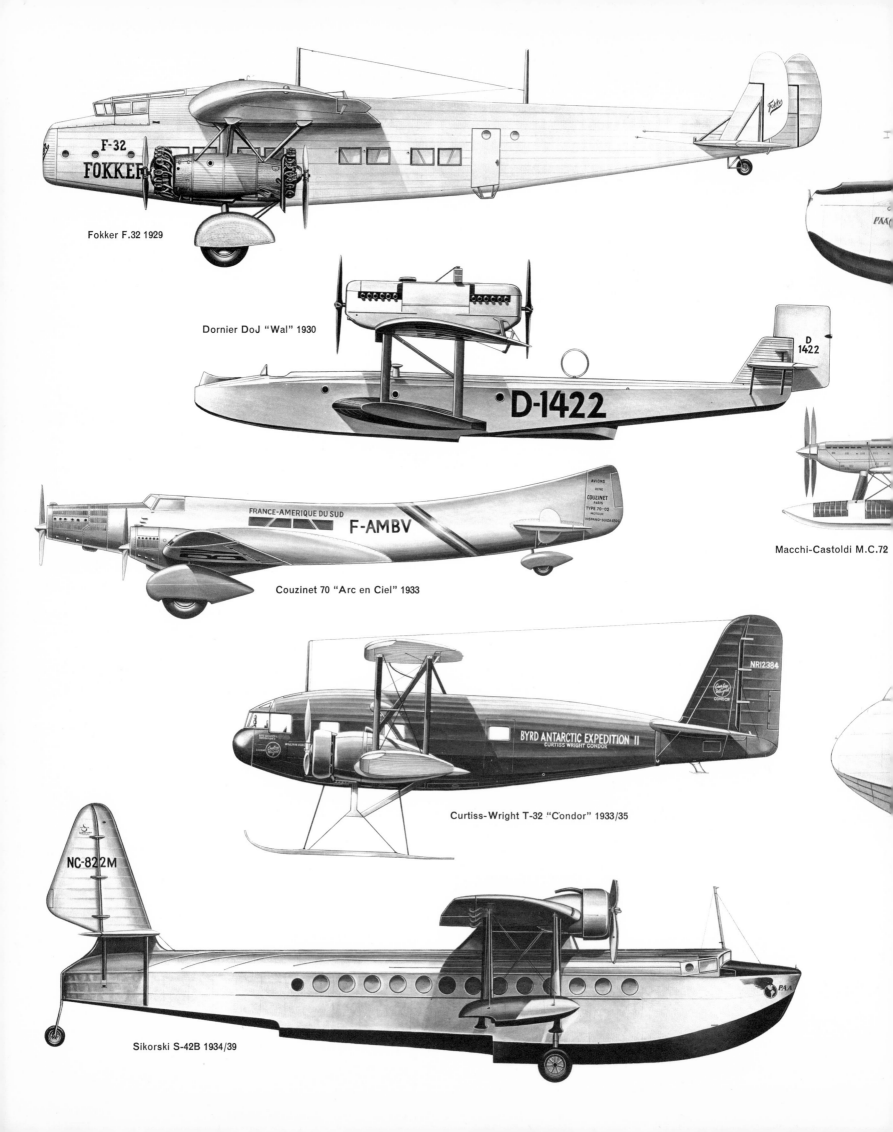

Fokker F.32 1929

Dornier DoJ "Wal" 1930

D-1422

Couzinet 70 "Arc en Ciel" 1933

FRANCE-AMERIQUE DU SUD
F-AMBV

Macchi-Castoldi M.C.72

Curtiss-Wright T-32 "Condor" 1933/35

BYRD ANTARCTIC EXPEDITION II
CURTISS WRIGHT CONDOR

NR12384

Sikorski S-42B 1934/39

NC-822M

Martin 130 "China Clipper" 1934/36

NC 14988 A-115

AMERICAN AIRLINES

Douglas DC-3 (C-47) 1935/68

G-·ADHM

IMPERIAL AIRWAYS
LO

Short "C" Empire "Caledonia" 1936

МГП-АНТ25
CANT-ANT25

Сталинский маршрут

ANT-25 "Stalinskij Marschrut" 1936/37

0 1 2 3 4 5 m

0 1 2 3 4 5   10 feet

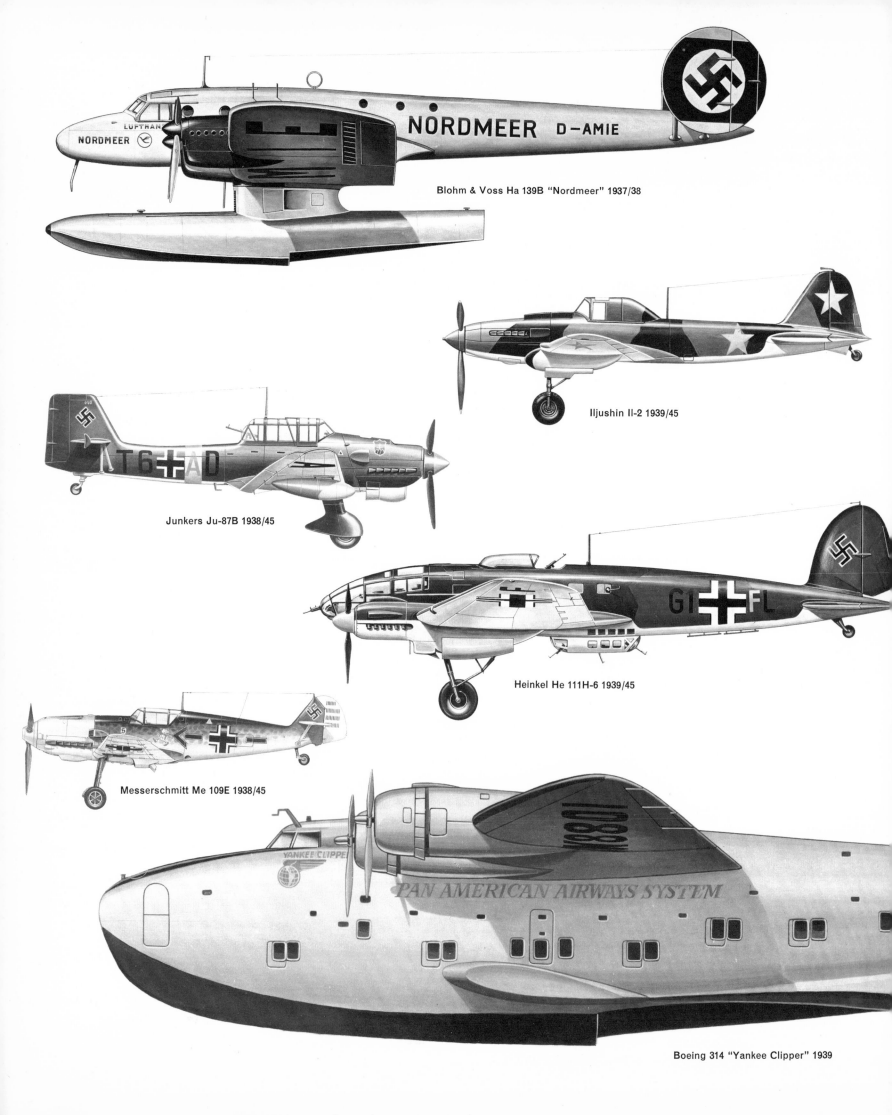

Blohm & Voss Ha 139B "Nordmeer" 1937/38

Iljushin Il-2 1939/45

Junkers Ju-87B 1938/45

Heinkel He 111H-6 1939/45

Messerschmitt Me 109E 1938/45

Boeing 314 "Yankee Clipper" 1939

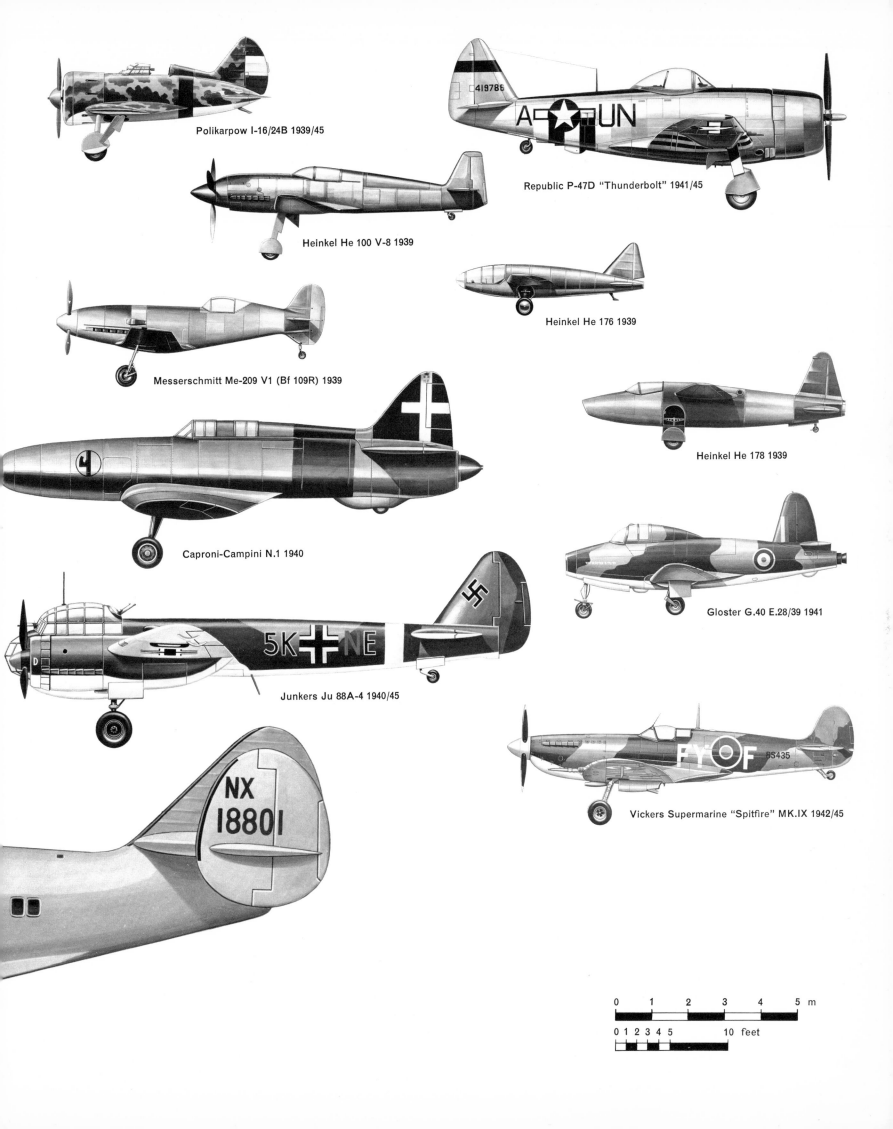

Polikarpow I-16/24B 1939/45

Heinkel He 100 V-8 1939

Republic P-47D "Thunderbolt" 1941/45

Heinkel He 176 1939

Messerschmitt Me-209 V1 (Bf 109R) 1939

Heinkel He 178 1939

Caproni-Campini N.1 1940

Gloster G.40 E.28/39 1941

Junkers Ju 88A-4 1940/45

Vickers Supermarine "Spitfire" MK.IX 1942/45

0   1   2   3   4   5 m

0 1 2 3 4 5   10 feet

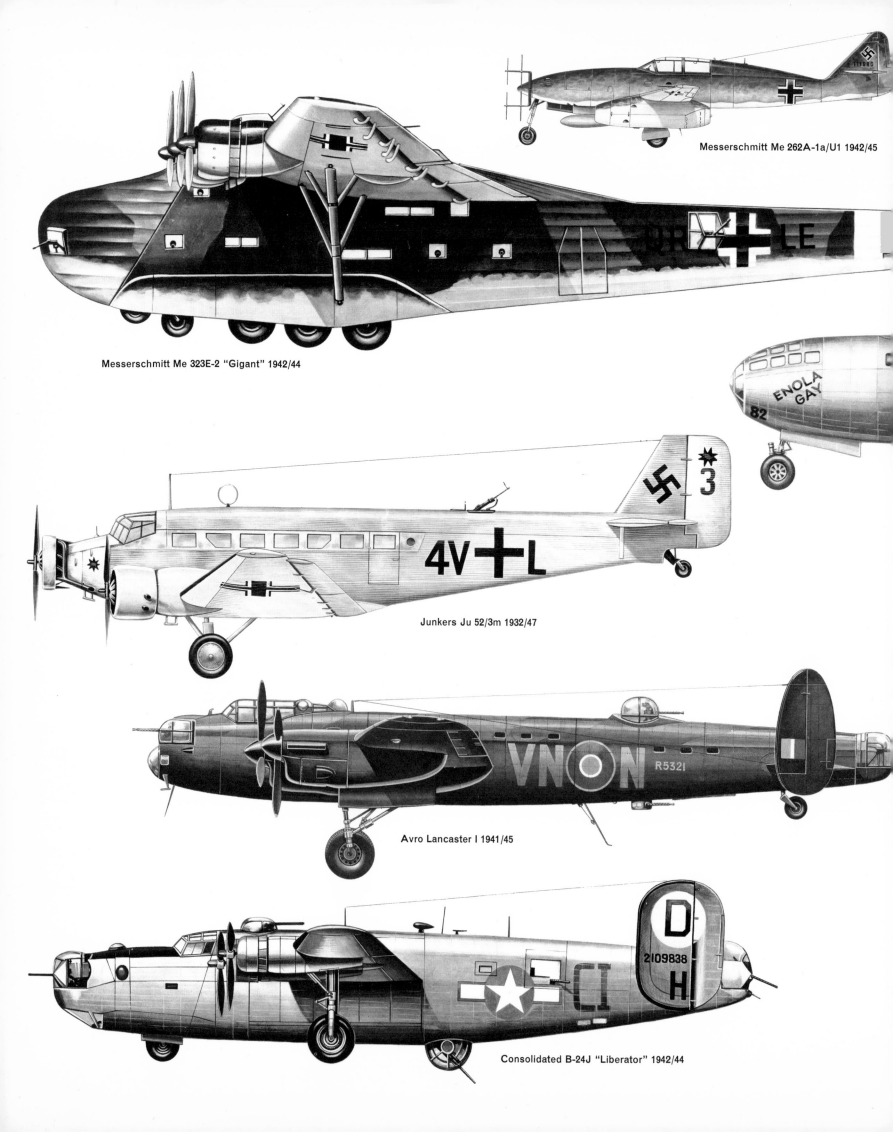

Messerschmitt Me 262A-1a/U1 1942/45

Messerschmitt Me 323E-2 "Gigant" 1942/44

Junkers Ju 52/3m 1932/47

Avro Lancaster I 1941/45

Consolidated B-24J "Liberator" 1942/44

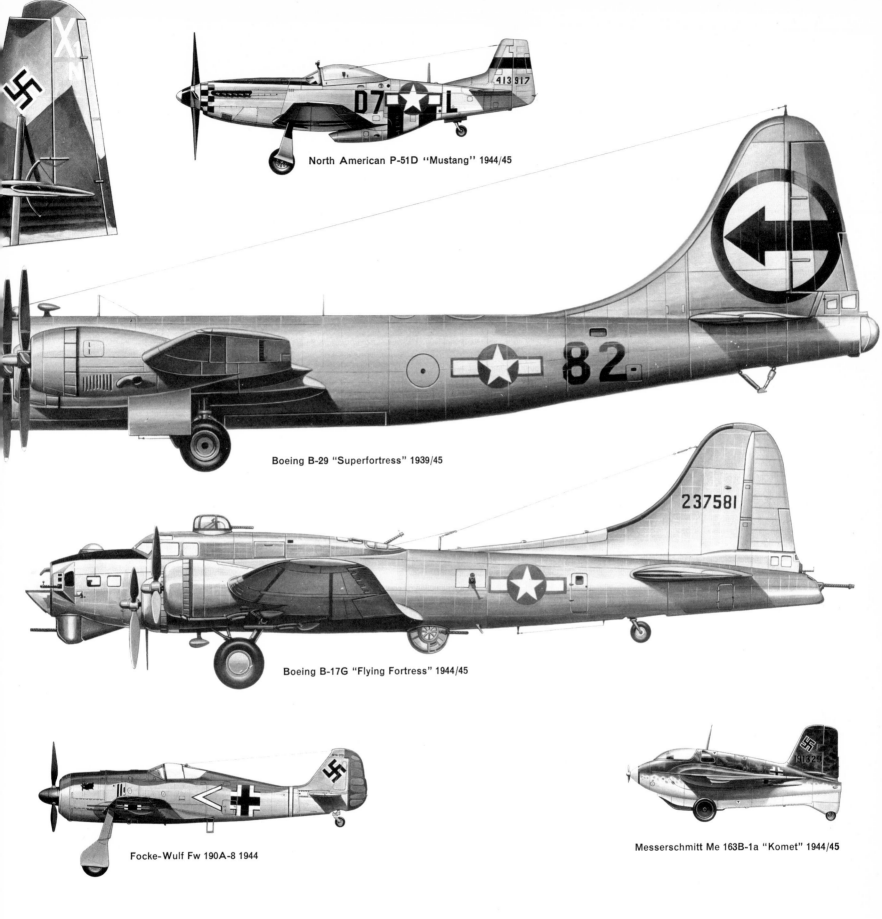

North American P-51D "Mustang" 1944/45

Boeing B-29 "Superfortress" 1939/45

Boeing B-17G "Flying Fortress" 1944/45

Focke-Wulf Fw 190A-8 1944

Messerschmitt Me 163B-1a "Komet" 1944/45

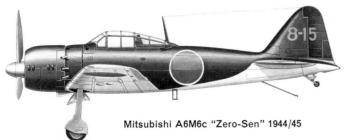

Mitsubishi A6M6c "Zero-Sen" 1944/45

LIST OF AIRCRAFT

The dates accompanying the captions refer to the year of construction of the illustrated machine.

INDEX OF PRINCIPAL NAMES

Note: Those numerals in italics indicate a page on which the name is to be found in a caption.

This book was produced by Edita S.A., Lausanne,
under the direction of Ami Guichard,
Joseph Jobé and Charles Riesen.

Printed by Imprimeries Réunies S.A., Lausanne.

Bound by Maurice Busenhart, Lausanne.

Printed in Switzerland